Craig Brown's Greatest H

Craig Brown was born in 1957. He is probably the most prolific journalist of his generation, with regular columns in *The Evening Standard*, *The Sunday Times*, *The Independent on Sunday* (as Wallace Arnold) and *Private Eye*. His books include *The Marsh Marlowe Letters* ('Funny and gratifyingly mad' – Michael Palin in the *Mail on Sunday*), *A Year Inside* ('it will grow curiouser, funnier and truer with the passage of time' – Matthew Parris in *The Times*), and *The Agreeable World of Wallace Arnold* ('outstanding, endlessly inventive and irresistible' – Lynne Truss in *The Independent on Sunday*).

He lives with his wife Frances and his children Tallulah and Silas in Essex.

Craig Brown's Greatest Hits

CRAIG BROWN

Century · London

This edition 1993

1 3 5 7 9 10 8 6 4 2

Copyright © Craig Brown 1993

Cover photograph © David Redfern

First published in the United Kingdom in 1993 by
Century
Random House, 20 Vauxhall Bridge Rd, London SW1V 2SA

Random House Australia (Pty) Limited
20 Alfred Street, Milsons Point, Sydney
New South Wales 2061, Australia

Random House New Zealand Limited
18 Poland Road, Glenfield
Auckland 10, New Zealand

Random House South Africa (Pty) Limited
PO Box 337, Bergvlei, South Africa

Random House UK Limited Reg. No. 954009

A CIP catalogue record for this book
is available from the British Library

ISBN 0 7126 5783 5

Designed by Behram Kapadia
Typeset by SX Composing Ltd, Rayleigh, Essex
Printed in Great Britain by
Clays Ltd, St Ives PLC

Contents

Acknowledgements

I am most grateful to my publishers, Random House, for agreeing to give this book a sophisticated, tasteful dust-jacket in keeping with its contents, and to The Wallace Collection for allowing them to reproduce the cover painting, which many argue is among Poussin's finest. I am also grateful to my publishers for allowing me to choose the title 'The Considered Overview: Steps Towards The Millenium' rather than falling into the trap of settling for anything vulgar or 'commercial'.

The articles on restaurants and television originally appeared in *The Sunday Times*. The political sketches, many of the parodies, the two long poems, the clerihews and the short whimsical pieces originally appeared in *The Times*. Most of the Wallace Arnold pieces first appeared in *The Independent on Sunday*, though 'She Took It Out Inch By Inch' was in *The Literary Review*. The longer profiles and the pieces on Dartington and Eton first appeared in *The Tatler*, except for 'On The Button' which was in *The Spectator*. 'A Thingy Sort of Bloke' first appeared in the *Times Literary Supplement*. All the Diaries first appeared in *Private Eye*.

Any freelance journalist who has managed to keep going for any length will be indebted to quite a few different editors. I am particularly grateful to John Gross, Ann Barr, David Robson, Ivan Barnes, Ian Jack, Ian Irvine and Shirley Lowe, each of whom gave me encouragement and, even more importantly, employment when I was starting out. Later on, Mark Boxer at *The Tatler* and Les Daly at *The Sunday Times* – both now, alas, dead – were extraordinarily helpful to me. As well as being fun to work for, both of them preferred the idiosyncratic to the useful and the offbeat to the dogged, pushing me in all sorts of directions I might not otherwise have gone. Finally, I am grateful to Helen Hawkins for all her help with my TV column, to Nicola Davidson for managing to extract various old articles from the News International computer, to Ian Hislop for letting me into *Private Eye*, and, above all, to my wife Frances for soothing my tension when the jokes won't appear.

FOR MY PARENTS
PETER AND JENNIFER
AND MY PARENTS-IN-LAW
COLIN AND SYBIL
FOR MY CHILDREN
TALLULAH AND SILAS
AND FOR MY WIFE
FRANCES
WITH LOVE

'Absolutely Flabbergasted'

Henry Bellingham's Blues

I couldn't remember what he looked like, nor could I remember his name. Henry Bellingham, Henry Bellingham. Every few months since the last General Election his name would crop up in conversation. He had been two years ahead of me at Eton. Henry Bellingham, Henry Bellingham. And he was now an MP. Henry Bellingham, MP, Henry Bellingham, MP. Aged 26, he had been selected to fight Christopher Brocklebank-Fowler's seat, aged 28 he had won it, and he is still only 29. But I still couldn't remember what he looked like, nor could I remember his name.

Others who had been with me at Eton were almost as hazy. One person couldn't remember his face at Eton, but was pretty sure that a flat cap usually sat on top of it. Another thought that he probably had something to do with the beagles. Another thought that he might have been one of those people who did geography for A-level. No one knew what house he had been in. Even those who couldn't remember the smallest detail about Bellingham seemed convinced that there was a certain humour in the fact that he was now an MP. The name of Widmerpool cropped up, as it always crops up.

Some of those who had been with him at Eton only became aware of him at Cambridge. Again, the flat cap rode tall in recollection, but it was now joined by fire extinguishers and champagne from the bottle and incidents with cars and more fire extinguishers. Hooray Henry recurred as a phrase. Stories about a shotgun recurred, but no-one could say exactly whether it had been youths or pensioners or friends or enemies who had been once peppered with light-hearted shot, or if it had every really happened. This was all that was known, and rather more than was known, about Henry Bellingham, Conservative MP for Norfolk North West.

The hand approached me at the end of an outstretched arm in the central lobby of the House of Commons. 'Henry Bellingham.' I had been expecting to recognise him, to have my memory jogged, but I did not and it was not, even though his face is distinctive. It is a little as if Michael Edwardes had suddenly lost weight and sprouted an aristocratic nose. He was wearing a double-breasted Admiral jacket, but would keep his hands in his trouser pockets so that the jacket was forced to part around his bottom. 'I thought we'd have a spot of lunch if that suits you.' Off we strode, Henry at the helm.

He ordered a sherry before lunch, and we talked about Eton, as Etonians do. I wondered what house he had been in. It was ACG. 'Do you know Charles Moore? Well, he was in ACG for a half before going to College. A few tugs had to wait anything up to a year before going to College . . . Anyway, I was a complete failure at Eton. Not very good at games, though I enjoyed them. No, I wasn't in Pop. Mind you, I think being in Pop did a lot of harm to some people. A lot of people I know who were in Pop have been extraordinary failures at what they've done . . . No, I never beagled at Eton. I come from a hunting family, but I never beagled. Ours was a social house. Bloody good lot in our house actually. I keep up with a hardcore of half-a-dozen, I'd say. What d'they do? Well, there's a stockbroker, and an estate agent, and a merchant banker, and one who sells computers, and one who's in the army and one who does nothing . . . Yes, does absolutely nothing, but I think he wants to be an MP too, eventually.

'Until the age of sixteen I was an absolute pain in the neck, but then I worked pretty hard, picked up the odd distinction and I think I ended up with two grade As, so I didn't do too badly.' His A-levels were: history, economics and, yes, geography. Then he went to Cambridge. His father and uncle had both been to Cambridge.

At this point in our conversation, he decided it was time to go from the bar to the dining-room, so he finished off his sherry and guided us out. He walked with ease in his environment, as Etonians do. I was grateful for the break in conversation: I didn't want to mention his alleged japes at Cambridge so early on. He had already asked if a little red tourist badge I was wearing on my coat signified that I was a member of the Socialist Workers Party and I didn't want to further any anxiety he might have with questions about improper behaviour.

'My mother was flabbergasted, absolutely flabbergasted when I told her I was going for the candidacy. She didn't know I was even vaguely interested in politics. I was pretty flabbergasted myself, to tell the truth. I always thought that one day, having made my pile at the bar, having settled down with a wife and family, well, then I might look around for a seat. I thought that I'd be at least 35 or 40 before the opportunity came up, but then the opportunity came up when I was 26, and, well, I seized it.'

The opportunity came up when Christopher Brocklebank-Fowler, who had been the Conservative MP for Norfolk North West for twelve years, defected from the Conservative party to the Social Democratic Party in 1981. 'Now, I had the absurd idea to apply for the seat myself, so I went to the agent, Keith Chester, a real larger-than-life character, and I took him into my confidence and I said, look, Keith, you'll probably think I'm round the twist but do you think I've got a chance? And he said, well, it'll do you no harm and as a local you'll definitely get an interview, so why not have a go?'

From this point on, like the Buddy Holly Story and the Martin Luther King Story before it, the Henry Bellingham Story is one of starting as a no-hoper and winning folk round to his point of view. '. . . So I went in there and I spoke for twenty minutes on How I Would Win This Constituency and, though I say it myself, I did pull out of the hat a performance . . . well, a performance I had never emulated before, and I don't imagine I'll emulate again. Keith rang me that night and said, Henry, you were something different: no one took you seriously as a prospective candidate before, but now you must go away and fight this one tooth and nail.'

Luckily enough, Bellingham felt the same on the main issues of the day as the selection committee. 'After Brocklebank-Fowler, they obviously felt they had to be more discerning. a) They were worried about law and order, and as it happens I do favour the restoration of the death penalty, b) they wanted total commitment to Margaret Thatcher, which I could certainly provide and c) they wanted a definite and determined commitment to the nuclear deterrent, of which I'm a staunch advocate.'

I wondered if he had any beliefs which were not shared by his constituency association. He paused for such a long time that I thought that he might not have heard the question, or, alternatively, that a fishbone had got stuck in his throat. In retrospect, I think that he was thinking that this was the type of tricky question that demanded extreme caution. 'Let us just say,' he responded, 'that there hasn't yet been one issue on which Henry Bellingham has fallen out with his constituency association.' He took another bite. 'But we're jumping the gun a bit. Let's get back to the selection.' His youth, he said, did not count against him: 'They just wanted someone totally different. It wouldn't have mattered if I was black even.'

Let us now skip two years to the General Election, where 'six hundred people rolled their sleeves up and worked as they'd never worked before'. Once or twice, he bumped into Brocklebank-Fowler. 'I said a courteous hello and he told me to take a running jump.' One day, Mrs Thatcher spoke in support of him in the village of Castle Acre: 'We had a bit of fun – we got this great big cattle truck and used it as a platform . . . we got great come-back from the villagers.' These were the results in Norfolk North West in the General Election of 1983: Conservative 23,358; SDP Alliance: 20,211; Labour: 10,139. Aged 28, Henry Bellingham was returned as an MP.

The next day, we met on the 8.36 a.m. train to King's Lynn from Liverpool Street. 'Staggering, isn't it, that BR don't invest in automatic window cleaners,' he said as we peered through the grimy windows of the carriage, 'staggering.'

His first day in the House of Commons was, he said, 'like day one at Eton – no one knew where to hang their coat.' He was initially 'staggered and flabbergasted' by the amount of constituency work which came his way, but whenever he feels overworked, 'one stops and reflects how many people would give a right arm and a left leg for the job. Some of my younger colleagues have become disillusioned after a year. They've discovered it's not all glamour, and a lot of it is humdrum, and they're frankly a bit browned awf, but I find that if you work flat out over the weekend you really make use of the little free time you have and you enjoy it all the more.' He enjoys mixing with MPs of all persuasions in the House of Commons bars, 'except for some of the new Labour MPs who've made quite a few enemies in terms of their behaviour. People have tried to welcome them into their new club but they're so militant that they shun any form of welcome. D'you know Nicholas Soames? He was at Eton. Anyway, he goes up to the most militant of them and makes a point of saying he'll drop in on him for a glass of champagne on his way home. He absolutely loves mobbing them up!'

Henry Bellingham lists his interests as Small Businesses, Northern Ireland, Defence and Agriculture. He is the Secretary of the Conservative Backbench Smaller Businesses Committee and he is also the Joint Secretary of the Conservative Backbench Northern Ireland Committee, 'a post for which there was admittedly not much opposition, ha ha.' He says that he thinks twice before speaking about Northern Ireland as his family owns land there. 'I take the view that if you go into the Commons with low expectations then if you achieve anything it's an extra bonus . . . Of the new boys, I'd say I'm not on the inside track, but I might be on the next track out, as it were.'

Elected in June, he did not make his maiden speech until November, by which time about two-thirds of the new members had already made theirs. 'I wanted to take the temperature of the water before plunging in,' he explains. The debate was on Small Businesses, which is, of course, one of his Special Interests, and he admits that he was working out what to say for weeks. 'My main point,' he explains, 'was how crucial small businesses are to the economy.'

After he had given me a copy of the *Hansard* containing his maiden speech ('Can I keep it?' I asked. 'Absolutely, very much so,' he replied), I thought that the time had come to mention Cambridge. He went up to read geography but soon switched to archaeology and anthropology ('the biggest skive in Cambridge') and from there went on to read law. In the last three weeks he 'did a mega-swot' and achieved a 2.1. He happily admitted to spending most of his time with horses and hounds, and he particularly enjoyed point-to-pointing. 'I used to bet a lot, and with some success.' I told him that his life-style at Cambridge had been described to me as reckless. He laughed rather loudly, as if interrupting a pause. 'Reckless! Ha! Ha! Ha! Well, I suppose the Magdalene bar was frequented on most nights, ha! ha! Practical jokes? Ha! Ha! Ha! One or two, I suppose, but in the best tradition of student pranks. We were never arrested. Or at least never charged! Ha! Ha! Ha!'

Could he remember his favourite pranks? He paused. 'Trying to think. Ummm. Well, there was the odd fire extinguisher . . . I used to do my practical joking with David Johnson. D'you know him? He was a practical joker par excellence and he's now a vicar . . . No, I'll come back to you on that one, if I may.'

His last two years at Cambridge were devoted almost all to riding. He was the joint master of the Cambridge university drag hounds, and in the Cambridge university point-to-point, his mount, 'At East', came in third at 40-1.

The train arrived at King's Lynn ('a lovely old town, really super') and as we walked towards his car, a modest Ford, I realised that Henry Bellingham was being furtively recognised by strangers. 'I try to keep a high profile,' he explained, 'I aim for two stories a week in the local press. It's still a marginal seat and I want to build it into a Tory stronghold.' There was a small collection of cassettes on the shelf of the car, among them *The Best of Boney M*, but he didn't put one on. He wanted his full concentration, and mine, for our tour of his constituency. We started with the factories. He had got used to them during the General Election.

'I'd go in and I'd say, quite frankly, of course I'm young, of course I've got no first-hand experience of the factory floor but you've got to take me for what I am. That was the basic line I took, and it seemed to pay awf.'

The Industrial Estate is so crammed with small factories that no matter how slowly he drove, his enthusiastic commentary, full of details about encouraging prospects and fresh orders, could never keep up. He seemed to have visited all the factories at one time or another. 'I ring them up and ask to come round and they love it – that's Wedgwood Crystal, and that's Frigoscandia, big company – you see, if you visit now, during peace time, it's ten times more effective than in the time of an election – and that's Berol, the felt-tip pen people, you've probably heard of them, and that's a food-processing company, and that's Dow Chemicals. As you see, there are a lot of thriving companies and once we've cleared up this nagging unemployment problem, as I have no doubt at all we will, there'll be no stopping us. They're an independent lot around here, and, my goodness, they're not scared of hard work.'

As we drove away from the factories towards the countryside, Henry Bellingham quite voluntarily set his mind to tackling the broader issues of the day. Ten years ago, he had been a moderate, vaguely a Heath-ite, but since becoming an MP and seeing the unemployed and such things at first hand, he was behind Mrs Thatcher all the way. These are some of the words he said as we were driving through the outskirts of King's Lynn that morning: 'Streamline . . . Economic efficiency . . . Overall growth . . . Incentives . . . Work Ethic . . . Conciliatory . . . Streamline . . . Economic Efficiency . . . Overall growth . . .' I can't remember saying anything myself. My eye had caught sight of a cassette he had taped himself. He had written the contents on the outside cover. They included *Like a Rolling Stone* by Bob Dylan and I sat pondering the choice. 'Strategy . . . Job Creation . . . Tax Thresholds . . .' he continued. We were now out in the open country. 'We are now out in the open country,' he told me.

In each village, Henry Bellingham has tried to cultivate someone whom he calls 'my eyes and ears'. 'They tell me what's happening in their particular village, so that if it's Mr Brown's Golden Wedding I can send him a card of congratulations. And it means a lot to people, you know. I had one old boy who rang me up the other week almost in tears. And they show my letter round the pub and that sort of thing. It's that sort of contact with people which gains one a personal following.'

We came to a halt at one village when Henry Bellingham spotted his eyes and ears walking along the street. 'Rowley!' he shouted, then we nipped out of the car and shook hands with Rowley. 'And you've met my son, of course,' said Rowley, bringing a tall and tough-looking young man to the fore. 'Yes, yes,' said Henry Bellingham, shaking him firmly by the hand, 'and how are you, Clive?' 'It's John, actually,' replied the young man, without a smile. Henry Bellingham changed the subject by asking him how things were going. John said that he was on the dole. The ends of Henry Bellingham's mouth made a swift commiserative detour towards his chin, and then we all piled into the pub, The Lygon Arms.

Henry Bellingham shook hands with the barman and the two locals at the bar before ordering us all a drink. He ordered himself a half pint of bitter. When a little of it dribbled on to his chin, he wiped it off with a white handkerchief from his trouser pocket. Another, coloured, handkerchief, in his outside jacket pocket remained stationary all day.

Over our drinks, Rowley told me that though he had been on the selection committee, he hadn't voted for Henry, but that he regretted it now, because he was a fine young man and a fine, hard-working MP. This view was echoed throughout the day by many people. As he was saying this, Henry was jotting down someone's problem in the little notebook he keeps with him. Later in the day, at the council offices, I saw a bulging file of letters from Henry Bellingham, MP. At the Conservative Association in King's Lynn, I looked at reports from the local press pinned to the board: 'MP sees Postal Posters', 'MP Sees Church Tower Danger', 'MP Comes To The Aid Of The Party', 'MP Meets Resident' and, under a photograph, 'MP Henry Bellingham trying on an army helmet for size'.

What will become of Henry Bellingham, MP now that his reckless days are behind him, now that he is conscientious and works flat out, now that old boys, tears in their eyes, pass round his letters in pubs, now that Northern Ireland has him in charge of its backbench committee, now that his eyes and ears are firmly implanted in every village in Norfolk North West, now that he is not on the inside track, but on the next track out, as it were? I would guess that Norfolk North West will return him as their member at the next election with an increased majority and that he will be their member for years and years. He will marry someone suitable. 'Any woman who's mad enough to contemplate the prospect of being married to me will know already that I'm a Conservative MP and all that it entails.' (At the moment, when asked to bring a woman to functions he brings his mother.) Perhaps, if things go right, he will become a Minister. Certainly, his contemporaries' initial astonishment that he should have become an elected representative of the people will fade as they grow used to the inappropriateness of their own success; before long, those who had forgotten him at Eton will start to remember him as a friend, A-levels in geography will be commonplace, and we will all be wearing flat caps. His own memories of his pranks will become everyone's, and flimsy rumours of guns and drunken driving will be forgotten.

Before I left him, I asked him to come back to me, as promised, with a couple of pranks. He had obviously been thinking hard. The first involved taking the wheels off someone's car and leaving it at Newmarket. The second found him and a friend entering a dance halfway through dressed up as gorillas and scaring the girls. 'That friend's also hoping to become a Conservative MP,' he added.

'Always a Little Bit in Love'

Barbara Cartland's Diary

As frankly one of the most popular members of the Royal Family and the only one let me add who has sold over 10 million copies of my books in Saudi Arabia, it is up to me to argue our cause on television and on the wireless until I am blue in the face.

I do not want to do it, of course I do not, I have much better things to do, but someone has to, so it had better be me.

The British people simply adore their monarchy. They need someone to look up to and they utterly crave the glamour and history of us all.

It is high time someone of my stature – read and loved by thousands of millions, with over 15 million copies sold in Saudi Arabia alone – began to sing the praises of our Marvellous Monarchy.

Prince Charles, for instance. There's plenty to praise there, if only people would quite simply make the effort to look.

He may not be tall. In my day he would have been called a midget or a dwarf, in fact he's not my idea of a Prince at all. He's also as bald as a cricket ball, dithers this way and that rather than just getting on with it, is frankly rather common – I suppose it's all that German blood, poor thing – and was utterly ruined for life by Gordonstoun and is probably queer to boot and his eyes are far too close together, which Englishwomen never like.

But it is simply disgraceful that he should now find himself the target of abuse from people who barely know him. So I hereby call on the nation to join with me in singing his praises, loud and clear, for all the other nations of the earth to envy.

However pathetic and sissy he might be, it is not for us to say so, or it might be the end of the Monarchy. I have written to every single Member of Parliament calling on them to pledge their support for poor Prince Charles, enclosing a postage-paid envelope for a speedy response, headed FREEPOST DWARF.

And what would you replace our marvellous Royal Family with? You answer me that. One would have to find some delightfully well-loved figure, preferably an exceptionally well-bred lady, a Dame perhaps, and with Royal connections, plus a great deal of experience in matters of the heart, a romantic novelist, maybe, or a ceaseless health campaigner, someone who's not afraid to speak her mind, someone with the mind of a seer and the body of a teenager, someone with a daughter ready and willing to take over when she abdicates. Nominations on a postcard, please, to me, Dame Barbara, or to my darling daughter, Princess Raine, c/o Buckingham Palace. Petitions, posters, round-robins, etc, also very welcome.

I receive a great many letters from men and women all over the world saying that they want above all to look like me and asking how to go about it.

The secret is to stick to pure honey, lemon rind, scrunched-up Malaysian spiders and Tibetan goose-droppings.

Rub two and a half pints of honey all over your face twice a day, pepper it with lemon rind and then mould the spiders and the goose-droppings to fill an area of circumference six inches all around your eyes.

Many world leaders have followed my advice including Mrs Gandhi, President de Gaulle (who was in love with me at the time), President Marcos (who proposed twice to me before breakfast) and President George Brush. And that is what keeps them all looking so young.

And I'll tell you something else.

I sell over 20 million copies of my works every year in Saudi Arabia alone.

A lot of nonsense is spoken these days about world peace by people who should know a great deal better.

President Brush has already had the benefit of my advice. I sent my pamphlet *Barbara Cartland on World Peace* to him, bound in ribbon, and have received his personal thanks in return. The same goes for Mr Yeltsnip.

I intend to offer my advice freely to the next President, Mr Clintop, as and when he needs it. He has already made noises in my direction, and like all the others he is a great fan of my books.

I will tell him this.

Women like their men to go to war, preferably in a smart, freshly-laundered uniform. They don't like the stay-at-homes one little bit.

Any woman who says differently is lying.

We Englishwomen like to keep the hearth warm, waiting beautifully turned out, with a hot meal in the oven, for our husbands to return from war perhaps with one or two minor head wounds and the odd scar.

What absolute rubbish to pretend otherwise.

As for these Bosnians and Suburbians and all their simply frightful tiresomeness, I have advised Prime Minister Major – who recently proposed to me three times before breakfast, incidentally – that they will get absolutely nowhere until they wear full-dress uniform rather than sloppy, ill-fitting 'genes' and so forth, which every Englishman knows are only worn by queers, footballers or similar.

By the way, I am terribly popular in Yugoslavia. I have sold over 40 million books there (50 million in Saudi Arabia, incidentally) and they love me for it.

Very dear friends who know all about these things tell me that the Bosnians have more copies of my books than the Suburbians and they refuse to lend them and that is the root cause of all this fighting.

Often, one can only discover the true reason for a war through talking personally to the experts. I used to be in constant touch with Chairman Mao, who was a little in love with me, proposing five times over a light lunch. This is what so many people simply do not understand.

While we are on the subject, it may interest you to know that my books sell over 65 million copies each year in Saudi Arabia alone.

I am often asked by my many admirers to list my proudest achievements.

But how does one measure achievement?

Which is the more marvellous?

- That I received 1,534 proposals for marriage during my first Queen's Charlotte's Ball?

- Or that I was instrumental in the invention of penicillin?

- That, working flat out at a secret location, I brought about a triumphant end to the Gulf War (General Schwarzenegger, Sir Edward Heath and Mr Saddam Hussein were all a little in love with me)?

- Or that, between 1930 and 1950, I received firm offers of marriage from over forty world leaders, including Stalin, Franco, Mussolini, the little American President whose name I forget and my very dear friend Sir Winston Churchill?

- That my books sell well over 100 million copies each year in Saudi Arabia alone?

- Or that I invented the concept of the EEC on an Egyptian cruise with Dickie Mountbatten in June, 1932?

- That I have twice been ranked the most dignified member of the British Royal Family by the National Home Furnishing Association of Colorado Springs?

- Or that Princess Diana found everlasting love and happiness through constantly reading and re-reading my books?

In the end, as any Englishman will tell you, it is none of these outstanding achievements, unequalled in our century, that matter.

No. What matters above all else is selflessness, serenity and humility.

And God – who has always been a little bit in love with me – has blessed me with all three.

'And Is There Money Still For Me?'

The New Vicarage, Grantchester

Just now the lilac is in bloom,
All before his little room;
Inside, the fax is buzzing strong;
Outside, the tabloid press still throng,
And in the flower-beds, I think
The lighting and the cameras wink.
And down the borders, well I know,
The men in raincoats lying low.
But foolhardily they roam!
Jeffrey Archer's not at home!
Here he is, sweating sick and hot,
Entertaining a dreadful lot
Of big-wigs in his penthouse flat
Some tall, some small, some thin, some fat,
Some in showbiz, some in art,
But nobody who isn't smart:
The odd dee-jay, a nob or two,
Perhaps a senior minister who
Might put in a word with the PM
To set him on his feet again.
To all he offers his winking eye
And large helpings of his shepherd's pie
Washed down with bubbly, cold and fizzy,
Never relaxing, always busy
But how he wishes that he were
In Grantchester, in Grantchester!
And as he beams to all these sorts
Harken to his secret thoughts:
God! I will pack and take a train,
And get me to Grantchester again!
I only know that you may lie
Day long beneath the Cambridge sky
(But would I lie? Oh NO! These lips

13

Are full of facts and tips and quips
But no lie has passed between 'em
Overstatement . . . yes, ahem)
But to thrust your book into the charts
Demands the exaggerating arts,
While latest sales figures buzz and burr,
Through the fax machine in Grantchester.
Ah, Grantchester! In Grantchester
I feel my latest novel stir:
Two men one rich, one poor
No: both rich, and above the law,
Each plotting to kill the other
Then: 'Hang on! Aren't you my brother?!'
Or perhaps three deadly foes
(No make that four: who knows,
With four the book could well be longer,
The chances of a series stronger)
Who kidnap each other and in the end
Each foe becomes the other's friend.
For sure, a good twist in the tale,
Does much to boost a healthy sale:
Maybe the hero could turn out a rogue
(The anti-hero's much in vogue)
Or the rogue become a hero
Allowing my silver pen to zero
In along my favourite tack
The guy who's been To Hell and Back
A bit like me! ('Did I ever tell you, Frank,
About the letter from the bank
Asking for a half a million quids!?
Well, frankly, Frank, I was on the skids,
Resigned my seat, did the honourable thing,
Then gave my publishers a ring,
Sat myself down and wrote a book,
Sold a million, and now look
Smart-suited, cheery, nicely tanned
I'm the richest author in the land!
Yes, I'm like a character from my fiction,
With simple grin and simpler diction,
Next to me, my characters seem real
Tell me, who would ever steal
Jeffrey Archer for a plot?
No reader would believe such rot!')

A cardboard cut-out! Untrue to life!
If you cut him with a knife
He would not bleed so much as crumble
And have you seen him playing Humble?
He comes on like Uriah Heep,
Resembling more a smirking creep!
('Good question, Frank, now ask another:
Do you know about my mother?')
God! I will pack, and take a train,
And get me to Grantchester again!
And Cambridgeshire, of all England,
The shire for Men Who Twitter Bland
But Grantchester! ah, Grantchester!
There's peace and holy quiet there'
(Not my rhyme, ed: if you take a look,
You'll see it comes from Rupert Brooke.
His rhymes are full of wishful thinking,
His homesick thoughts so often sinking
Into sentimental reverie, eg,
'And is there honey still for tea?')
In Grantchester their skins are white:
They plug by day, they plug by night,
Practising journos' Christian names:
Frank, Libby, Melvyn, Jemima, James,
Must make sure they don't ignore yer
(Breathe not a word about Victoria!
Two thousand to an unknown vagrant!
Nonsense! With a wife so fragrant!)
The women here do all they ought;
The men observe the Rules of Thought.
They love the Good; they worship Truth;
And did you know my name's Babe Ruth?
Ah God! To see the branches stir
Across the moon at Grantchester!
(That rhyme's better, but didn't Rupert err
Attempting to rhyme 'stir' with 'ster'?)
Amidst the chirp of yellow-hammer,
The author struggles with his grammar:
'The villain that was with his gun
What fell when he begun to run
Wished for his revenge and fast
And all because of what had passed
Between them and him and her and he.

He got hit twice, and then he flee,
Saying as he began to die:
'You may get her but you won't get I!'
'My goodness, what a ripping yarn'
Thinks Jeffrey, but then 'Oh! Darn!
Perhaps that 'I' should be a 'me'
And ought that 'him' to be a 'he'?
And perhaps that 'flee' should be a 'fled'
And that 'saying' should be a 'said'!'
Oh! Who would be given the author's lot!
(Or should that 'given' be a 'got'?)
Say, does he still call Smith Square
To find out why he isn't there?
And does he charge about the place
(Forgetting now his fall from grace)
To rally Tories through the land,
Into giving him a helping hand
To regain Mrs Thatcher's ear
And perhaps oh gosh! be made a peer?
Say, does the digital watch still peep
To call the author from his sleep
And does he jog around the lawn
In track suit 'till the break of dawn?
Stands the church clock at ten to three?
And is there money still for me?

'At Ease'

The Carlton Club (Wallace Arnold I)

Might I add a small *postatis scriptatum* to the sundry farmyard noises that conspired to drown the merits of poor Mr Major's excellent Carlton Club speech on equality and classlessness? I regret to say that many of my fellow commentators on this newspaper, as on so many others, have been encumbered since birth by sizeable chips on their shoulders. Just because the portals of the Carlton Club are not thrown open to such inky representatives of the Great Unwashed as themselves, they exact their revenge by publicly suggesting that it is in some way an 'elitist' place, full of 'snobs' and 'upper class toffs'.

A correction, if I may. As has been widely reported, I have, for the past fifteen-odd years, enjoyed occupying the lustrous position of Hon. Entertainments Secretary to The Carlton Club. From this superb vantage point, I have witnessed a Carlton Club at ease with itself, a Carlton Club in which people rise through their own merits, good luck and hard work (particularly good luck), a Carlton Club which, in common with Mr Major, I have come to believe is a veritable paradigm (dread word!) for the British Society we both wish to create.

'Snobbish' indeed! I once saw Mr Jeffrey Archer walking down the main staircase, and even Lord Tebbit himself is a Member (though I hasten to add he has been discreetly dissuaded from using the Members Dining Room whilst others are eating, and a tapestry screen depicting Victorian hunting scenes is generally placed around him when he sits in the Library, as much for his own benefit as for the convenience of other Members). Poor Mr Major has, of course, been fully accepted as a Member, and will continue to be so right up until his very last minute as Prime Minister, when his immediate resignation from the Club will be accepted with the utmost regret. At the moment, he enjoys unrestricted use of the Club's facilities, though we do ask him to keep his voice low in the Upper Billiards Room, as complaints have been received from one or two of our elder members who have been disturbed by some of his more *outré* vowel sounds.

As I say, the Classless Society is already alive and kicking at the Carlton, and some of our major initiatives in this direction are at present being studied by the special task force from Central Office, led by Sir Norman Fowler, who has been granted temporary membership of the Club, provided that upon entry he removes the somewhat common and unsightly brass 'buckle' from his shoes and pursues his perambulations employing only the back staircase. As a fully-fledged Temporary Member, Sir Norman is, of course, welcome to enjoy luncheon at the Club on any weekday before 12 o'clock, on condition that he brings his own sandwiches and light refreshments and consumes them within the confines of the cubby-hole provided for that express purpose on the lower-ground-floor, one along from the boiler. The lavatory facilities of the Club are also at his disposal, though he has been expressly asked to give priority in this area to Full and Life Members who might wish to avail themselves before him.

I have it on good authority that Sir Norman and his team have been bowled over by the bold classless initiatives we have undertaken at the Carlton Club. To encourage a more relaxed atmosphere between Members and Staff, for instance, we have recently granted the Servants permission off kneeling during the pouring of Members' cocktails, and they now need only enter a room backwards, whereas before they had been obliged to depart backwards too. Also, any Member requiring a Servant to dress up in Maid's Clothing for purposes of a sound whipping must apply for written permission from the Secretary before so doing, though the same rule need not apply, of course, to Members who wish to dress themselves in Maid's Clothing, as long as they provide their own uniform, tip the Servant the recommended sum and confine their activities to the Lower Morning Room. These, you will agree, are all bold pioneering steps towards a classless society, and anyone wishing to help the Club in this important field should apply without delay to The Hon. Secretary (no tradesmen please).

'Authentic Lives'

Kate and Eilish Holton

Usually, one television programme leads on to another, and we take them as they come, unaffected by their random juxtaposition. A comedy can follow the news, and we don't find the comedy any less funny or the news any less serious. But on Tuesday night, after watching ITV's *First Tuesday*, a documentary about Irish Siamese twins, I switched over to Channel 4, where *Salute to Kirk Douglas* was about to begin. If I had seen them at different times on different nights, I would have made no connection between them at all. I might even have enjoyed all the corny back-patting on *Salute to Kirk Douglas*. But the *First Tuesday* documentary about the love and courage of an ordinary, unsung Irish couple and their struggle to do what was right by their Siamese twin daughters had the effect of withering the *Salute* into an unctuous sham.

The story *First Tuesday* had to tell was extremely harrowing. A day before Mrs Mary Holton gave birth, she was told by her doctor she must expect Siamese twins. It turned out that Kate and Eilish were joined all the way down from their shoulders to their abdomen, with just two legs between them. Before the programme began, I had been squeamish about watching it, but within minutes I was agreeing with Mary Holton when she said, 'I'm amazed at how normal it is.' The three-year-old twins were so pretty, and so cheerful, and each so individual, that one adapted to them in an instant; indeed, there were times – in a swing, blowing out candles on their birthday cake, in their high chair – when their togetherness seemed to make them sweeter than ever.

They were blessed to live in a friendly Kildare community which treated them with easy affection. The failings of Roman Catholicism are regularly – even relentlessly – portrayed on television, but its belief in the unique worth of each human being was gloriously alive in this community, and the sight of it was humbling. In the early part of the film, it was the matter-of-fact decency of ordinary people that was most touching. 'How are yez, girls?' chirruped the cashier at the local supermarket, smiling at their two little beaming faces.

For a year, a camera crew under the direction of Mark Galloway was at hand. The crew recorded the girls' progress – early words, movement classes, blowing bubbles – together with the hopes and fears of their parents. The great question shadowing Mary Holton and her husband Liam during this year was whether or not the girls should be separated. What risk, if any, should be taken? Was it simply social pressure, in a world formulated for individuality, that made separation seem so important? What if the risk were greater to one girl than the other? 'How do you carry that cross lightly, or with meaning?' was the way in which Liam summed up his spiritual quest. Throughout, he showed no trace of self-pity.

This was different from almost all the television I have ever seen, in that it added a dimension of seriousness to life rather than taking one away. In concentrating on the plight of Siamese twins, a part of the human race too small even to classify as a minority, the film managed to raise questions in my mind – questions about individuality, about love, about parenthood – far beyond the ostensible remit of its subject.

At the end of last year, the doctors advised the parents that, although the operation would be the most complicated of its kind ever undertaken, the chances of both girls surviving were very strong indeed. Eventually Liam and Mary decided upon separation: joined together, the twins' suffering would increase immeasurably with age and adulthood.

In the weeks leading up to the operation, the cameras showed the poor, brave parents trying to ease their children's way, showing them dolls joined together and then happily separated, keeping them cheerful through a fog of medications and injections and deprivations. 'After the operation, you can eat all the sweets you want,' said their father.

The documentary then leapt in time to a week or two after the operation. The news was very sad. 'Eilish turned her head to look where Katie had been and she cried,' said her mother. Kate, the more outgoing of the two, had died from heart failure four days after the operation. Through his sadness, Liam said that they drew comfort from knowing that both twins could have died from Kate's weak heart had they not been separated. A few weeks on, he said he felt that in a funny way Kate's spirit was living on in Eilish, who had acquired a new giggly, outgoing side to her personality.

The film was made all the more moving by the tact and reticence of the film-makers. Scenes that more mawkish and cynically 'caring' film-makers would have elbowed their cameras into – the minutes before the operation, for instance, or Kate's funeral, or the tears of the parents – were simply not shown. This wholly admirable propriety meant that sentimentality was eschewed. The lasting impression of this film was of the vast depths of grace to be found in one Irish couple. They are both of them, in their way, saints, in that their example, transmitted through the unlikely medium of television, can act only as a beacon for good. I can't remember ever being so affected by a television programme.

And then 10 minutes later, *Salute to Kirk Douglas* from the Beverly Hilton

Hotel. The occasion was the presentation of the American Film Institute's Life Achievement Award, 'the highest honour our industry can bestow. Ladies and Gentlemen – Mr Kirk Douglas!' The diners, painted and pomaded and polished to a sheen most morticians would envy, rose to welcome him, each mild swing of their dainty handclaps tugging ever so gently at the foundations of their facelifts.

'Kirk, you've raised four wonderful sons,' cooed Lauren Bacall. Michael Douglas, the most famous of the four wonderful sons, compèred the tributes, and then added a few more of his own. 'You put celluloid in our genes, Dad,' he said. Or perhaps he said, 'You put celluloid in our *jeans*, Dad,' for each of those wonderful sons looked unnaturally stiff, as if awaiting delivery to the front window of a leading department store.

'Dad, you gave us your drive, your caring and your hunger for excellence,' said Michael, introducing an array of clips, in all of which Kirk Douglas seemed to be exactly the same, bar the occasional change of costume to show that he was now, say, a Roman gladiator rather than a Chicago gangster. This astonishingly unvarying quality was described by the president of the Institute, whose name I did not catch, as 'a unique intensity'.

'There is only one Kirk Douglas', 'Kirk, you've given us some of the most powerful moments ever seen on the screen', 'Those of us who act, yearn to share a scene with you': the tributes came in fast, and very thick. The oddest gushers seemed to mistake his more heroic screen roles for his character. Thus, they would praise him for his lifelong struggle against tyranny, offering a clip from *Spartacus* as their evidence. Television has an eerie propensity to salivate over the bogus. *First Tuesday*'s Katie and Eilish proved that, once in a while, it can also pay tribute to authentic lives, in all their pain, and in all their glory.

'Bang Bang Bang'

Rod, Gun and Max

Anyone who has served time on a grouse moor will have noticed the peculiar collective personality that comes over the shooters. Recently, Martin Amis has shown the general reader how a darts board draws out the lout in man; now Max Hastings shows how a shoot draws out the buffoon in him.

With engaging honesty, Hastings recalls entries in his lifelong gamebook in which he urged himself to be less awkward, to fit in: 'If I want to get more invitations,' he wrote as a young man, 'I must learn to shoot straighter and fit into company more gracefully.' Perhaps just one more step in this campaign, his new book of essays fits in with aplomb. Whether read by the bedside, as the publishers suggest, or by the fireside, as the author suggests, *Outside Days* will make snug reading for the company of fishers and shooters and hunters. Those who have no understanding of field sports will find it a more baffling, even off-putting affair.

It is tactfully written in the language of the buffoon, mixing the bluff with the babyish, the hearty with the heartless. For a language that is constantly slapping itself on the back for its down-to-earthness, it is choc-a-bloc with euphemism. Birds 'crumple' after being 'dispatched' once you have 'taken a punt' at them. You 'joust' with a fish. The author writes of 'doing something like justice' to a pheasant, which means killing it. There is something almost camp about such banter. When Hastings applies it to women, the reader might well feel that he is reading the work of a wickedly satirical male impersonator, a latter-day Burlington Bertie. 'By far the most skilled and important challenge for the sporting wife,' declares Mucker Max, is to produce 'a delicately roasted partridge.' Such music-hall absurdity reaches fresh heights of sauciness with the declaration that, 'One of the tests of relationships in sporting households is to discover who does the plucking.' Boom! Boom!

The author has a passion for Victorian sporting literature, and places his own book in a line with this genre. He finds great happiness in the countryside and relishes adventure. He is a good writer, though overkeen on the comma. He might, then, have taken the genre one step further, exploring the elemental urges that lie behind rod and gun, and the deep, primitive satisfaction men gain from hunting in packs. Instead, he has retreated into pastiche; a good pastiche, but a pastiche nonetheless.

The shooting argot, which Hastings employs so gracefully, is the argot of the public-school prankster. Hastings writes of duffers and flukes and going the whole hog. A sweet photograph on the back of the book's jacket shows the author standing in waders, a large salmon in each hand, a bashful, lopsided smile playing over his boyishly spectacled face. This is a man on holiday from adulthood in a country full of Crunchie bars and japes and fellows who say 'Let's go and have a bang at quackers' when they want to kill a duck; a country where women act as school matrons to their charges; a country full of the laundered kiddie-speak of prep-school comics. 'Bang, bang, bang, bang' is one of the sentences in *Outside Days*, and so is 'Grrr'. 'But, heavens, it was fun!' is another. A comparable tone of voice can be found in the Duchess of York's new children's books about Budgie the helicopter.

The regressive instinct squares ill with the writing instinct, and throughout this book Hastings retreats from the possibility of a writer's perception into the blather of upper-class rah-rah. But occasionally a glimpse of the real oddity and complexity of field sports emerges from behind the blanket of clubbability. At one point, Hastings is in the midst of an exciting, Buchanesque description of stalking a stag. He shoots the stag and kills it. 'He walked two steps,' writes Hastings, 'lurched and keeled over to bounce in the heather. He looked at me once, from where he lay, as I came up to him, then that was that.' One half expects Alan Bennett to be chipping in with 'I got a glimpse of his face, and, you know he smiled', but in fact something far odder happens. Hastings sips coffee from a Thermos, and meanwhile, 'I talked to the beast as the sun started to appear over the hill, because I felt an intimacy with him at the moment that no grouse or trout could match.' From the world of Budgie the Helicopter, we are plunged into the strange, twilight world of Dennis Nilson, chatting away to those to whom he thinks he has done something like justice.

Small wonder that such a bizarre sport has clothed itself in the protective armour of English upper-class banter. Hastings gives us this armour, beautifully polished, but how much more interesting it would have been to take a look at the body it protects.

'Behold I am Vile'

Job's Resignation

My Dear Almighty,

Behold I am vile. It has been a great privilege to serve under you these past few years. I recall with particular pride the many personal kindnesses you bestowed upon me.

During my period as your faithful servant, I have had the honour to have a great wind come from the wilderness and smite the four corners of my house. It is with particular pleasure that I recall the fire you sent from heaven, burning up my sheep and consuming them.

Your generosity has known no bounds. I was especially grateful to have been the recipient of sore boils from the sole of my foot unto my crown, and I wish to personally thank you for clothing my flesh with worms and clods of dust as and when I needed them. During all these brave and far-reaching initiatives, I have been privileged to rent my mantle and fall down upon the ground and worship.

I thank you also for taking me up by the neck and shaking me to pieces. During my time in office, I have been happy to play my part in allowing you to put my brethren far from me, and mine acquaintance verily estranged from me.

As you know, I am now keen to pursue plans outside office, for my days are swifter than a weaver's shuttle, and are spent without hope. I now look forward to supporting future policies from the back-benches.

Yours ever, Job.

My Dear Job,

It was characteristically considerate of you to put your office at my disposal; throughout our time in Government together you have always been willing to abhor yourself and repent in dust and ashes, and this has gained you the respect of all your colleagues.

I should like to thank you most warmly for your unrivalled service in helping me to tread down the wicked in their place. Your contribution to the reception of sore boils, worm and clods of dust has been second to none. He that reproveth the Lord, let him answer for it.

I will greatly miss the extraordinary sense of humiliation and total self-abasement you brought to your time in office. With every good wish. We look forward to turning fresh terrors upon you in the very near future. Gird up now thy loins like a man.

Yours ever, Almighty.

'A Bit of a S★★t'

Alan Clark's Diary

Bumped into a ghastly little woman at reception the other night. Took her to be one of the waitresses; common as muck, foreign look about her, nasal voice, not a bad bust, decidedly alluring to be frank, tidy-poo hair-do, had her marked down as a cleaning lady, obviously fancied me something rotten, kept giving me the come-on by asking me questions of the 'What exactly is it that you do, ooh that must be interesting' variety.

Was just plotting to offer her tuppence ha'penny an hour to clean out the stables when I suddenly found myself getting the hots for her. Must have been her feet – two of 'em, one on each side, quite small, well shod, not bad at all. So I put my arm round her shoulder, volunteered her my broadest grin, and whispered into her ear, 'If you really want to know EXACTLY what I do, why don't we bunk up together for a few mins in a little Ministerial cupboard I spotted out in the corridor – let me 'Minister' to your every urge, know what I mean, hur, hur?'

At this point, an oik in pin-stripes sidled over to the cleaning lady and said, 'Your Majesty, may I present Lady someone-or-other?' Crikey, I thought, how utterly spastic of me – I've been trying to have it off with the Queen. Smack botties for Alan. Silly really, because I hardly ever fancy Krauts; no sense of humour. Mind you, if my memory serves, I rather think I had it away with that daughter of hers, Anne Thingummyjig, some time in the late 70s, bit of a boot face but quite a goer, and Margaret's quite a pole-vaulter, of course, and that Fergie looks a lot of fun in a tarty way, and Princess Michael could f★★k the hind legs off a grand piano, even if she is a bit of a nouve, and of origin unknown.

On the way to the Ministry, spotted a blind man plus begging bowl. Bit of a moral dilemma, but I finally removed the money from the begging bowl, stuck my tongue out at him and gave him a bloody good kick in the shins. Felt a bit of a s★★t, who wouldn't, etcetera, but what other options were open to one? I simply felt in all honesty I had to teach him a thing or two. This is the real world. It's no good all these snotty little liberal buggers getting on their high horses about this sort of decisive action if they can't come up with a half-way decent alternative. Lucky the poor bugger wasn't a blind woman, or it wouldn't only have been my tongue that I stuck out, arf arf!!

Saw that fat loathsome incompetent oaf Ken Clarke. 'Lovely to see you Ken,' I said, 'You're doing marvellously at the Home Office. Highly impressive. Keep it up.'

'Jolly nice of you to say so, Alan,' he replied, sick-makingly.

What a first-class hypocrite! What an utter five-star shit! The slimy toad must have known I didn't believe a word that I was saying. Yet without so much as blinking he came out with utter crap, piss and balls like: 'Jolly nice of you to say so, Alan.'

What a lying git! How pukey can you get? And how spassy and nouveau of him to think I wouldn't see through it! Who does he think I am?

Talking of ratbags, that Dalai Lama's a prize shit, oily and loathsome little creep of the first order, awful churchy holier-than-thou-air about him.

'What's your game then, baldie?' I said to him when we met at a parliamentary reception back in '89.

'Velly nice meety you,' he replied.

'Cut the cackle,' I said. 'Just tell me why you insist on poncing about like a prize ninny in those godawful robes. Who'd you think you are? Mrs Gertrude Shilling?!'

'Solly, no understandy,' he answered.

What a sanctimonious little charlatan, all smiles and deep bows and sweaty hands clasped together in prayer, talking non-stop balls. Nouve, too: no gentleman ever wears orange. I could see through him a mile off. 'I can see YOU never went to Eton!' I said – and that saw him off pretty damn quick.

At an opportune moment, I took Margaret Thatcher – never lovelier, good uplift to her bra, under-rated BTM too, oozing with controlled sexuality – to one side. 'See the little bloke over there, Margaret,' I whispered. 'Definitely not to be trusted. Been talking the most frightful gibberish about loving thy neighbour, learning to live together, not killing each other and similar complete balls. I think he must be up to something.'

'But who can we trust these days, Alan?' said Margaret, using my first name – a sure sign that a woman's trying to lure one under a table for a quick one-two.

I took the bull by the horns. 'Personally, Margaret, I've always thought Saddam Hussein seriously under-rated, but then when you've been a military historian as long as I have, you can't help but admire the fellow. He's got balls, Margaret. And missiles. Okay, so he might be a bit moody, but Christ, who wouldn't be, stuck in Bongo-Bongo land with only nig-nogs for company? But his heart's in the right place. If I were you, Margaret, I'd sack that fat spastic twerp Ken Clarke and put Saddam in the Cabinet. So it might not be popular with the pinko brigade, but what have they ever done for you?'

Her bountiful globes rose with her every breath. 'Yes, yes . . .' she said, distractedly, and motioned away from me with a nod of her head, a sure sign a woman's got the absolute hots and is gasping for it.

I arrived back home rather late that night – and between these four walls I wouldn't be at all surprised if Margaret didn't too! I'm not saying anything happened, but I'm not saying anything didn't happen either! She obviously loves a true aristocrat, a man of sophistication, class and understated distinction. Cwor! Oy, oy! Way-hay-hay! Wheeee!

Of all the disloyal little creeps, none come more disloyal than my fellow Ministers under Thatcher. What a shower! No sooner had I told everyone what the others had said behind closed doors, than they'd pass it on!

For instance, I once told Michael (Heseltine) that Tom (King) didn't think that Michael (Howard) thought much of the way Leon (Brittan) was going round telling tales on Willie (Whitelaw) for spreading rumours that Cecil (Parkinson) was gossiping about what Kenneth (Baker) had said to David (Young) about there being too much backbiting in the Cabinet – and he immediately went and told Norman (Fowler) who went and told Michael (Heseltine)! But then it's absurd to expect my own high moral standards to be reproduced in a Cabinet full of the most ghastly riff-raff, some of whom have only two houses, if that! No wonder they wouldn't let a man of my proven integrity and position into their oiky Cabinet! Am overcome by a mad urge to piss over the lot of them from a great height. Instead, decide to publish my diaries.

'Brush, Brush, Brush'

The Concerns of Alan Clark

This blissfully unpleasant book should do much to restore the reputation of Simon Raven; indeed, it is almost as if Alan Clark were once Raven's earthly representative at Westminster. The memoirs and diaries of other politicians carry the implicit message, printed over every page, 'Don't Blame Me'. The message of Clark's *Diaries*, darker, nastier, funnier, truer, is best conveyed in his own acid words: 'There are no true friends in politics. We are all sharks circling, waiting for traces of blood to appear in the water.'

The *Diaries* have already been attacked as unsound by his fellow politicians, notably David Mellor, who for some reason forgot to point out that his own character sketch on page 239 though short and in parenthesis is horribly to the point – '(. . .everyone loathes him).' Certainly, many individual politicians will curse at every mention of their names. The adjectives 'poor' or 'little' (little Douglas Hogg, little John Smith, poor dear Tam, little John Moore, poor old Jeremy Thorpe, oily little runt Hussein, etc, etc) are the very best that they can hope for. Clark's abuse of other politicians is made to measure. Dame Janet Fookes, for instance, is damned for her 'vast arse', David Penhaligon (on the day of his Memorial service) for cutting 'an unmemorable figure, really, with his (demi-bogus) West Country vowels and *homespun* philosophy' and Nigel Lawson for his dodgy coiffure: 'There is a suspicious henna tinge to his hair. Is he tinting, or rinsing?'

There are far more embarrassing revelations in the Clark *Diaries* than in all the other Ministerial memoirs of the Thatcher years put together. Reports of others 'blubbing' are frequent, including Jerry Wiggin on being sacked, and both Leon Brittan and Cecil Parkinson when things got too much for them at the Department of Trade and Industry. Even those rare beings touched by Clark's admiration find themselves equally damned in due course. I suspect that Lady Thatcher, the only politician Clark wholeheartedly admires, will flip through her references in the *Diaries* with growing irritation. Her courtiers would be best advised to shield her from the Clark account of the Westland crisis, in which he bursts out laughing after reading just a few paragraphs of her statement – 'I'm sorry . . . I simply can't keep a straight face' – before singing her praises for her 'shameless' performance: 'How *can* she say these things without faltering? But she did. Kept her nerve beautifully.' Later he tries to reassure the perplexed Ian Gow. 'Ian's trouble . . . is that he is, *au fond*, a man of honour. Personally, I don't give a blow. Lie if necessary.' Somehow, I doubt whether the Clark account of Westland will be inserted in the bibliography of Lady Thatcher's own memoirs, to be published in the autumn.

Yet I would guess these *Diaries* will unnerve most politicians less for their cracks at individuals than for their self-portrait of the terrors and drudgery of political life. Though adamant in his proclamations of social grandeur – vulgarly, almost desperately, (some might even say inaccurately) adamant – Clark is entirely conventional, even pooterish, in his Ministerial worries, soothed neither by wealth nor by aristocratic languor, made remarkable only by their very public admission. Stuck as a junior Minister, Clark is simultaneously bored stiff with each post and terrified that he will lose it. 'As for the Dept, I never want to go through its doors again. Total shit-heap, bored blue' he writes. Yet his dreams are pathetically similar to his nightmares. On holiday in Zermatt, 'I fantasised, deluding myself that I might be going to go "sideways" into Ray Whitney's old job.' This would have taken him to the full majesty of Parliamentary Under Secretary at the Foreign Office. Similarly, when he is with the Prime Minister, he is every bit as anxious for her approval as those he professes to despise. 'Yet she is NOT forthcoming to me. Distantly abandoned me in the lobby on entering, and started talking to Dykes of all people. She used to be so friendly when we were in Opposition . . .'

What is unnerving about these diaries is not their eccentricity, but their normality: Clark enjoys setting himself up as a pantomime devil ('Am I always to be thwarted? Surrounded by nincompoops and inadequates?') but, at least within the field of politics, the portrait he paints is really of just an average middle-ranker, huffing and puffing in the race for preferment, one foot always ready to trip over those who edge ahead. 'I retoy with the idea of supplanting him (Tom King), and promptly . . . My present solution is to move TK to Health, where he could be pinkly affable and repair some of the damage caused by my 'abrasive' namesake. But that could only happen if Clarke has a nervous breakdown – unlikely in one so fat – or – perfectly possible at any time, he must make the Norwich Union wince – something 'happens to' him. One mustn't be uncharitable (why not?) but this after all is the roughest game, at the roughest table.' Could this be Sir Norman Fowler, or Lord Whitelaw, or Lord Tebbit writing? Of course it could be, but it isn't: the bad fairy gave Alan Clark a career in politics; the good fairy gave him candour.

Two other points should be made, neither wholly apparent in the numerous Benny Hill-style extracts that have been serialised. The *Diaries* are often hilariously funny, and the footnotes, in particular, are comic masterpieces, beautifully juxtaposing the conventions of high seriousness with the lowest comedy. On page 110, for instance, he writes, 'Then I will walk again, saying brush'. An explanation comes in the footnote: 'The Clarks believed that when constantly (but inaudibly) saying 'Brush', the features compose themselves in an expression of benign concern.' Or the joke can be reversed, as on page 195 when he spots but fails to name 'that dreadful little tick with curly hair and glasses, four foot six or thereabouts, I've never seen him smile.' The footnote reads, simply and solemnly, 'Dave Hill, Director of Communications, Labour Party'.

And, as in the novels of Simon Raven, threaded through the human comedy – the sneering, the plotting, the blubbing, the ogling – is the stark thread of human mortality. Clark is forever counting the days to his death ('Two thousand? Three thousand at most') and looking in the mirror, grimly cataloguing his increase of jowls. The book is haunted, frighteningly and beautifully, by the ghosts of the First World War ('I can get carried back to the summer of 1914, or worse, the year following when the telegrams started to arrive thick and fast, pedalled up the drives of the Great Houses by sly sideways-looking postmen, and Kipling lost his only son at Loos'). A career in politics is ideal for those with a disposition towards death, for the struggle is so damnable, the peaks so footling, the final fall so assured. Out of office, politicians evaporate, leaving little trace that they were ever there. It is still possible to spot one ex-Prime Minister pottering through the Central Lobby in The Palace of Westminster. Few tourists can remember who on earth he is, and neither, it is said, can he. Alan Clark's one earnest political initiative, The Fur Labelling Order, was squashed flat on his desk by his great heroine and the furriers of Finchley. Politically, he is dead. But his *Diaries* stop time in its tracks, and will forever show, in their wicked delight, the ploys employed by a group of senior politicians in Westminster in the 1980s as they plotted and pranced and elbowed their various routes to oblivion.

'Chat Among Yourselves'

The Ballad of Dartington Hall

Daydream on miracles. What's the most wonderful possible one? Think of a small side-effect of it and carry it out yourself.

This was one of a hundred projects on a sheet of paper given out to the staff and pupils after a democratic meeting this summer. The list was entitled, 'PROJECT WEEK OR ANY WEEK TAKE THE BRAKES OFF YOUR BRAIN IF YOU DON'T LIKE THESE THINK OF SOMETHING BETTER GOFORITGOFORITGOFORIT-GOFORITGOFORITGOGOGO'.

If anyone at Dartington had daydreamed on disasters last year it is unlikely that their imaginations, so little acquainted with pessimism, would have come up with the Blackshaws. Lyn and Beth were the Christian names of the Blackshaws, but now they are just known as the Blackshaws. They are probably the only people ever to have passed through the school to have been condemned to this ultimate punishment.

Take any newspaper story. Go and see the people involved. Find out what really happened. Write the truth for once.

I went down to Dartington to see the school and also to find out what really happened. For half a day I was playing it by ear and asking about syllabuses and so on. Occasionally, a teacher or pupil would refer in passing to 'the Blackshaw business' or 'the awful summer' or even 'the dictatorship' before whizzing on to something cheerful. Early in the afternoon, the new headmaster, Roger Tilbury, blurted out, quite un-prompted, 'I expect you'll want to know more about the Blackshaw business but I'm afraid we're not legally allowed to talk to you about it. Both sides have signed undertakings not to talk about the other side.' I tried to look as if the thought of talking about the Blackshaws had never crossed my mind. Then he added, 'We wouldn't get into much trouble, but he would.'

Plan and carry out a legal publicity stunt. See how many inches you get in the papers.

The basic story, culled from the papers, was this:

CRIME AND SEX SHOCK
AT 'FREEDOM' SCHOOL
★ ★ ★ ★

THE HEAD'S NUDE WIFE
★ ★ ★ ★
HEAD QUITS OVER PORN PHOTOS
★ ★ ★ ★
BARE-ALL BETH IS BARRED
★ ★ ★ ★
DARTINGTON BOYS
ADMIT BURGLARIES
★ ★ ★ ★
EX-HEAD STILL AT SCHOOL
★ ★ ★ ★
NEW DARTINGTON HEAD CALLS ON
PUPILS TO MAKE IT A BETTER SCHOOL
★ ★ ★ ★

Adopt a threatened species. Make it your personal mascot. Figure out how to get it flourishing everywhere.

Roger Tilbury was the Deputy Head of Dartington for 14 years, and was twice passed over for the headmastership, before the trustees – without reference to the staff or pupils – made him and Eric Adams joint headmasters on Blackshaw's resignation. Adams is the school bursar and seems to carry less sway amongst the staff or pupils, tending to defer to Tilbury. Even on the touchy subject of how many places at Dartington remain unfilled, Adams says, 'You'd better ask Roger that one.'

Roger exudes dependability and, in the wake of Blackshaw, is quite content to lack charisma. He sings 'bom-di-bom' as he jumps down the stairs with a little both-feet-in-the-air leap at the bottom, wearing sandals with socks underneath. His office is reassuringly unimaginative, with a line of French textbooks, a filing cabinet, a maroon leather briefcase (with locks) and, on the wall, a school curriculum and paintings by pupils of cars and motorbikes. When he gets serious, he talks in the sociological jargon of the Sixties which the more conservative magazines always find so rib-ticklingly offensive. 'You can't end up with a dysfunctional community,' he says, concluding a forgotten point, and then he talks of validity and treadmills and orientation. He shares David Frost's habit of pronouncing 'T' like 'D', so that 'better' comes out as 'bedder'. The minute you set eyes on him you know that he has never and will never pose nude. 'Chat among yourselves, ho, ho,' he said, leaving me alone in his room, as he bounced off to talk to parents whose boy had had to be constrained the day before. He is a decent man with an appreciation of the ridiculous. We were going to send Koo Stark to take photographs of Dartington, and when told of this he laughed enthusiastically. The next day, he rang me up apologetically and told me that the pupils had so disapproved of the idea that he was afraid he'd have to say no.

Despite his conventionality his commitment to the ideals and practice of Dartington is quite obviously absolute. What are those ideals? 'Other people believe that children are evil and must be prevented from making choices because they'll choose wrong. We believe and expect them to be reasonable for most of the time, and we allow as much freedom of choice and freedom from an imposing authority as possible.

'. . . people always foist on us the question of how many children get to university. Well, actually, quite a few (last year 18 out of 28 in the sixth form). But we think we'd be failing in our duty to the children if we stuck rigidly to the O-level, A-level and university treadmill.'

Tilbury blames the 'stranglehold' of exams on the diminution of progressive education in recent years. Two progressive schools – Wennington and Monkton Wyld – have closed, and many which were once considered progressive – such as Bedales and Frensham Heights – he now refers to scornfully as 'Liberal Grammar Schools'. 'But there's obviously a market for that sort of thing, so good luck to them.' He believes that another reason for there being fewer and fewer progressive schools (only five in the whole of Britain, according to senior master David Gribble) is that, since Dartington was founded, in 1926, other schools have incorporated many of its original ideas, such as co-education, an arts department, no corporal punishment and persuasion rather than coercion. During the worst days of 'that awful summer' he admits he thought that Dartington might be the next to go. Now he does his best to exude a cheery confidence, but 10 per cent of children were removed by their parents during that awful summer, and others have shied away since. He was a little furtive about giving me exact figures, but it seemed that the maximum capacity of the school is 270 pupils, and, this summer, they had only 210.

Check out the local council bylaws. Find an abysmally stupid one. Find out what you would have to do to get it changed. Go for it.

Most of the rules at Dartington concern the procedure for getting the few real school rules changed or abolished. The real school rules include: 'No one will be allowed to keep a car at school unless they have passed their driving test.' All school rules go through Senate, which consists of staff and elected pupils, and, to quote the school's somewhat ambiguous prospectus, 'all the School's 20-odd basic rules have been voted through Moot at some stage'. Moot consists of as many of the staff and pupils who want to attend. Post-Blackshaw, there have been three amendments to the rules of discipline, tightening up on drugs and stating, 'Crimes against people are intolerable in the school . . . Complaints against individuals over such things will be considered by a group, including the pupil, the tutor and the Houseparents. The pupil will have a right to have a friend present at the meeting and parents will be informed of the outcome or may be asked to be present.'

Sex, so loved and loathed by Fleet Street, does not appear to feature in the school rules at all. An old girl I spoke to told me she loved everything about Dartington except for the compulsory sex, but, when I raised the topic late in my visit, Roger Tilbury did his best to suggest nonchalance. 'The sexual temperature at single-sex schools is a lot higher than in co-educational schools,' he said. 'By and large, inter-pupil disapproval deters people from going too far. They know it disrupts a group if two of them start having an affair, so generally speaking they don't.'

But what if two sixth-formers wanted to consummate their relationship? What would he do? He paused, thinking hard. 'It obviously depends on the quality of the relationship, but if two pupils had a deep and loving relationship and were dead set on pursuing it further . . . well, what would I do? Hmmm. If I really believed it to be a deep and loving relationship, I think that after consultation with their parents I . . . I . . . I might advise them to get a flat in Totnes and become day pupils. Or something of the sort.'

Take the headmaster's role for a week. Report on it. Take any other role for a week. Report on it.

The children can wear what they like and say what they like. As I was walking along with Roger Tilbury, a group of children started teasing him about his James Bond-type sunglasses. I would like to have joined in but I was too scared. He took it in good heart, smiling bravely. I know that they would have teased him, and he would have smiled bravely, whether I had been there or not. The children's clothes are very varied, though no-one is outlandish enough to wear a tie. A pretty 12-year-old girl was wearing a T-shirt dress with large letters printed on it saying 'WOMEN ARE ANGRY'. Roger Tilbury later told me that her mother had given it to her. The girl had recently worn it to a school concert and a shy Welsh mother, noticing it, leant over to Tilbury and said, 'I expect men are a little peeved too.' Most people were wearing jeans and there seemed to be a crazelette for girls to wear jewels on the side of their noses. Some of the classrooms had been painted by pupils. The maths room was bright blue with various murals of cats. In large letters on one wall it said: 'Cheap labour by Occi Saya and Mole'. 'Who's Mole?' I asked one of the children. 'Oh, he used to be a skinhead,' I was informed. Most of the boys' haircuts were shortish, as is the norm in the outside world, but I noticed one girl whose hair was half shaven and half bright purple. She had a sensible-looking face. Two boys I spoke to said that after last summer they had been thinking of selling Dartington Hall T-shirts to the public.

There is a lot about Dartington which looks the same as a lot of other public schools – the building, the remoteness, the classrooms and corridors and loos. The clothes are an obvious difference, and you can approve of them or disapprove of them but their obviousness is a distraction from the fundamental difference between Dartington and other schools. I had never before been to a school where there was no suggestion of fear: no one to find you out, nothing to be found out for. I had expected to cram this article full of first-class jokes about liberalism run wild. It has run wild, and there are first-class jokes to be cracked – jokes about jargon, about misplaced trust, about a passé belief in free expression, about the Blackshaws, about poor-to-average exam results, about a chink here and there in the armour of progressiveness – but perhaps to give children childhood, to suggest to them that their choices are more varied than to beat or be beaten, is worthy of something a little more gracious.

Find a bit of wasteland in a dirty city. Landscape it.

'This school is for adventure', were the opening words of the first prospectus for Dartington when the school was opened in 1926. It was founded by the American millionairess Dorothy Straight and her husband, primarily because they couldn't find a suitable school in England to educate their own children. 'The Devil has left Moscow and come to live in Dartington', the Bishop of Totnes said from the pulpit during the first year. Straight away, many progressive thinkers – among them Aldous Huxley and Bertrand Russell – sent their children to Dartington. At the moment, famous parents include the bass guitarist of Led Zeppelin, Jeremy Sandford and the late Joseph Losey. On the question of famous ex-pupils, the teachers are a little tetchy. 'A lot of people ask about famous Old Dartingtonians,' Roger Tilbury told me, 'but it's not a game that we're into. We don't judge our success, or our pupils' success by the standards set by the outside world.'

When another teacher asked me whether I'd send a child to Dartington, and I said that I'm sure any child would have a great time there, but what about afterwards? he replied, 'It depends on your social values. You shouldn't send a child here if you'd be worried if he ended up looking after syphilis victims in the East End.'

Perhaps because they still feel under siege, the teachers tend to overstate their case, and if one smiles in the wrong place they quickly clam up. 'Are there any old Dartingtonians on the staff?' I asked Mrs Tilbury over lunch. 'Let me see,' she replied. 'No, not at the moment. At least not on the teaching staff. There are one or two on the domestic staff.' I waiting for a smile from her. It didn't come. I nodded diligently.

There are a lot of beards in the staffroom, a lot of them hidden behind copies of the *Guardian*. There are also a lot of children in the staffroom, lingering quite happily. I was sitting in the staffroom drinking a cup of coffee when a child came up and put me through a questionnaire on smoking. One of the few rules at Dartington concerns smoking. It is not banned, of course, but there are certain non-smoking areas, and there have been calls from some of the children to have these extended. 'By and large, the children are much more reactionary that we are,' one teacher told me. 'They are often lobbying to increase restrictions, and they tend to be much more vindictive when it comes to fining for anti-social behaviour.' The staff are more liberal. Their cars have stickers saying things like 'Ecology Party'.

Identify what you think is the very worst/nastiest/most screwed up aspect of the world as you understand it. Identify the very first step you can take to doing something about it. Take the step. See what happens. Can you take another?

'I still suffer from success orientation,' Roger Tilbury confessed to me as we went on a tour of the school's facilities. His own son, Nathan, works in one of the shops in the Dartington Hall Estate. 'He enjoys contact with people. He's not into the money game or the success game.' His reticence in condemning the more conventional public schools where the success and money games prevail is not shared by the rest of his staff. In the staffroom, the mere mention of Denis Silk, the headmaster of TV public school Radley, produces screams and guffaws. David Gribble, the Old Etonian senior master at Dartington, seems the most passionate enemy of the traditional public school. He once taught at Repton, but left after a boy he had reported for eating a sweet in class was then caned for the offence. 'I remember once at Repton a master obviously lost concentration while writing a boy's report and wrote by mistake, "I could do better." I think that he'd unintentionally hit upon a truth about himself and his position. At Dartington, when a child does badly, we question our own ability to create conditions in which he will thrive.'

Roger Tilbury showed me along a corridor where an educational poster on reproduction was illustrated by two humans copulating, into the biology department. 'As you know, we don't set much store by medals and prizes, but we were all pretty excited by this.' He pointed out a certificate announcing that Dartington Hall had won the first prize for bee-keeping in the Devon County Show.

Because the outside world believes in success and money orientation, there is a ravine between it and Dartington, a ravine crossed rarely, and then only by bees. Committees have recently been set up to bridge this gap, with five teachers and three pupils on each committee. I asked a group of children what the committees were. 'Living – that's to do with the environment – learning, caring, spending, and erm, what's the other one?' 'Selling, or something like that.' Occasionally, the real world intrudes. During lunch, a boy got to his feet and announced to the assembled school that his bicycle had disappeared and unless it had been returned to its former position by the end of the day he would be contacting the police. 'We always think that letting the children make their own announcements informally works much better than channelling everything through a member of staff,' explained Roger Tilbury.

Invent your own religion. Draw on available ones if you want.

Leaving the dining-room, with its choice of peanut butter or chocolate spread for tea and its colour photographs of last year's school trip to the Glastonbury Festival behind me, I loitered by another noticeboard.

Guest Service in Totnes United Free Church

'You are invited if your previous experience of church has bored you to tears if you believe in God but don't think that going to Church is particularly important . . .

Tessa Peggy Len Oliver Judy'

Next to this notice were others advertising new choices in classes: 'Vegetarian Cookery Course' 'How to buy and maintain your first car'. On the land near the geography classroom, a Malaysian pupil was pointed out to me. 'He keeps chickens and sells the eggs to the staff,' I was told.

Would I send my child there? This was the question they all kept asking, staff and pupils alike, when they began to realise that I was friendly to their aims. I would consider it as seriously as I would some other public schools. If one's child is eventually going to fall to Earth, will it make him less or more happy to have known Eden?

At the end of my first day at Dartington, Roger Tilbury offered to drive me to my hotel. His car was parked in front of the school. I accepted. He reached for his keys and unlocked the car.

Postscript: Not long after my visit to Dartington, a pupil was murdered by an outsider. Within a few months, the school was closed down.

'Colonic Irrigation'

Fergie's Whoosh (Wallace Arnold 2)

I fear that faced with Miss (Ms!) Lynn Barber 'sounding off' (dread words!) on the page opposite we are none of us going to get much peace o'er our bacon, eggs and bangers upon a Sunday morn. Frankly, I ascribe that lady's desire for shocking and 'poking fun' to those far-off years when, as wife of Mr Heath's Chancellor of the Exchequer in the early Seventies (disagreeable decade!), she was expected to bottle up her emotions and keep smiling.

Still, there was little excuse in a family newspaper for Barber's unseemly revelations last week concerning the admirable Duchess of York. If the Duchess has indeed signed on for a course of 'colonic irrigation', that is strictly between her and her irrigators. I myself have made it perfectly clear from the start of this affair that I have not the slightest intention of prying into whatever may or may not go on in the sensitive area of the Duchess's rear quarters.

I am glad to note that other senior commentators have followed my lead. Bernard Levin, for instance, in his trenchant defence of Wagner last Wednesday, made only a passing reference to the revelations, comparing the final triumphant chorus of the assembled Valkyrie in *The Ring Cycle* to the 'glorious whoosh – at once cleansing and victorious – that one might expect to hear emerging through the door of the Duchess of York's specialist during a successful colonic irrigation'. Wisely, he ignored the matter entirely on Friday in his trenchant tour-de-force on apartheid, merely stating towards the end of a closely-argued piece that, in the new South Africa, comparatively minor issues such as compulsory seat-belts, restraints on tobacco advertising and the pros and cons of the colonic irrigation of the Duchess of York would probably take low priority in the debating chamber.

That most sensitive yet forthright of opinion-formers, Mr Paul Johnson, has also seen fit to leave the issue tastefully to one side, urging readers to make up their own minds and to write to their MPs. In his only piece directly tackling the question, headed, 'An Entirely Private Matter', he argued persuasively that 'it is only too easy to pour cold water on the Duchess'. He then went on to suggest that forcible colonic irrigation could well hold the answer to the 'so-called joyriding, wanton vandalism and downright thuggery that is now rampant in our inner-cities. In future, the British Bobby on the beat must be armed with the very best anal syringe that the finest British craftsmanship can provide'.

In a more whimsical piece for *The Spectator*, Johnson defiantly wrote of other issues entirely. Previewing his forthcoming exhibition of watercolours, he revealed that 'the imagination of the watercolourist is instinctively drawn to the copse and the vale, to the play of sunlight upon water, to the ripple of wind through the wheat field and, in my own case, to the supreme visual pleasure of the colonic irrigation of one of the nation's most bonny young Duchesses.' He was otherwise at pains to avoid any mention of the matter.

My old *confrère* and quaffing partner Peter Jenkins, who keeps his ear well to the ground, revealed in our sister newspaper that 'sources close to Mr Major confirm that he has not yet ruled out the possibility of discussing with his Cabinet the colonic irrigation of the entire Royal Family'. Peter admitted that it was 'a vexed issue' which 'could not be swept under the carpet'. However, he did not expect to see it on the Agenda at Maastricht, at least not in the first few days.

Peter's rival columnist on *The Daily Telegraph*, Bill Deedes, devoted his Tuesday piece to an unashamedly nostalgic look at the enemas of days gone by. 'A lot of nonsense is talked these days about "class",' he began. 'Well do I remember that marvellous sense of community spirit that existed during the General Strike. People from all stations would pop into each other's houses after luncheon (or "dinner") and before dinner (or "tea") to offer one another colonic irrigation. In those far-off days of colonic camaraderie, it was still true to say that one's neighbour's enema was one's truest friend . . .' I only hope that the tabloid press follows Bill's sensitive handling of this delicate matter in the weeks to come.

Compare and Contrast

Meg Mortimer and Margaret Thatcher

Earlier this week, Michael Fallon MP attacked the television drama series *Neighbours*. He claimed that it was junk, that it dulled children's senses, and that they would be better off doing their homework. In a rare display of solidarity, Labour's shadow education secretary Jack Straw agreed, dismissing the series as 'pretty trashy'.

I myself was brought up on the predecessor of *Neighbours*, *Crossroads*. This, too, was often attacked by politicians. Only Mrs Mary Wilson had the courage to break ranks, writing an enthusiastic foreword to *My Life at Crossroads* (1975) a memoir by the show's star, Miss Noele Gordon. Headed *10 Downing Street, Whitehall*, her foreword notes that 'many women see Noele Gordon in the character of Meg Mortimer as the type of woman they themselves would like to be – understanding, sensible, able to cope with any situation'.

Oddly enough, if I compare what I remember about *Crossroads* to what I remember about geography homework, *Crossroads* emerges the clear winner. I have a recurring nightmare in which I am faced with a geography exam full of questions such as 'Explain, with use of diagrams, the workings of a Blast Furnace' or 'Describe day-to-day life on a coffee plantation in Kenya'. I stare at the exam paper in blank horror. If, on the other hand, I were to be faced with an exam paper headed '*Crossroads* 1969-77' ('Compare and contrast the characters of Amy Turtle and Bernard Booth giving dates where applicable' 'Describe day-to-day life in the Crossroads Motel hair salon, with particular reference to the relationship between Diane and Vera') I have every confidence that I would still, fourteen years on, gain at very least a beta plus.

(At this point, I should state my educational advantages. During the period in question, I lived in Hampshire, on the borders of Southern and Thames Television. By some much-envied freak of the airwaves, we were able to watch the same episode of *Crossroads* twice every evening, first on Southern at 5.00p.m. and then, by a twiddle of the knob, again on Thames at 5.25p.m. Our house was rightly known at the time as the Peterhouse of *Crossroads* studies.)

No doubt such revelations will cause grief to Mr Fallon. But is knowing all about a fictitious Midlands Motel (or, in the case of *Neighbours*, a fictitious housing estate in the suburbs of Melbourne) any less use than knowing all about Blast Furnaces and Kenyan Coffee Plantations? If only Mr Fallon had spent more hours with the former and less with the latter, he might have gained insights into the political life that would prepare him well for the years ahead.

During the year or so I spent writing the Parliamentary Sketch for *The Times*, I was struck by how both MPs and political journalists were infinitely less interested in what Mr Benn calls 'the issues' than in the classic soap-opera question, 'What happens next?' Every day would see some new twist to the plot – will he resign? has he been silenced? who will take her place? – and everyone would wait, spellbound, for the next episode. That the scripts were junk and the acting pretty trashy, was, by and large, irrelevant: what mattered was the neverending story.

The character of Mrs Mortimer, the well-turned-out, coping proprietor of Crossroads, was, I think, a precursor of the character of Mrs Thatcher. The parallels between the two verge on the uncanny: apart from obvious physical and sartorial similarities, both had difficult children, a boy and a girl, both had millionaire businessman husbands, both spent their time fighting takeover bids, both relished a challenge, both had to deal with tantrums from male colleagues ('What's up with 'im, then?' Meg's son Sandy would always be saying as yet another senior member of her staff stormed out of her sitting room, rudely slamming the door) and, alas, both were to find themselves unexpectedly written out of the plot when the ratings began to plummet.

Incidentally, it might interest Mr Fallon to know that, following the dismissal of Mrs Mortimer, *Crossroads* never recovered. Within a couple of years, it was dropped completely. Those of us who forsook our homework for the University of Unreal Life have learnt to deal with such upsets. But poor, swotting Mr Fallon (majority: 2,661) has been sheltered for so long from the cut-and-thrust of soap opera that I fear that for him, as for so many other Conservative MPs, The End may well come as a shock.

Postscript: Michael Fallon lost his seat at the next General Election.

'CounterBlasts'

Maggie Drabble and the Mortgage Tax Relief

Chatto & Windus is shortly to publish a series of polemical pamphlets called 'CounterBlasts'. Among the most enticing must surely be the forthcoming pamphlet on Property and Mortgage Tax Relief by leading novelist Margaret Drabble.

Readers can avoid overnight queues by reading today's exclusive extract.

Chapter One

It was January 9, 1989, and all England, that fractured, divided and broken land, seemed to be talking of one subject, one feature, one item. 'What about that Anthony Howard leaving the deputy editorship of *The Observer*, then, madam?' said Liz's fishmonger. 'Shocking business, eh? Shocking.'

Liz gazed into the fishmonger's mirror; a solitary fly buzzed around its circumference, jaded, dispirited, perhaps suicidal. The face which looked back at her had lost its use, warts protruded from the nose, a bushy moustache could be detected above the lip. It was the fishmonger's face. Would life have been better, more good, gooder, if she had been a fishmonger rather than a best-selling novelist married to a leading biographer, wondered Liz.

Hadn't Kierkegaard – Soren Kierkegaard – written something on the topic, the theme, the matter? She would probably never know.

The clouds parted ruthlessly as Liz stepped out on to the pavement, cruelly disgorging a burden of rain. 'Hello, Liz; how's James?' It was Charles, who had married Suzie on the rebound from Claudia. Liz had never forgiven Charles's second wife, Karen, for what Rupert, her third son, had done to Jemima after he had left Claudia, who had not recovered from divorcing Frank after his all-too-public affair with Araminta, abandoning Heriot to a lifetime of loneliness with Geoffrey. Still, life was like that.

'The Falklands War is so horrible, so very horrible,' said Charles, his face wracked with misery. 'How long do you think it will last, Liz?'

'It finished seven years ago, Charles,' said Liz. Time seemed to mean nothing to Charles these days.

'That's super news,' said Charles.

'Why don't you come to a party tonight I am giving with my current husband, Tom?' asked Liz. 'It is on the theme of Property and Mortgage Tax Relief. Dress Casual.'

Chapter Two

The tide of the country is flowing to the right, thought Liz, as, that late evening, that early night, that post-duskish part of the day when the world seems to erupt in an iridescent, timeless yet volatile phase of tranquillity and harmony, she placed some Estee Lauder Skin Softener Applique No 6 on her right cheek preparing for the party.

Downstairs, her guests were already enjoying the avocado and whelk dip, words fluttering between them like avaricious hamsters.

Esme Pricket, the Kleinian analyst, was wearing her Ralph Lauren sarong, real diamonds sparkling in her ears, as she spoke of the iniquity of home ownership to Melvin Osprey, the editor of the influential weekly *Serious Issues*, whose third wife, Louise Parfait, the famous actress, was discussing mortgage relief with dynamic television presenter Brian Shallow and his mistress, Melissa String, the darts commentator.

'I wonder if the concept of evil can be maintained in a truly socialist society,' pondered Nigel, as he helped himself to an anchovy vol-au-vent.

Chapter Three

'The wonderful thing, wotsit, thingamajig, about your parties, Liz,' said Hubert Nash, five-times-married theatre director, whose current production, an all-mime version of *A Long Day's Journey into Night*, had divided, separated, split the critics, 'is that they are not so much parties as intense discussion groups. Now tell me, what do you think about the dependency of a have and have-not economy on the oppressive leverage of mortgage interest rates?'

Outside, the tremulous roar of the moon seemed to cast its sonorous impact on the freshly mown lawn, the recently-dead grass lying twisted and mauled, ravaged for a reason it knew not, nor would ever know. In many ways, thought Liz, it echoed the mood of the nation.

'A handful of the wealthy is being subsidised by this divisive government while the poor are getting poorer, less well off, more out of pocket,' said Frank, as he slipped his right hand into Liz's white lace bra, bought at a Harvey Nichols sale in 1984.

The words of Liz's fishmonger, Bert, came back to her: 'Shocking business, shocking.'

Of course it was shocking, the squalor, the degradation, the misery that so many best-selling novelists felt in this nation, this country, this cluster of isles. Liz watched as Frank's left hand plunged in after his right hand in a vain attempt to release his little finger from a sharp piece of wire she should have seen to months ago. Beneath her, the floor seemed to shake and tremble with disgust at Thatcherism. But it was only Jemima, stepping on some cashew nuts, falling flat on her face. Life was like that.

'Critics Criticising Critics'

D. J. Taylor and The Literary Life

M r D.J. Taylor has written a book in which he attacks various literary critics, among them those who have attacked the critics on the *New Review*. Now Mr Taylor has himself been attacked in the reviews of his book. This means that we have a critic who is criticised for writing criticism of critics who have criticised other critics. In turn, the *New Review* often devoted pages to reviewing works of criticism, often by critics who disagree with a critic such as Leavis. So we in fact have a critic who is criticised for writing criticism of critics who have criticised other critics for criticising criticism of criticism.

This might be a little difficult for the general reader to take in all in one mouthful, so I have cut it up into handy little bites for the purposes of this introductory lecture on the nature of contemporary criticism. Here are the seven stages of criticism:

Stage 1: After a prolonged period of writer's block, the neglected novelist Burnt Oak writes his first sentence for more than 10 years: 'The cat sat on the mat.' His publishers, Totteridge and Whetstone, declare that this sentence is sufficiently long to be regarded as a short novella, and publish it accordingly.

Stage 2: In a book of criticism, Professor Hornchurch states that Burnt Oak's novella, *Cat*, in its 'audacious brevity, its resounding, essentially monosyllabic rhythm, its almost painfully brutish realism, constitutes the high mark of the work of a major, if in many ways minor, author'.

Stage 3: In the *New Review*, Professor Hornchurch's book is praised for its 'profound and often provocative criticism of post-war European culture . . . combining a love of the classics of Belgian neo-structuralism with a very real appreciation for the "brutish realism" of lesser known authors . . . a book to read and re-read, and perhaps even re-re-read'.

Stage 4: Two years later, the rumbustious critic Colonel Upminster Bridge, reviewing a selection from the now-defunct *New Review* in *The Spectator*, complains that the magazine was run by 'a corrupt Arts Council coterie of leftish writers, dedicated to thrusting their own cult of the unreadable on to an increasingly reluctant tax-paying public. This arrogant clique of die-hard obscurantists will be remembered for declaring as "profound and often provocative" the purely perverse.'

Stage 5: Mr D.J. Taylor, distressed at what he sees as the middlebrow conspiracy among critics on today's weeklies, attacks Colonel Upminster Bridge's *Spectator* dismissal of the *New Review*'s appreciation of Professor Hornchurch for 'petit-bourgeoise small-mindedness, the enforcement of out-moded conservative values of cosiness and decorum on to a world that has been made virtually incomprehensible by a decade of Thatcherism and the nuclear threat'.

Stage 6: Critic and travel writer Colin Dale, reviewing Mr Taylor's work of criticism in *The Sunday Times*, declares that it is 'ill-judged and naive, bitty and poorly conceived'.

Thus we arrive at the stage reached in the opening paragraph. But, of course, this is probably only half the story, for it will inevitably be followed by:

Stage 7: On a late-night television arts programme, Colin Dale's review in *The Sunday Times* is attacked by fellow critic Cromwell Road as 'intemperate and perhaps probably almost unnecessary'. Meanwhile, up-and-coming television critic Perry Vale watches the programme and, the following Sunday, devotes a space to take us to:

Stage 8: In which he wittily castigates Cromwell Road for his upper-class accent, disgraceful dress sense, his habit of crossing and re-crossing his legs and his 'incoherent splutterings against some new book or other'.

Stage 9: On a Radio 4 review of the week's television critics, Perry Vale is described as possessing 'an acidic wit and coruscating turn of phrase'. Hurrah! We have now reached the stage where a critic criticises a critic for criticising a critic for criticising a critic for criticising a critic for criticising a critic who has criticised critics for criticising the criticism of a critic's criticism. Of course, if Mr Taylor then complains about his treatment in print he will be a critic criticising a critic criticising a critic criticising a critic criti . . . but then this might only complicate matters.

'Dis Inderesdin Concept'

Arnold Schwarzenegger and Roger Scruton

Twenty years ago, it might still have been thought possible for a British Television presenter to extract gasps of wonder from his audience by telling them he was in New York. Now, with everything but the Queen's Christmas message beamed live from New York, everybody knows those days are over. Everybody, that is, except the presenters.

'Surely the most exciting city on earth – ladies and gentlemen, welcome to New York!' said Jonathan Ross on Monday, without, so far as I could detect, his usual undertow of irony. He then introduced live from New York, the most unexciting act on earth: Alma the Parrot Lady. Amid much kerfuffle, Alma dressed up her parrots to look a tiny little bit like Michael Jackson and Madonna. The audience struggled manfully to applaud. Ross looked suitably embarrassed and so, to their credit, did the parrots.

New York became even more exciting on Wednesday with the arrival of Terry Wogan (or was it a parrot dressed up to look like Terry Wogan?) In a bizarre example of keeping up with the Joneses, Wogan had also flown over to 'possibly the only place to be on the planet'. This was the opening of a grim-looking new celebrity restaurant in Manhattan to which Ross had not been invited. Half an hour earlier on Channel 4, the uninvited Ross had delivered a hardcheese commentary on the opening, concluding: 'Glad I stayed home in bed.'

Wogan sat opposite Sylvester Stallone, Arnold Schwarzenegger and Bruce Willis in a back room of the restaurant for half an hour while they joshed around in the sluggardly, butch manner they obviously feel contrasts so winningly with their divinity. I suspect a deal had been struck whereby the Wogan show guaranteed them 15 minutes to talk of nothing but the restaurant they were selling. No 15 minutes has ever lasted longer.

'It's a new kinda concept,' said Stallone.

'We have here dis inderesdin concept,' said Schwarzenegger.

'We got excited by the entire concept,' added Stallone.

And so they went on, while poor old Wogan sat opposite nodding nervous encouragement, cravenly giggling at their macho non-jokes, looking for all the world like the original man who fears having sand kicked in his face. If this is New York, how I long for Stoke Poges.

The Late Show's live coverage of the *Booker Prize* also had something of the air of a restaurant launch. Everywhere the camera turned, people were eating and drinking and wiping their mouths. Back in the studio for the heavyweight discussion before the announcement of the winner, the backdrop was an aerial view of yet more people eating and drinking and wiping their mouths.

Each year, the studio discussion of the Burper Prize features a Big Bad Wolf presumably chosen to keep all the little piglets on their toes. Last year it was Eric Griffiths, the year before Howard Jacobson. This year it was the poet Tom Paulin, who added a new dimension to the pantomime by sympathising profusely with the poor authors while simultaneously biting off their heads with gay abandon.

It was a performance of breathtaking hypocrisy. Paulin described William Trevor as 'repro and archaic', Martin Amis as 'bone-headed stupid', Timothy Mo as 'free-floating and tedious' and Rohinton Mistry as 'kind of tedious', before righteously declaring, after the presentation of the prize: 'It's terrible to see six writers thrown to the lions in this awful spectacle.' In a funny way, Paulin reminded me of Jeremy Beadle last week, telling Des O'Connor of the tremendous love he feels for those he so tenderly chooses to humiliate.

Of course, Martin Amis is himself a dab hand at abuse, and though he acted the fawn when interviewing Norman Mailer for *The Late Show* his Olympian *New Statesman* review of Angus Wilson in 1973 (' . . . the scruffiness of so much of the writing') haunted Wilson until his death last May. By that time, Wilson was something of a forgotten figure, though not half as forgotten as Nigel Williams sought to portray him in *Bookmark*.

Williams set out to explore how a writer's fame can nosedive within a matter of years. To push his point, he was forced to exaggerate the extent of Wilson's neglect. He staged a phone call to Wilson's hardback publishers, where a girl in the publicity office had never heard of him. He then tried to connect the isolation of Wilson's last days in a Bury St Edmunds nursing home with the Thatcher years and the backlash against liberal values.

As a thesis, it was just too pat. At the time of his death, Wilson had written no new novel for 11 years, hardly the fault of his publishers. Almost all his novels were still available in paperback. He had received his knighthood in 1980 when Thatcher was in power. The TV adaptation of *The Old Men At the Zoo* had been produced at the beginning of the 1980s, and at the end of the decade he had been the subject of a TV documentary. Such contradictions to his thesis Nigel Williams chose either to play down or ignore.

If Angus Wilson was neglected towards the end of his life, it was primarily because he wrote less, and he wrote less because of physical and mental deterioration, an awful state no government, however liberal, no publisher, however efficient, and no public, however loyal, could hope to cure. Nevertheless, the programme did serve as a memory of his enchanting presence and his great talent for mimicry ('Blood everywhere! Never laughed so much in my life!' he used to say, imitating his father returning from a bullfight), though it emphasised the cruelty in his writing at the expense of its far more evident humanity.

What outrage Angus Wilson would have felt at Roger Scruton, and what fun he would have had at his expense! There were times during Scruton's contribution to BBC2's series *Think of England* when I felt that Scruton must surely be a German spy parachuted into England with snow still on his boots, dutifully mouthing patriotic catchphrases swiftly acquired from some outdated primer. Roaring around on a motorbike, his anger buttoned up, Scruton spoke stridently through pursed lips in his odd, clipped vowels, about how 'we English' are so very gentle, unassertive and averse to extremes.

'Our weather has made us patient, phlegmatic and gentle ... Our landscape is like us – varied and individual but unassertive . . . In its subdued pageantry, its uniforms and its phlegmatic togetherness, the brass band represents something typically English.' It was as if Scruton had learnt all he knew of the English countryside from a close reading of the early works of Godfrey Wynn. If only an aeroplane had suddenly appeared through the typically English clouds, I felt sure he would have been flushed out, and we would have caught him screaming '*Schweinhund! Donner und Blitzen!*', shaking his fists to the sky. Alas, nothing appeared to interrupt his recitations of such nonsense as 'We English expect a show of dignity when it comes to Evensong.' I would advise those of my fellow country-dwellers who live in terror of the approach of Scruton's motorbike to switch around all local sign-posts at the earliest possible opportunity.

I would guess that Professor Scruton is not among the addicts of *Blind Date*. 'Hello and welcome to the day we've all been waiting for,' said Cilla Black, introducing the *Blind Date Wedding of the Year*. Alex and Sue, who met on Blind Date in 1988, were getting married. 'So follow me, gang!' said Cilla.

For most of us the prospect of kicking off our wedding day with Cilla gasping, 'This is it. The big day has arrived. So how're yer feelin'?' exists only in the realm of nightmare, but it seemed to further Alex's happiness. While he was vowing to love and to cherish, there was Cilla beaming over his left shoulder. The whole programme should have been ghastly, but in fact it was defiantly sweet and rather moving, showing that true love can conquer all, even primetime TV.

'Do You Live Here?'

Michael Heseltine (Political Sketch 1)

'Can I say hello to you, I'm Michael Heseltine, do you live here?' Mr Heseltine was pacing the length of Kensington High Street struggling to find someone – anyone – able to vote in the Kensington by-election. Striding due east from Safeways, men from the local party offices with microphones and portable telephones running hard to catch up with him, he would not let anyone pass.

'Can I say hello to you, I'm Michael Heseltine, do you live here?' Alas for Mr Heseltine, those who live in Kensington seem wise enough not to tackle its High Street for fear of heavy traffic, bustling crowds and looming politicians. Seeing the approaching chariot, the arm of Michael Boadicea outstretched in front, innocent passers-by would dart into the nearest shops. But others did not see him in time.

'Can I say hello to you, I'm Michael Heseltine, do you live here?' A security guard had been caught. 'Ye-es,' he said, visibly shaken, and the Conservatives surrounded him. A local at last! 'Ooh, good,' said Mr Heseltine, shaking and re-shaking the security guard's hand: 'May I introduce your Conservative Candidate, Mr Dudley Fishburn?'

There was no stopping them now. Mr Fishburn thrust out his hand. 'So whereabouts in Kensington do you live?' he asked. 'Shepherd's Bush,' replied the security guard. 'Ah,' said Mr Heseltine. 'Ah,' said Mr Fishburn. 'That's just outside our area,' said Mr Heseltine, 'Nice to meet you.'

Onwards, ever onwards, in search of a Kensington resident, the wheels of high politics span mercilessly round. Five elderly women at a bus stop found themselves unable to escape. 'Can I say hello to you, I'm Michael Heseltine, are you going somewhere by bus?' Having isolated their motives with uncanny precision, Heseltine pressed on with his interrogation. 'And you live here, do you?' No, they all lived at the other end of the bus route. 'Oh, well, nice to meet you.'

'Can I say hello to you?' Recognising the familiar face from the television screen, two men with moustaches dived into the safety of the Arab Bank. The familiar face looked elsewhere. 'Do you live here?' No, everyone lived somewhere else – Swiss Cottage ('That's a bit North'), Clapham Common ('That's a bit South'), Norway, Paris, anywhere but Kensington.

They thought the other side of the street might prove more profitable. 'Dudley! Dudley! Over here, Dudley!' A Conservative helper had tracked down an elderly Kensington resident emerging from Marks and Spencer. Mr Heseltine reached her seconds before Mr Fishburn. 'What about this poll tax?' asked the elderly resident. 'May I introduce Dudley Fishburn, your Conservative candidate,' said Mr Heseltine.

Three tourists from Korea wished to take Mr Heseltine's photograph. He gave a thumbs-up sign to the camera, beaming happily. He approached a woman selling flowers. 'Do you live here?' 'No, Chelsea.' 'Ah, just down the road.' On to the next woman. 'Can I say hello to you, I'm Michael Heseltine.' 'No speak English.' 'Ah.'

Outside Pizza Inn, a Kensington-based Conservative voter was located. 'Delighted we've had a chance to meet,' said Mr Fishburn, but he couldn't think what to say next. They strode on. 'Yes, I live here,' said a Greek man outside Body Shop. Mr Heseltine shook his hand vigorously, his eyebrows quivering in the breeze. 'But I do not vote,' he added.

30 June 1988

'Double Yolker Zits and All'

An Old Codger Remembers (1): Simon Raven

Simon Raven's novels, particularly those in his 'Alms for Oblivion' sequence, have about them a sort of gleeful nastiness. While his characters plummet deeper and deeper into a dark pool of turpitude, their creator, whizzing around on a punctured lilo, cannot help but giggle.

In his autobiographical writing, which started with *The English Gentleman* in 1961, Raven has never sought to distance himself from the iniquity of his creations; in fact, rather the opposite. Raven begins the 'Apology' which opens *The English Gentleman* by declaring 'I myself am not a gentleman'. He then confesses, with some inkling of shame, how, by the age of 30, he had 'successfully disgraced myself at three fine institutions' (homosexuality at Charterhouse, laziness at King's College, Cambridge, gambling to the point of total ruin in the King's Shropshire Light Infantry).

It did not take Raven many books before his shame had taken on the full dress uniform of pride. He was soon parading his various misdemeanours before the public like so many rosettes. Just as the reader of spy thrillers feels greater confidence in an author who can hint at a past in the secret service, so Raven must have realised that his readers would like evidence that he was no armchair sinner, but the real thing, expulsions guaranteed.

By the time his first proper volume of autobiography, *Shadows on the Grass*, was published in 1982, the real-life characters behind the 'Alms for Oblivion' series were well-known. Rare were the newspaper profiles of Jim Prior or William Rees Mogg that failed to mention their somewhat less cosy lives as Raven creations. Unhappy the Carthusian circa '41-'45, destined to spend the rest of his life with the Raven perched upon his shoulder, cackling away at his every achievement!

Lent an unaccustomed gentleness by its cricketing theme, *Shadows on the Grass* was gossipy and – a favourite Raven word – spunky, but it was tinged with affection, if less for its subjects' deeds than for their misdeeds. Though one or two illustrious contemporaries (Hugh Trevor-Roper: 'a conceited, angular and predatory young man') were spiked on the Raven hook, a great many – Prior and Rees Mogg among them – escaped only slightly tarnished. Raven himself emerged as a bad hat, but a bad hat set at a jaunty angle. Mischief had yet to turn septic with misanthropy.

53

Eight years on, the merriment has stopped, the glee has departed, and only the diablerie remains behind, spitting in the dark. *Is There Anybody There? said the Traveller* is remorselessly nasty about everyone and everything, not least its own author. 'Memories of recent events should, of course, be the most reliable of all,' Raven writes at the beginning. 'But in my own case, being those of a man on the edge of old age (62) they are rendered less so by spite and spleen; by envy, resentment and sulk'.

Hatred abounds, and it is relayed in language dripping with a grotesque mixture of baby-talk and locker-room bravado. 'Little Willie Wee-Wee' Raven replies to a woman who wonders how he has managed to ejaculate into her so quickly after having sex with another. Scummy, fluky, deadly, scabby, soppy are favourite adjectives of Raven and his contemporaries. Mountbatten is 'the sort of chap that would cut off your private parts and keep them as a souvenir'. A Negro is 'an uppity sambo'. The political columnist Peter Jenkins is remembered for his 'stubby little stalk'. Athens is 'a huge honking ordurous Gehenna of smouldering streets, proletarian breeding boxes and brutal granite blocks'. Even The Lamb of God is dismissed as 'painfully wet'.

Throughout the book, Raven's sense of disgust at the world and its inhabitants, prime among them himself, veers beyond the candid and into the absurd. It would be hard to imagine, for instance, the following description of Goa failing to win first prize in a weekend competition for a Raven parody: 'In the scabby bungalows nearby, divorced wives of English dons and lawyers injected themselves with heroin and nagged at their twelve-year-old daughters until they threw their virginities away on beachcombing Indian youths of the lowest conceivable caste.'

Sex is hardly a spiritual activity in the rest of the Raven *oeuvre*, but in *Is There Anybody There?* it is as grim and joyless as can be. 'I lusted for Sidney, double-yolker zits and all' is a typical line, though at one point Raven, with uncharacteristic priggishness, concedes that 'rutting with a skeleton' may well be 'not wholesome'. Bodily fluids from virtually every orifice seem to seep on to every page, and even into a summer luncheon served in a Corfu villa to Lord and Lady Glenconner.

Every good autobiography is aware of the vicissitudes of memory. Raven's stated aim is to create 'a work of comparison: how did such a place, such a poem or such a picture, such a pastime or (above all) such a person seem to one when one was in one's salad days? then again at the age of forty . . . or yet again at sixty . . ?' Incidents that took place in the same location but years apart are juxtaposed in the hope that some pattern or contrast might emerge. The exercise soon proves fruitless, for all Raven's memories are swathed in the same bitterness, and all are presented with astonishing clarity and seemingly total recall. Much of the book does not ring true, particularly those passages repeated from previous volumes, but now with different characters in different locations. Perhaps it is wrong to expect to trust an author who has spent so much energy in proclaiming his untrustworthiness, but in many respects Raven's autobiographical world seems less consistent and far more contrived than his fictional world. Certainly, his rendering of real characters is considerably more wooden, for Raven shows them no mercy, allows them no decency and, on a technical level, forces them all to speak in remarkably similar tones.

Lingering darkly at the back of this book is a love story, a story of a 13-year affair that ended with Raven being spurned ('Your mere presence is intolerable'). For Raven, honesty can only be brutal, banishing all emotion. But spite is a poor conduit for the communication of passion, even passion rejected. The book is thus infused with an unarticulated wrath. It reads as an act of revenge against his lover, and against himself, and against a world which he feels is no longer deserving of his pagan mirth.

'Dream Dreams'

The Liberal Party Assembly (Political Sketch 2)

'I for one,' they all say at some stage during their speeches: I for one think this, I for one think that.

Mr Cyril Smith spoke early in the day. 'I for one,' he said – and observers were tempted to demand a recount – 'I for one consider David Steel handled himself very well in a very difficult situation.'

David Steel! We had almost forgotten about him. Liberals have a remarkably short shelf-life. Left for more than a week or two, they either go right off or disappear. Senior Labour and Conservative MPs need only put their heads around the door of the House of Commons once in a blue moon and they still remain famous, but if a Liberal so much as nips out for a breath of fresh air, before he reappears people start wondering which one he was, what he is doing now, and whether he is dead. Perhaps to compensate for the speed with which they dematerialise, the Liberals speak in ever grander phrases. After 'I for one' come the words 'dream', 'vision', 'the 21st century', 'regeneration' and 'principles', in no particular order, and often all at the same time.

'Have courage! Dream dreams! Have vision!' said Mr Smith. For a moment it seemed that he was about to burst into a rousing medley of the greatest hits of Peter, Paul and Mary, but instead he waddled back to his seat, stretched his small hands across the vast globe of his belly, smiling openmouthed at the applause he was receiving.

Though the day in the conference hall lasted eight hours and saw 55 speakers, there was only one speech, and that repeated every five minutes. It began with regrets for the results of the last election, continued with a plea not to give up hope, asked everyone to give the new party a go and concluded with something along the lines of: 'Let us look beyond the present to the future, beyond the future to the past and into the present by way of the future,' followed by long and sympathetic applause.

'What an adventure! What a challenge! Let's take it!' were Mr Des Wilson's concluding words. His face is Famous Five out of Brer Rabbit, his words roughly the same. It is hard to think of sitting in a committee room for three months with Mr Bob Maclennan in quite such enthusiastic terms, but everyone at the Liberal Assembly is Bob mad.

What do you call a man with no arms and no legs swimming in a sea of

Liberalism? The answer, of course, is Bob. He appeared onstage halfway through the afternoon, as pristine as a shaved peach, vaguely reminiscent of a junior member of the Royal Family, a retired princess maybe, or even a defrocked viscount. But in real life he is leader of the SDP, a man dedicated to challenges.

Throughout the day he had the opportunity to observe his future colleagues. Mr Richard Holme, looking more than ever like a bogus major specialising in defrauding spinsters in forgotten seaside towns, spoke of the good times they'd have together. Mr Alan Beith spoke of being entrusted with the freedom of future generations. Mr Simon Hughes spoke of the Earth and its fruits.

With so much goodwill pouring out towards mankind, young and old, male and female, rich and poor, Bob could feel excused for feeling slightly nauseous. 'It has been a very hard road to hoe,' said Mr David Alton, exposing his inner-city origins, before quoting Martin Luther King, second only to The Tolpuddle Martyrs in this year's name-dropper's Conference Manual.

Next came Michael Meadowcroft. 'We need have no inferiority complex,' he said, though looking at him, skilled observers found it hard to think why on earth not. In the auditorium, people shuffled to and fro, saying thank you and sorry as they bumped elbows and knees. 'I for one,' said the next speaker, and everyone sat comfortably.

16 September 1987

'11 in 68'

Douglas Bader and Me

What was an elephant's eye doing in a bubble-gum tree? This was the sort of question that troubled me most throughout that momentous year, 1968.

Over the last few weeks, anyone who did anything in 1968 has been paid to reflect on what they got up to 20 years ago. Anyone who took a daytrip to Boulogne in 1968 has been asked to reminisce about his part in the Paris riots, and anyone who pecked a girl on the cheek has been able to sell an article pointing out the folly of free love. The common conclusion seems to be: 'How much wiser we all are now. Thank goodness we have all grown up.'

My own reminiscences of 1968 are somewhat different. While everyone else was setting fire to Paris, shopping at Apple, appearing on Dee Time, meditating, hallucinating or learning the sitar, I was trapped inside a prep school near Basingstoke. Even as an 11-year-old, I realised that for a full appreciation of the zeitgeist, this was not the place to be.

'I looked in the sky where an elephant's eye was looking at me from a bubble-gum tree.' This song, a top 10 hit, tormented us with its mysterious lyrics. 'And all that I knew was,' the group chorused, 'the hole in my shoe which was letting in water.' We could understand each separate word – elephant, bubble-gum, shoe, etc. But we felt excluded from their overall meaning, a meaning that was surely a vital clue to being grown-up in 1968, a meaning barred to boys aged 11 wearing short hair and short trousers, learning Latin and maths and rehearsing HMS Pinafore for the end-of-term concert.

Sensing that we were in the wrong place at the right time, we grabbed at the intermittent and often faulty news from the exciting, hippy, psychedelic world outside. We usually got the wrong end of the stick, even on issues of some significance. I well remember a dormitory debate on the matter of sex, a very Sixties issue. We all knew that it happened in bed, but a boy called Hudson maintained that the man and his wife stayed awake while it happened, while the rest of us felt pretty sure that, if they were in bed, then most surely sex happened while they were asleep. At times, I privately suspected that the whole idea of sex was pretty improbable, as babyish a rumour as those stories the junior boys would dream up about the games master being a Russian spy, flashing secret messages from the roof at midnight to passing planes.

On more adult matters, I felt myself better informed, having changed my subscription from Look and Learn to the Disc and Music Echo. Through scrutiny of the photographs, I understood the importance of flares. Alas, however hard one tugged at the bottom of a pair of shorts, the meagre flares it produced compared very poorly with those of the Beatles.

A boy called Macaulay had an elder brother who had bought a triple album by Donovan called 'A Gift from a Flower to a Garden', and the younger Macaulay knew many of the words by heart. Listening carefully to his recitations, we came to realise that the majority of the childish fads we had spent so much time and energy growing out of – not just girly things like flowers, but elves and fairies and cuddly toys as well – now formed the main tenets of the hippy philosophy from which we felt so excluded.

Direct contact with the outside world in 1968 invariably ended in tears. I sent a letter to Chip Hawkes of The Tremeloes asking if he would like to make the speech at our school prize-giving, feeling sure that the school authorities would rejoice at the engagement of someone so famous, but received no reply. The post was filled by air ace Douglas Bader who, having presented me with a prize, told me that my tie was not straight – something that Chip Hawkes would never have done.

Perhaps influenced by the teachings of the Maharishi Mahesh Yogi, I brought a joss stick back to school at the beginning of the summer term. I put it in a jam jar and watched it smoke away while having a bath one evening. Always alert to the danger of fire, the geography master hurled himself into the bathroom and, believing himself to have chanced upon the still greater peril of drugs, marched me straight to the headmaster's study. I explained that a joss stick was not a drug and the headmaster, a fair man, struggled hard to believe me. But if it wasn't a drug, he wished to know, then what exactly was it for? I stared down at the floor in silence. I knew that it was a joss stick, but nobody had ever told me what it was for.

I still don't really know what a joss stick is for, what the elephant's eye was doing in the bubble-gum tree, or why I had to be II years old in 1968 when everyone else was 22. By the time I eventually managed to become a long-haired university student in 1976, everyone else had gone punk. Anyone who was the right age in 1968 should begin to realise that they have a lot for which to be thankful.

'Etartnecnoc'

Anthony Burgess's Diary

Breakfast, literally speaking the fasting of one's breaks or, from the early Nordic 'Brrr – eat fast', as the Vikings would say when the weather was chilly, is not only one of the few words in the Anglo-Saxon tongue to possess an 'ak' immediately followed by a 'fa' at its epicentre (another such word being akfa, a probably mis-spelling of aqua, meaning the opposite of no-water) but it is also my preferred meal.

The British Establishment – largely and probably unknowingly trans-vestitic and certainly increasingly cannibalistic – has never understood breakfast. They go for slices of pig and the encaged remains of an unfertilised embryonic bird to set them on their feet. Coming from a long line of Lancashire Roman Catholics, I stick to porridge, or, rather, it sticks to me. Por-ridge, or, etymologically speaking, 'pour-ridge', is rightly ladled in a pouring motion all over the ridges of one's visage or face, and this tradition I maintain every morning. Porridge poured everywhere is good for the brain and for the skin, and its multilumpitextuosity accounts for the splendour of my hairstyle, which retains some oats first poured in the year of our Lord 1935.

I have always found the look and smell of a bottle of Heinz tomato ketchup powerfully erotic, in that noble word's original sense of 'tasting slightly of tomatoes'. In the contemporary sense of the word, it is not erotic at all, or at any rate not nearly as erotic as a can of tinned peaches in heavy syrup one of which I remember taking to the opera and courting successfully in the spring of '48, only to be turned down when it came to bed because it had become suspicious of my infatuation with a beautifully ripe pineapple. All full-blooded Englishmen, particularly those of Irish descent, have found sexual desire within their loins for the suppurating convexities and soft, skeiny protuberances of the fruit (originally 'froo-it', owing to the fact that, if it had an unrelenting central core, it was hard to bite froo it), and this explains why the Establishment has never allowed a law to be placed on the statute books forbidding full intercourse with any type of fruit.

The English, by which I mean to say those who live in England, have always made the mistake of wearing wellington boots on their feet when it is wet. I have a sturdy pair of wellington boots myself, but I wear them on my head, never on my feet, and then only when it is sunny. In my 43rd novella, *The Wellington Boot Wearer*, I portrayed a Lancastrian working-class Catholic battling with the inherent forces of evil who takes to wearing wellington boots, but ill-advisedly not on his/her (the man is a transsexual) head but on the feet. The book closes with his death at the hands, or rather mouth, of an escaped lion, a symbol of the deity, perhaps, who has been fed for over 20 years solely on wellington boots. I wrote the novel with the intention of suggesting that if the unnamed hero had followed my advice to wear his wellingtons on his head, and then only when sunny, he might still be alive, for it was rainy when the lion escaped. But did they listen? On my frequent visits back to this beleaguered isle, I am amazed by the continued wearing of wellingtons on feet, despite my prophetic warning. But then the English have never understood serious fiction, sending those of us who are its foremost practitioners into exile, forcing us to write for the *Daily Mail*, denying us knighthoods, turning our creations into musicals.

People say that my failing is that I cannot concentrate – interesting word, spelt backwards emerging as 'etartnecnoc', a meaningless jumble of letters – but this is intolerable and untrue. They also say that I am a master of the *non sequitur*, leaping from one subject to another when they do not follow. For the past year I have not been following the patchy progress of my neighbour Graham Greene, a very undistinguished writer and a grumpy old bat, with whom my argument escalates, though the escalator, or, in French, *escalateur*, goes down as well as up, echoing, in a quasi-mysto-mechanical way, the descent and subsequent ascension of Lord Jesus Christ, who was, of course, not a Lord at all, as the Anglo-Saxons, being riddled with snobbery, like to think, but a carpenter, in fact I believe in this country there is a sporting commentator called Harry or Harold Carpenter, though whether he has ridden on a moving staircase or not we have no way of knowing. Where was I? Ah, yes: *concentration*. There is a concentrated orange juice – Ki-Ora, now there's a funny word, and Bivouac, there's another – but when we talk of concentration we mean something more than orange juice, moving staircases, sporting commentators, Graham Greene, or even Jesus Christ, but now I've lost my thread, which is, incidentally, an anagram of 'dearth'.

I make frequent appearances on what in this country is known as the *television*, often to talk about my latest opera, novel, cookery book, hymnal or work of literary criticism. I have recently extended my range so that I am now available for cabaret turns, golf club dances, and bar mitzvahs, singing a selection from *Showboat*, reciting the seven French nouns whose plurals end in 'oux', demonstrating New Developments in the Handjive, presenting a course of lectures on Michel de Montaigne or all at the same time. In the summer, I will be touring the country in the company of my barber and a leading manufacturer of porridge oats, and at the end of each show the audience will be invited up on to the stage to taste my hair while I read extracts from my new six-hundred-page *magnum opus*, which details the tribulations of a homosexual Cardinal in Singapore confronted by a triumvirate of Yahweh, an Unnamed Force and Destiny as he performs his ablutions upon the lavatory, though it is finally established that they have called at the wrong address. It is, in its oblique way, a chronicle of our century. I look forward to seeing you all there.

'Eton made me'

The Wind Changes

One of the reasons that autobiography is necessarily false is that it lends retrospective significance to events which at the time seemed no more pertinent to life than anything else. This falsity also has something to do with the way Etonians live their lives. They get used to being alive more quickly than others. From there on, it is a matter of plotting a course, of making sure that the world adapts to your needs. People become characters, the untoward becomes experience, everything, and everyone, begins to fit in.

I spent the morning of my last day at Eton, in July 1975, writing parodies of the Bible to an A-level standard. Only five of us had been studying for theology A-level, two of us – Nick Coleridge and myself – because we were clever, the other three because they were not. While the three had revised hard, forcing the words of God into their brains, occasionally looking up, their eyes closed, to repeat five times a line like, 'For I reap not neither do I soweth saith the Lord', Nick and I had long realised that there was no need for such labour, and that no examiner would be able to tell the difference between what was God's word and what was ours. Every quote in both our papers was made up as we went along. We gained the highest grades. When you are bright and eighteen and Etonian, there is no one easier to parody than God.

By the time I left Eton, I had a confidence in my own cleverness, but I was wary and standoffish in those areas traditionally allotted to Etonians. I was not socially assured, and I felt scorn for those who were. In the Eton pub, 'Tap', boys would josh and swagger, hurling each other's Christian names noisily across the room. They spoke with the twangs of their parents whereas I, wishing to be outside this cliché, muttered things quietly with cynicism in my tone. The real Etonians in Tap were decorated with scarves and hats and blazers and ties, fresh from beagling and boating and supporting their House, and they always seemed to be served before me. I dressed scruffy, determined that the uniform would never fit me. I remember an enemy housemaster ambushing me in the street. 'I have a private bet with myself,' he said, 'that your hair will soon be so long and your coat tails so short that they will meet in the middle. Take this as a warning.' A few years ago I learnt without sorrow that this housemaster had become an alcoholic and had been forced to resign his house; at about the same time I had begun to go bald.

The real Etonians had an awareness of the world which grew more accommodating as it expanded. Even those who had been caught drinking aged fifteen and who had once spat their housemaster's nickname – Soddy, or The Ripper, or Wetty – with venom, now, three years on, would speak of him as a 'good man', mixing their affection with the condescension they judged his social due. They would return from sherry with him, tipsy from the twin pleasures of stealing an extra glass when he was out of the room and employing his Christian name when he was still in the room. It was as if for them the world was, quite rightly and properly, a system of secret codes for which Eton provided the necessary keys; once unlocked it would prove commonsensical and well-ordered, tricky only for those whose lesser schools had provided faulty keys, fit only for unlocking uneasy systems. Some time after I left Eton, I met a young ex-grammar school geography master who had just joined the staff. He told me that finally the boys could scare him more than he could scare them because in times of stress they could always thrust their trump card into his face, and on that card was illustrated the fact that the outside world was theirs, and not his. Sometime between being young and being grown-up the wind changes direction and the face you are pulling is the face you are left with. Etonians know this, so they start pulling superior faces as soon as they possibly can.

I was suspicious of grown-ups, not being able to think of anything to say in their company, and this separated me from my contemporaries, who realistically saw them as future versions of themselves and therefore worthy of sympathy. In my gloomy blushing silence, I would listen to their chatter – I am thinking now of the holidays – and I would be unforgiving to the frivolity which they brought to anything serious and the seriousness they brought to all frivolity. In their slightest noise or action, I would be alert to hypocrisy, and in any of their game attempts at jollity I would see only pathetic charades to deny our destinies of death. When the kinder among them turned their attention to me, the sullen youth in the corner, I would enjoy summing them up in my mind as they spoke. While someone was telling me of her sons of about the same age as me, I would be thinking 'you stupid old bitch, you shrill and ugly cow' or something akin. I was not nice, and I am glad that the wind did not choose to change direction just then.

I went straight from Eton to the drama course at Bristol University. Even now, I feel that I have to add the word 'straight' to that sentence because if you are Etonian you are expected to go to Oxford or Cambridge, and if you go anywhere else it is because you failed the Oxbridge exam. But by inserting the word 'straight', I am hoping to convey that I did not take the Oxbridge entrance and that I went straight to Bristol of my own free will.

I suppose I must have been different from the others to have gone to do drama at Bristol, even if I only went to Bristol in order to prove the difference. When people think of Old Etonians, they tend to think of Oxbridge-educated Old Etonians, though they might also be thinking of very stupid Old Etonians. The two groups (there is some overlap) have in common a belief in the appropriateness of their position in society and a confidence in its continuation. They are both novelist and hero: the worries of the world might well be an entertaining backdrop. They were much quicker than I to notice – or is it to invent? – a scheme in things, revelling in *A Dance to the Music of Time*, matching their contemporaries to the characters, getting it all sorted out, life, and other people, and providence.

Visiting my Eton friends at Cambridge in my casual Bristol attire, I found it hard to believe that everyone was serious. Nostalgia seemed to be scripted, rehearsed, polished and enacted before taking its place in each student's canon. People were starting magazines, not because they had anything they particularly wanted to put in them but because this was the kind of thing they would like to reminisce about in later life. On they went with elaborate practical jokes involving lots of dressing up; though they never quite worked, this never impeded the legend. There seemed to be no present at Cambridge: everyone lived for the day before, converting it into something simpler, grander and more effective for its reappraisal in years to come. Our first three years at Eton had been spent in trying to overcome the embarrassment of changing from calling friends by their surnames to calling them by their Christian names, and now I found that awkward effort undone overnight: I was 'Brown' again, ironically, embarrassedly, then confidently and finally matter-of-factly 'Brown'.

After Eton, the drama course at Bristol seemed like an adventure playground, with little bits of acting and writing and lighting and designing and studying Howard Brenton all mixed together, so much so that by the end of the first year I was bored stiff with it, visiting the department only between 5 and 7 on Tuesdays. I left Bristol towards the end of the second year, one last attempt at recoil from the attraction of lethargy. The intensity of experience forced upon one by Eton, and, I suppose, by adolescence, was such that any divorce from it, whilst initially enjoyable, would come to seem like divorce from life, as if one were to be trapped forever away from everything. But my unconventional manoeuvrings did not bamboozle my Etonian friends, who had now become so adept in their classification of the dramatis personae of their lives that every move to evade their Powell-trained eyes to them made me all the more classifiable: the character who struggles to be different is a conventional figure in the novel.

After Bristol, I became a freelance journalist. I didn't bother with local papers or training courses or the NUJ but went straight to the *Sunday Times* and magazines such as this one; having qualms about most attributes Eton gives her sons, I was only too happy to skate along on the arrogance I had gained from her, and it saved me much boredom and drudgery. And with arrogance comes a necessary complacency: I have never believed myself to be a journalist, but a novelist or a playwright, and though, of course, no great or even small novel or play is being produced, I have always trusted my innate complacency gradually and tactfully to deflate my expectations of myself. When does the wind really change? Perhaps only when we acknowledge that we are pitiful versions of what we intended to be, that life, like a servant turned thief, has let us down.

While my friends at Cambridge settled down to another two years of wisecracks and crucial experiences, lovingly preparing charts on who had been influenced by whom and who had had sex with whom and who had never had sex at all and who had been approached by MI5 and who had over-reached himself; and as the real Etonians crashed ever more cars and let off ever more fire extinguishers and drank more and more and more, I shambled confidently around newspapers and magazines and pubs gathering work. I hadn't been a journalist long when I fixed up with *Harper's & Queen* to write a profile of Jeffrey Bernard. He suggested we meet in the French Pub, 'and we'll go onwards and downwards from there'. I had never been to the French Pub before, but for two years it was to be my home from home (my actual homes being a series of flats run by aggressively clean girls and squats inhabited by liberal television watchers).

The French Pub is situated in Dean Street in Soho. Outside, it was called 'The Yorkminster', but its inhabitants called it The French in much the same way as lovers have secret names for each other. Its unmarried companion, an afternoon drinking club called 'The Colony Rooms', just up the street and then up a thin staircase, was similarly always known as 'Muriel's'. It is hard to find adjectives to describe its inhabitants – world-weary, wry, charming, intelligent, occasionally bitter, acerbic, wounded, paternal – without betraying condescension, and perhaps that condescension deserves to be betrayed, because I must always have been conscious that for me it was an early episode, an 'experience', whereas for them it was a statement, a conclusion. I remember one night which summed up the French Pub so well that I knew it was summing it up well even while it was happening. I dropped in just before closing time on a quiet night when there were only four people down the educated end of the bar (one end was educated, the other was pornographers and advertisers). There was a publisher, an antiquarian book-dealer, a painter and a burglar. Even the burglars in the French were of a better class – this one had once burgled a leading politician's house, declaring himself 'reeely shocked' when he read in the *Telegraph* the next day the amount she was claiming off insurance, and he had always admired her, too. I noticed that the four of them were being unnaturally quiet and conspiratorial, and that Gaston, the publican, seemed to be paying particular attention to them. As I approached, Gaston said, 'We'll let him have a little' and brought out a bottle of Absinthe, vintage 1917 – the year before it had been declared illegal. To stand with these four sniffing, sipping, swallowing, savouring vintage Absinthe seemed to me the true vision of life represented by the French Pub, a world where wit and depression were as close, dependent and mutually restrictive as Siamese twins.

A couple of times I saw Peregrine Worsthorne, clean-shaven, brightly-socked, dapper, in the French Pub. On both occasions he carried with him an air of just browsing, and stayed perhaps twenty minutes. He told a friend of mine later that he always felt waves of resentment washing over him as he stood there, but I think he might have misinterpreted the signs. There were definitely richer people than Worsthorne among the regulars, and definitely quite a few painters and actors who were more acclaimed: what jarred was his spritely self-confidence, evidenced not by anything as ungentlemanly as loudness, but by an aura he emits of being in control of life, a notion fundamentally false to the character of the French Pub; perhaps those waves, whatever they consisted of, were just the water struggling to reclaim the fish.

Etonian friends would visit me in the French, popping in, enjoying the party, and popping out again. It bemused me that they could take it so lightly. One of my closest friends, Napier Miles, told me that it offered such a complete view of things (he was reading English at Oxford at the time) that he felt one would either have to surrender the rest of one's life to it or else treat it as an occasional joke. I had never been drawn to analysing my attraction to the French, and I disagreed with him. Some time later, my long-standing girlfriend, who had, in lots of ways, been my life, left me, and when I knew for sure it was forever, I choreographed a trip by myself to the French Pub. I told my friends there that she had gone, and they were so generous, so compassionate, so penetratingly understanding, that as I left I knew that I would never be going back, and nor have I. I did not wish to live with their understanding of things. I began gradually to see the merits of bright socks and a dapper exterior, and to see that even for me the wind would one day change.

One of the most valuable lessons an Old Etonian can draw from Anthony Powell is that he must expect to bump into other Old Etonians at inconvenient times in inconvenient places for the rest of his life. I still see ten or so Etonian friends regularly, another ten I would like to see from time to time but don't, and then there is a pool of about a thousand which every few months provides an unexpected face to loom up in the street or at a party, producing varying degrees of embarrassment and effort. Brief and improved curricula vitae are exchanged; one asks the other if he still sees someone else.It is all skilfully handled on both sides, and so is the speedy parting. Perhaps it is because between every class at school the Etonian has to pass in the street about a hundred people he knows, and nod at them, or smile at them, or exchange banter with them, that the Old Etonian is so proficient at wheedling in and out of conversations; sometimes it is confused for charm.

But there are odder meetings too. It must have been during my French pub years that I was walking near Lincoln's Inn around lunchtime when a figure came out of a law building whom I instantly recognised as one of the senior boys at Eton I had most loathed. His name was Ryder and he had been my House Captain in my second year, occasionally interrogating me over petty offences by spotlight, and sending me on semi-ridiculous fagging errands, but nothing really cruel or upsetting. I hadn't thought about him for years, and seeing him didn't open any old wounds. In the normal course of things, we would have passed by, pretending not to notice each other, but we had exchanged glances, and I thought he had recognised me, so I said a cheery hello. He looked a little confused, so I said who I was, and asked him whether he was now a solicitor. He didn't answer the question, but straightaway said, 'I feel I owe you an apology. I don't think I knew how to handle authority, and I think I misused it against you. I've been thinking about it a bit recently, and I think I was wrong.' I suppose I said, 'Oh, don't worry', and managed a chuckle before we both hurried off to our grown-up lives, perhaps never to stumble across one another again. It was an admission of guilt and of failure, both alien to the Etonian ethos. I came away thinking two things: that I was physically taller than him now, and that his gesture was in some way pathetic. That it was also decent and brave did not enter into it. Radical, Bohemian, scruffy, I had learnt more from Eton than Ryder ever had.

When people think of Old Etonians, they tend to think of successful Old Etonians, because they are the ones who make themselves most evident. Oddly enough, the people who became drug addicts and who one occasionally hears about having just entered or exited or re-entered Broadway Lodge are, by and large, not the ones who showed no House spirit and skulked around listening to Captain Beefheart instead of playing games: no, they are the beaglers and rowers, the ones who shouted each other's Christian names across Tap in their blazers, the much valued members of their houses, the boys who were happy to retain the twang of their parents' voices. I don't know why this should be. At Eton, they might have enjoyed an illicit cigarette, but if ever they had come across anything to do with drugs they would have speedily reported it to their housemaster, such was their sense of responsibility. In my third year at Eton, I joined a voluntary experimental class called 'social studies'. It was called this so as to prevent the more conservative masters rumbling the fact that it was actually sociology. I suppose the ten or so of us who enrolled on the course were leftish anyway – certainly none of us were keen games players – and so we might have been prepared for the conclusive statistics to what we had half suspected: that most people are much poorer than Etonians. Anyway, during the course of one week, nearly half the class was expelled on different drug offences. As far as I know, none of them went on to become an addict; no doubt they are holding down good jobs in the city. So why did the addicts come from the ranks of the real Etonians? Perhaps they missed Eton, perhaps they needed drug-induced visions of an entire world dressed in tails singing 'Jerusalem' in College Chapel to keep them going; perhaps without the props they had so loved, they grew to sense their own dullness; perhaps they just had a lot of money and time on their hands.

I have never missed Eton because I never felt comfortable there. It is an extraordinarily forceful place. No matter how high you climb, there will always be vast amounts of people above you. Even the headmaster is sixth or seventh from the top and seems to be on trial throughout his tenure. The few times I have gone back, I have felt nothing like love or hatred, but the same apprehension that ran in my blood when I was there. As a pupil, I never felt in the right place at the right time wearing the right clothes in the right way; I was always avoiding people, and making excuses, and not managing to learn things, and feeling anxious that around the next corner I would be found out. I never felt in place because I could not work out where my place was, and it became even more difficult to ascertain the higher I rose. It is Eton's genius that it accommodates its rebels, and it accommodated me well, giving me the run of the theatre and of the school magazine, but the apprehension never left me. I used to be proud that this awkwardness and anxiety dominated my memories of the school, thinking that they freed me from it in a way that friends like Napier and Nick, who loved it, could never be free, but happiness has no copyright on nostalgia: I see more and more clearly the way Eton, however much I try to ignore it, has dominated the way I think and the way I am, its force and intensity and worldliness growing like roots in my brain. Maybe one day I will learn to relax and enjoy it all like the others do. People who were not in the same house at the same time as Nick and Napier are as mystified at their conversations as those who were never at Eton at all. Granville, Dentley, Oakes: what are they? They could be Midland towns or makes of water biscuit, but they are in fact names of boys whose different shortcomings have been mythologised by Nick and Napier, an ideal palliative to their own occasional moments of self-doubt. And so it goes on, Eton boys, masters, sayings, from ten years ago making the present ever more interesting and the past ever more present.

It is often said that Etonians have better manners than anyone else. If this is true (I think that they also have the worst manners, but can always choose which set to employ) then it is another indication of the control which they have grown to assume they can exert over their own lives and their own actions. Wealth allows the beginnings of control: locations and people can be changed at will and the number of people for whom one has to modify one's behaviour grows smaller. But other sides of Eton also promote in its sons the suggestion of divinity. You cannot walk around two towns in tailcoats for five years without coming to some decision as to your importance in relation to the untailcoated pedestrians, and it would be a saint or madman who emerged from these five years with ideas of his own inferiority or even equality still instinctively intact. Five hundred years of Old Etonian prime ministers and great writers further encourage the Etonian to feel apart, above, and in charge. After five years of living in such a powerful and well-established fantasy, however uneasy one might have felt, the outside world looks as paltry as a stepping-stone, handy, maybe, but only for where it can get you. It has been said that if an Etonian meets someone else coming towards him in the street, he will greet him, be charming and carry on chatting to him as they both walk down the street in the Etonian's direction. Etonians do not just have charm, they employ charm. 'You are welcome to look around the house,' says the charming man, indicating that the house is his and not yours. Etonians control it all; they are what they imagine themselves to be; even if they are considered failures, like Cyril Connolly, they are considered failures because they have passed orders to the world to consider them in that way.

The wind changes, and we are prepared. Past failure of morals or – so much more noticeable – of taste, are reclassified or forgotten. I remember Nick Coleridge having a hippy poster on his wall at Eton saying 'War – It's a Dying Business'. He had forgotten this until I reminded him. In the same way, I remember being bullied a bit in my first year or two at Eton, and if anyone now asks, 'Was there much bullying at Eton?', I sometimes tell them of the few occasions on which I was bullied. But I have been recently reminded that this was not the whole picture. A couple of years ago, about six of us went out for dinner in a Chinese restaurant in Holland Park with our old housemaster, Giles St Aubyn. On these occasions Napier Miles sets the ball rolling by saying, 'Any news of m'dame?' to which we all chortle, because our dame was an unattractive figure, and someone whose well-being in retirement is of jocular unimportance. (A dame at Eton is a sort of matron: as is well known, at Eton most essential functions are protected by code.) Giles then says something like, 'She continues to write happily from Bangor' (or wherever it is she's ended up) and an ironic smile plays across his mouth, ergo more chortles. Napier then continues with, 'Any news of X? Any news of Y?' and we all giggle helplessly as more and more ridiculous people are pulled out of forgotten hats. We were playing this game at the Chinese restaurant when Napier said, 'And what news of Dentley?' and the giggling multiplied: Dentley was a junior boy with a soppy voice, parents who ran a donkey sanctuary (this still seems very funny to me), and a collection of ties, all hideous, which he would attempt to sell for a bit of pocket money, all the time bleating, 'Buy a tie, buy a tie', a phrase everyone would chant as he approached. I can't remember whether Giles's news of Dentley was good or bad; perhaps it was bad. At any rate, Giles suddenly said that we had all been cruel to Dentley, teasing him, bullying him, and making his life a misery. I remember spending the rest of the evening feeling deeply ashamed: I knew that *I* had once *been* bullied, and I knew that we had all treated Borwick's existence as a joke, but I had never seen myself as doing the bullying, myself as a bully. The subject was soon changed, and conversation bubbled once more.

There are worse stories, of course – a friend of mine who went to Shrewsbury remembers them all nicknaming one boy 'Mumsdead' after his mother had died halfway through the term – and I don't want to apportion my own moral duplicity on to Eton, but I think that Etonians are rather more adept than others at incorporating an expedient hush into their moral biography, and this expediency has something to do with charm, and something to do with manners, and it all has something to do with the confident belief that one can plot one's own life, that it is just a matter of setting the right face towards the wind and then waiting for the wind to change.

A few months ago, I was walking down the King's Road in the evening with Nicholas Coleridge. We were cracking competitive jokes, as usual, striding along in search of a restaurant. Coming towards us in the distance we saw someone we had known quite well at Eton. We had both seen him since Eton, and he had been funny and rascalish and a keen drinker and fun. I was glad that he was approaching. While he was still out of earshot, Nick, who knows these things, told me that this old schoolfriend had recently emerged from an alcoholic clinic, that he had no job and was living by himself somewhere. As we drew level, I felt embarrassment. The old schoolfriend, who was carrying some groceries, also looked embarrassed, perhaps sensing that we knew, or that we might find out. A year before, I would have asked him to join us for dinner and seen if I could do anything to help. We spoke awkwardly: he didn't suggest we drop round. We didn't exchange phone numbers. We carried on walking, he in his direction, we in ours. It was a windy night.

Soon afterwards, I began writing this.

'Exactly The Same'

Richard Branson's Boundless Ambitions

Some people possess the odd quality of looking exactly the same in every photograph. Richard Branson is one of them. Branson as a hippy, Branson as a businessman, Branson in goggles, Branson joshing about, Branson on his boat, Branson in his balloon: the same straightforward, easily excited expression beams out, its grinning eyes and carnivorous mouth facing head-on to the camera. It is as if Branson were a child putting his head through a splendid variety of cardboard fairground cut-outs, ever anxious to be someone other, a cowboy maybe, or perhaps an astronaut. But, when the photographs are developed, does Branson experience the child's disappointment when he discovers that, underneath it all, it is still him?

I suspect that this quality of always looking the same has something to do with dullness, possibly the same dullness which turns those who possess it into adventurers, the dullness that enables those touched with it to see the world as a pretty normal sort of place, a place of few problems and fewer mysteries, a place which is there to be got the better of. Esther Rantzen always looks the same in photographs, and so do John Moore and Jeffrey Archer.

The blurb on this first biography of Branson claims that he is 'all the more intriguing for his apparent simplicity', which is rather like saying that a sheet of paper is all the more intriguing for its apparent blankness. Branson's biographer, Mick Brown, seems to realise that Branson's interest lies elsewhere. He writes in his introduction that 'Branson's rise is a paradigm of the changing face of Britain over the last 20 years'. That thesis – the shift from idealism to pragmatism, or, if you would prefer, from sloppiness to efficiency – simmers quietly throughout the biography, though Brown wisely never lets it bubble over.

Branson was born into a lower-upper-middle-class family from Shamley Green. His father's family had been in law for three generations. His father sounds like a kindly English gentleman while his mother is something rather more exotic and pushy. She was the youngest of Cochrane's Young Ladies in the famous dance revues, and later became one of the first air stewardesses. Her ambitions for her son were boundless, and, in their furthest reaches, have yet to be realised. 'One day Richard will be prime minister,' she told friends, when he was still a child.

At Stowe, Branson was outstanding not for any aptitude at work or games but for that most ungentlemanly of public school attributes, being keen. Aged 15, he wrote to the headmaster a detailed memorandum suggesting improvements to the school ('we can cut down on the Italian and Spanish waiters by at least half'). During school holidays, he embarked on money-making schemes. He grew Christmas trees and bred budgies, neither with much success.

Still at school he founded *Student* magazine, his first real success. He managed with ease to solicit contributions from all sorts of famous people – le Carré, David Hockney, even Jean-Paul Sartre – turning down articles sent in by Robert Graves and Yehudi Menuhin as 'too boring'. He left Stowe early, before the first issue appeared, explaining to the headmaster that, by doing so, he would be able to 'give more to Stowe and Britain'.

Keenness, attached to whatever art or politics were going begging, became his distinguishing feature. At one moment, he would be writing to President Johnson asking him for a good luck message to print in the first issue. At the next, he would be chanting, 'Hey, hey, LBJ, how many kids have you killed today?' as he marched alongside his early mentor, Vanessa Redgrave, to Grosvenor Square. Recently, when Miss Redgrave asked him for a contribution to a Workers' Revolutionary Party scheme, he politely refused. Like all keen people, however hirsute they may be, or however many jerseys they wear, he likes being on the winning side. 'Richard would cheat at snap,' an anonymous friend sneaked to Branson's biographer.

The Virgin mail-order record business took Branson into the bottom reaches of the big time. John Varnom, his associate, explains the delight they took in 'selling things to hippies while pretending to be hippies ourselves'. While others slopped about in kaftans, expanding their minds, the soft-spoken and appropriately inarticulate Branson expanded his Coutts bank account and studied the pages of *Country Life* in search of property. For relaxation, he quietly eschewed smoking dope in favour of the more traditional joys of throwing bread rolls and letting off fire extinguishers. When head of his own record company, he found it hard to remember which rock star was which, often warmly congratulating minor road managers on their latest albums.

Non-stop doers are most revealing by what they do not do. Having sacked his sagging hippy artistes in 1976 and revitalised Virgin's image by signing the Sex Pistols in 1977, Branson still refused to allow Malcolm McLaren to call the Sex Pistols/Ronnie Biggs single 'Cosh the Driver', though he turned a blind eye to McLaren's claim that the bass-guitarist was the otherwise reticent Martin Bormann. Earlier in his career, he refused the offer from the Beatles of a giveaway disc to go with *Student* on learning that it was a recording of the dying heartbeats of Yoko Ono's miscarried baby. Branson has always been aware of the parameters of taste, and in that sense he has remained closer to big business than to rock culture, ever the bright-eyed boy from Shamley Green.

Mick Brown's *Richard Branson* is that rarest of things, a biography which meets its own claims to be both authorised *and* critical. While Brown has an obvious admiration for Branson's pluck and drive, he does not skate over some of his dodgier or more disastrous dealings. The book is obviously aimed at the aspirant businessman as much as at the celebrity-fancier, and Brown's descriptions of quite complicated business transactions are admirably lucid.

Brown has sought out a large number of Branson's friends, colleagues and somewhat bitter ex-colleagues. Only when Branson is given his own say do the eyelids begin to droop. On politics: 'Economically, Mrs Thatcher's got it about right. The dead wood needed to be trimmed. But there's a lot of room in this government for a more caring attitude.' On sex, post-Aids: 'You're never going to stop people making love. And I don't see why people shouldn't have four or five relationships before settling down . . . ' Small wonder, with thoughts of such tedium, that the keenest, most restless boy in school should seek his excitement from balloons, business, boats – anything but himself.

'Fish Finger Nation'

The Tell-tale Splash of Ketchup

BLESSED FISH FINGER
A Haunting, Angry New Lament by Heathcote Williams

The shape of a fish finger
Is the shape of a
Bungalow
If you removed all the windows
(From the bungalow
That is. Not from the fish finger.
Fish fingers don't have windows, of course:
If they did, they wouldn't taste
Very nice).
If you removed all the windows
And flattened the roof
And then covered the entire bungalow in
Breadcrumbs and fried it in butter
Or sunflower oil
Then you would have something resembling a very
Very large fish finger.

But too big for a plate.
In the sea
The fish finger flaps about
Basking in its ocean heaven
Whilst above her Cap'n Birdseye
Hangs his dreadful net.
No human being has ever heard
A conversation between one fish finger
In the wild
And another fish finger.
They speak in silence
Of the threat of man:
The tell-tale splash of ketchup on plate

Harkens them to their doom.
Couped up in a packet
24 piled into a box measuring
Nine inches by four
Emblazoned with the gaudy pictures
Of human kiddies beaming inanely
And the beard-encrusted
Not to be trusted
Face of
Cap'n Birdseye.
Homo Sapiens
Has long had a taste
For the fish finger.
Once, long ago
He worshipped it.
Fish fingers were placed on the altars of the Eskimo
To be paid homage
By man.
See fish fingers now
Four abreast on a plate
Sandwiched between a dollop of
Alphabetti Spaghetti
And a couple of
Potato Croquettes
Their solemn dignity
Reduced to the nick-nacks
Of everyday conversation: 'Have you finished your fish fingers,
Bert?' 'Not as yet, Doris: one more to go, thank you.'
Her domain under threat
The fish finger prepares to be eaten
Without a murmur.
In her silence, a rebuke to
Man's infidelity.
Fish finger! Fish finger! Fish finger!
Never again will I eat you
Unless I'm really, really peckish.
And there are no
Baked Beans
In the larder.

Notes on the Nature of Fish Fingers

'I have always maintained that a hearty Yorkshire fish finger takes quite some

beating, and I have long been its stoutest advocate.'
Roy Hattersley: from 'On Fish Fingers and Freedom and Other Essays'
(1983)

  DAVE (A Man In His Thirties): (Pause): 'I'm not a fish finger.'
  FARRELL (A Man In His Forties): What are you, you bastard?'
(Hits Dave)
  DAVE: (Pause): I'm a fish finger.
  FARRELL: That's more like it. (Pause).

Harold Pinter: extract from *Fish Finger Music* (1989).

Dear George, A veritable cracker of a missive! You raised the richly enticing
question of whether or nay the goodly Bard ever wrote a halfway-decent part
for a fish finger. Quite a puzzler: if memory serveth, I would hazard that I
remember Ellen Terry play the doughty Lady MacB as a fish finger a good
many moons ago at the Old Vic. (Incidentally, try as I may I can find no
reference in the dread Lawrence, DH of that ilk, to fish of any type, though I
might add that his less healthy characters tend towards a surplus of fingers!!!

From *The Lyttleton-Hart Davis Letters*, Volume 23

The long still hot weary dead fish finger lay discarded and forgotten in the
crusted shiny still gloomy pan perhaps contemplating in misery and torture
its fargone longlost days when she was a young fish fingerette the days when
her still unsullied flesh remained undefiled by the breadcrumbs of defeated
yet persistent cooks and she felt a slow abiding rage grow and rise and burst
from deep within her.

William Faulkner: *Requiem for a Fish Finger* (1936)

In the past decade, over 10 million fish fingers have been culled each day by
the human race. The world could be encircled four and a half times by man's
weekly consumption of fish fingers laid end to end, though this would
obviously constitute a major road hazard.

From *The UNESCO Report on the Plight of the Fish Finger* (1987)

'Flambé'

The Kitchen Inferno (Table Talk 1)

Now that Harrods resembles nothing so much as an airport shop, and Peter Jones is Never Knowingly Overstaffed, The General Trading Company may well be able to claim the title of the last smart shop in London. Situated at the Sloane Square end of Sloane Street, it is full of that combination of peasant fibres and expensive tags that Chelsea dwellers find so irresistible. Though often chock-a-block with the royal family, it is, nevertheless, a relaxing place in which to linger, one's mind vaguely occupied with modest fantasies of buying a small cushion.

Sloane Ranger women, of whom there are still plenty about, tend to treat the General Trading Company as their office, and shopping there as their job. 'Hard day at the General Trading Company, darling?' their husbands ask them in the evening.

'Absolutely whacked!' they reply. 'Two cushions, a Peruvian bedspread and a new chest of drawers – and that was just *before* lunch.'

'Poor love. Have a drink.'

The General Trading Company has a little café in its basement, run by the ubiquitous Justin de Blank. It is distinctly un-posh, even slightly hippyish, and could quite easily be transported lock, stock and barrel into, say, the ICA, without anyone batting an eyelid. Down one end, there is a counter with pastries and so forth looking a little despondent; behind the counter, there is a grill, of which we shall be hearing more later. Down the other end, there is a glass wall leading to a conservatory. The room itself is wood-lined, rather like a half-hearted sauna bath or a tree house. As is now the norm in upmarket breakfasting establishments, newspapers hanging from hooks are available to those who wish to catch up on the previous day's disasters over a nice cup of coffee.

Though the store itself has a number of pleasant posters and children's wallcharts on sale, the restaurant has no pictures whatsoever. Instead, it has the most extraordinary proliferation of notices, most of them warning customers about imminent felony. WHO'S AFTER YOUR BAG? BE SURE IT'S SAFE reads one poster, while the silhouette of a pair of hands snatch at a bag. No less than four copies of this poster are displayed. There are also two posters saying SMOKERS ARE REQUESTED TO USE OUTSIDE TABLES and others saying

THE PROPRIETOR CANNOT ACCEPT RESPONSIBILITY FOR HATS, COATS, UMBRELLAS, ETC and PLEASE LOOK AFTER YOUR HANDBAGS AND OTHER VALUABLES. Oddly enough, one sign beginning PLEASE LOOK AFTER . . . had fallen over, a victim of neglect. In many ways, breakfasting at the General Trading Company is like sitting in the visitors' wing of a high-security prison.

I was having breakfast with a friend, but everyone else was breakfasting alone, all lined up on single tables along one wall as if about to break out into a morose Thirties song for a Dennis Potter spectacular. The clientele, at least for breakfast, seems to consist of single women with heavily lacquered hair, expensive coats and small dogs. Judging by the surrounding signs, half of them are genuine millionairesses and the other half are confidence tricksters, and it is up to each person to judge for themselves which is which.

We ordered cooked breakfast at roughly 9.10 a.m. A croissant and a brioche came virtually straightaway, but gave every indication of having been baked the day before, or even the day before the day before, or even the day before that. Now that one can buy perfectly light croissants in bags at supermarkets, Justin de Blank should be able to do better than to offer such doorsteps. Or perhaps they were there not to eat, but to frighten off any mugger before his slippery fingers start inching towards one's handbag. The jam, though, was pretty good. (THE JAMS SERVED IN THIS CAFE ARE SOLD IN THE KITCHEN DEPARTMENT reads yet another notice).

For the next 20 minutes, we chatted away in merry anticipation of our cooked breakfasts to come. Oddly enough, when I had ordered a poached egg instead of a fried egg, the friendly waitress had explained that the only eggs they did were boiled, which is a fat lot of good with bacon and sausages. Close scrutiny of the premises revealed that they only had a grill to work with, and that a proper cooker was nowhere to be seen. How, then, do they boil the eggs? And if they can boil an egg, why can't they poach one? Such mysteries are sent to try us.

Anyway, after 20 minutes waiting, our conversations began to flag and our stomachs began to rumble. Perhaps, I suggested to my companion, someone had stolen our breakfasts, and a sign should be erected immediately bearing the legend, WHO'S AFTER YOUR BREAKFAST? BE SURE IT'S SAFE. THE MANAGEMENT CANNOT ACCEPT RESPONSIBILITY FOR BACON OR MUSHROOMS.

Just as I was finishing this modest witticism, the grill behind the counter, upon which our breakfast had been cooking so very slowly, burst into flames. These were not sparks or flashes, but real large yellow flames, two or three feet high, sprouting from the grill and billowing out into the room. Conversation, or what little there was of it, came to an abrupt halt as all eyes turned towards the inferno that had once been our breakfast.

I was expecting someone to reach for a baby fire extinguisher and that, I thought, would be that, but there was obviously no fire extinguisher to hand. Instead, in an attempt to remove the grill-pan from under the grill, one of the cooks placed brown paper around the handle, at which point three or four of us shouted, 'Not with paper!' and he swiftly removed it before it, too, burst into flames. I can't remember exactly how the grill-pan was removed, but after much commotion it was. All that was left of our breakfast was a few charcoaled shreds.

'Sorry about that,' said our waitress, bravely, 'I'm afraid your breakfast has been delayed. More coffee?'

Our breakfasts eventually arrived at 10 a.m., a full 50 minutes after we had ordered them. The sausage was too salty, the bacon too streaky, and I missed my egg like mad. Even the choice of two different types of mushrooms failed to cheer me up. In normal circumstances, I would have concluded by saying that breakfast at the General Trading Company would never set the world on fire, but now I am not so sure.

'Flyaway Hair'

Cecil Parkinson's Diary

It is a very great pleasure for me to be given this opportunity to put forward the Government's position on a number of important topics. Very kind people – some of them attractive young ladies! – tell me that I am what they call a 'natural communicator'. I accept the compliment with grace. If I have such a quality, it derives from my great belief in this Government's frankly first-rate policies, and the terrific team we now have. All I have to do is to state these great assets clearly and smoothly, and the next election will be ours, and it is indeed gratifying to think that I can do the 'communicating' job better than, say, John Selwyn Gummer, that slimy little twerp about time she got rid of him and as for that bloody Howe and if that Baker does that smile once more I'll kill him the bastard. To employ a nautical expression, with a steady hand such as mine on the anchor all should be well.

I have always considered what I call 'personal grooming' to be of overriding importance. I have long held to the opinion that if people can't respect your hairstyle then you equally can't ask them to respect your policies. Luckily, I have a very full head of hair, and I'm happy to report that the compliments tend to flood in concerning its body, general tidiness and overall grooming. Might I seize this opportunity to pass on a few tips?

a) Do remember to wear a hair-net upon retiring to bed. I regret to say that a number of my Cabinet colleagues – first-rate team, incidentally – have overlooked this advice, resulting in flyaway hair, poor quality partings and general lack of body. Small wonder that Lawson went for the proverbial Burton. I know he'll forgive me for saying this – Nigel's a very old friend of mine, and I have the greatest respect for his now alas gravely discredited economic abilities – but his hair was often disorderly and never anywhere near as spruce as mine. Why? Simple. He forgot his hair-net. So much for the fat slug, who is, incidentally, a much-valued colleague and old friend of myself and my loyal wife Ann.

b) I never forget to place a seawater fish – cod or turbot are both readily available from your high street fishmonger – underneath my hair-net before 'turning in for the night'. The excellent oils and aromatic properties permeate from the fish through into the hair and scalp to afford perfect manageability in the morning, and my steadfast wife Ann is more than grateful for a cod lunch around mid-day, first removing any of my stray hairs from the gills, of course.

I am delighted to have been given this opportunity to show you what one might call the more 'human' side of 'yours truly'. It can be a great burden, you know, to be lumbered with the title of 'the great communicator', as it prevents people from seeing the more warm and rather private side of what has been described as my 'terrific personality'. You'll no doubt be wondering how I came by the above knowledge of personal grooming for men. Before entering the worlds of industry and politics, I served an apprenticeship at a prestige gentlemen's hairdressing salon in South Audley Street. As well as learning the finer points of trimming, perming, pruning and so on, one received a valuable education in how to present oneself in an attractive manner while looking in the mirror at one's client. Nowadays, when I am asked by the Prime Minister to present the 'human face' of the Party on the small screen, I pretend to myself, as the studio manager 'cues in', that I am back in that salon, with the camera as the mirror and you, the great British electorate, as my client. As you can judge for yourself, this works beautifully, though I think Peter Sissons might have been a little surprised at the close of a recent *Question Time* when I found myself asking whether sir required anything for the weekend.

Pedicure is another of my talents, my Diploma taking pride of place on my office wall. It is a skill much valued by the Prime Minister. It was at the end of one of the crisis meetings of the Inner Cabinet during the Falklands Conflict that I first suggested to the Prime Minister that she should relax with a pedicure, and she took to it like a duck to water. Now, in our full Cabinet sessions, she takes care to place her Secretary of State for Transport in the chair opposite, so that, when the urge overtakes her, she may throw off a shoe and place her foot under the table in my able hands, all the while holding forth about the grave issues of the day. 'Other people bring me problems,' she once told a mutual friend, 'but Cecil brings me pedicures.'

This remark arouses some jealousy amongst my absolutely first-rate team of Cabinet colleagues, of course. Ken Clarke is so ham-fisted he couldn't pick his own nose without first consulting an expert, and that little prick Gummer looks like something you'd file out of a toe-nail, so my position at the feet of the Prime Minister seems assured.

Might I just put in a word on the need for Cabinet loyalty? 1990 has so far been a particularly trying year for myself and my colleagues in Government, and now, more than ever before, there is a desperate need for Ministerial solidarity. Many of my colleagues, alas, do not abide by these rules, little realising that stray off-the-cuff remarks about, say, Waddington's overpowering body odour could prove most unhelpful.

Happily, I inspire tremendous loyalty from my colleagues, who have thankfully put my little 'local difficulty' of 1983 behind them, and are now more anxious than ever that I take the 'driving seat' in the run-up to the next election. Cabinet memos confirm this. At the last Cabinet meeting, I intercepted a memo from Clarke to Baker while Margaret was droning on. It was tremendously heartening: 'Cecil holds the Keays to the next election!!' it read, to which Baker's memo soon came back, 'Conservatives Flor-a Great Victory!!' Soon, Howe had chipped in with a memo of his own stating, 'No Flies on Cecil!!' On the evidence of such overwhelming support, I can safely say that any problems I may have had are in the past and that my role in Cabinet can only grow stronger.

One final tip, if I may. Kind supporters often ask me how I get my head to bounce about uncontrollably in sudden jerks in that attractive way on television and in Westminster. The answer, of course, is a discreet electric-shock machine secreted in one's collar stud. It serves both to stimulate the hair follicles and to ensure a smile appears in the area of one's mouth every 25-30 seconds, with little or no damage to the brain.

'Frankly Rather Common'

The Redbrick Rons (Wallace Arnold 3)

The ever-beady eyes of Arnold have been much overworked of late, I fear. On Thursday evening, shortly after dinner, they bore witness to the second episode of a new series on the dread gogglebox, *The Camomile Lawn*. Alas, within minutes they were twitching well nigh uncontrollably.

Have the Redbrick Rons who now populate the BBC no sense of how the upper classes behave? With mounting horror, I watched as one dreadful solecism followed head-over-heels upon another. No gent, for instance, has ever taken cream in his tea, yet there was Paul Eddington pouring away. Similarly, sunbathing to get brown is a recent craze of the middle-to-lower classes, while napkins would never have been displayed in rings, and would most certainly not be referred to as – most dread of all words – *serviettes*.

My old quaffing partner Mr Philip Howard had sounded the alert in an important article in the previous week's *Times*, pointing out that gentlemen would never wear stick-up collars with black tie, nor eat at a table at which the pudding spoon and fork were positioned at the top of the place 'setting'. You may note that I have included inverted commas around his word 'setting' for, in all honesty, no gentleman would ever use such a word, a favourite of under-maids, journalists and what one might call the 'cleaning classes'. Nevertheless, Philip's conclusion was spot-on. 'Television dramas,' he wrote, 'are made by the shop assistant classes.'

Might I list one or two further howlers in *The Camomile Lawn* that poor Philip, for whatever reason (presumably breeding – or lack of!) failed to spot? In the late 1930s, the English (please, never *British*) upper classes would have rather died than have the lawns mown from left to right. Indeed, this rule gave birth to the phrase, highly popular at the time, 'He's a bit of a left-to-righter', to describe the encroachng *nouveaux riches*.

Again, the wooden leg worn by the Paul Eddington character afforded me a great deal of bother. In the 1920s and 1930s, it was considered an awful mistake within the upper echelons for a man who had lost a leg to be seen to replace it with a wooden leg. This is not to say that wooden legs could not be worn. Far from it; they could be worn, but only by those who already had two legs of their own. Indeed, in the early 1930s, the then Prince of Wales ensured that wooden legs became all the rage when he wore one to a party given by the Marquess of Bute in 1931. By the spring, Wooden Leg Parties were being thrown all over London, and it is said that Wallis Simpson originally caught the Prince of Wales's eye by wearing no less than *two* wooden legs – one on either side of her real legs – to a garden party at Knole. But no one-legged gentleman would ever be seen with a wooden leg, as my dear old friends Hoppety Metcalfe and Off-Balance Ogilvie would be the first to attest.

And why, may one ask, did the producers of *The Camomile Lawn* allow their female characters to be heard repeating, again and again, that awful word, *button*? 'I'll just do this button up, and then I'll be with you,' I heard one of them utter within the first ten minutes. It should go without saying that upper-class women in the 1930s had been brought up never, under any circumstances, to employ such a word, and a fair amount of the social intercourse of that era was directed towards avoiding its mention, an awkward process as there was no ready alternative. To solve this linguistic problem, many of the grander houses would not allow their tailors to place buttons on any garment, which some historians suggest accounts for the rash of arrests for indecent exposure among the upper classes at the time.

A few final errors, if I may. In those days, no gentleman would have lived in a house overlooking the sea. The existence of the telephone was not acknowledged by the English upper classes until way into the 1960s, though some members were employing them as effective ice-cream scoops as early as the late 1940s. A proper lady would never have countenanced a croquet-hoop on the lawn, the splayed prongs being considered too suggestive for visiting tradesmen. Gentlemen have never worn swimsuits for bathing, preferring the warmer combination of jacket-and-tie. As we move inexorably towards our Classless Society, methinks we would do well to remember such things.

'Frightfully Fatty'

Vince Hill in the Land of Vermeer (Table Talk 2)

In every European country, and even as far afield as Africa and America, you can be breezing along thinking how very untouristy and real everything is, and how happy you are to have left Britain miles behind, when you turn a corner of a quaint little street and all of a sudden you are confronted by a sign saying 'The Admiral Nelson Watneys Draught Darts Snooker A Big British Welcome From Mine Hosts Johnny and Sally', decked from top to bottom with Union Jacks and pictures of Andrew and Fergie.

Inside, taped muzak of Old Tyme Music Hall hits such as 'Down at the Old Bull and Bush (Bush, Bush)' played on a piano accordion seeps through the speakers while Mine Host Johnny, replete with handlebar moustache, is leaning on the bar boasting to a man in a naval jacket with shiny buttons of the great tax advantages to be gained from foreign domicile, and how he spent Christmas Day on the sand, sombrero on head. Suddenly, the microwave pings, and out comes a swollen-looking object with a Union Jack cocktail stick wedged into it which turns out to be OUR GREAT BRITISH BANGER.

There will be those for whom such unexpected apparitions merit much rejoicing, but to be quite honest they fill me with gloom, reminding me of Jimmy Tarbuck in the land of Tintoretto, or Vince Hill in the land of Vermeer. I mention all this because there are little parts of London where the same must happen in reverse, where Italians on holiday stumble across Italian restaurants, and Americans gasp as they come across a McDonald's. There are enclaves of more offbeat populations in nooks and crannies of the city, one of the smallest and most chummy of which would seem to be the Portuguese enclave around Golborne Road, to the far north of Notting Hill, in the shadow of the infamous Trellick Towers. The place mills with Portuguese. Within a few yards of one another, there is a Portuguese delicatessen, a Portuguese pâtisserie and, last but not least, Casa Santana, a Portuguese restaurant.

Casa Santana is a spit-and-sawdust sort of place, though I suspect that they long ago wrote off sawdust as too poncy by half. The ground floor has a bar to the right and two or three tables to the left, with a colour television in the corner playing non-stop videos of Portuguese Val Doonicans and Peter

Gordenos. Lots of bits and pieces hang fairly haphazardly over the walls, including a straw boater, a couple of woolly hats, ashtrays bearing the legend 'Madeira', helmets, swords and plates painted with rustic scenes. Sitting on the bar, a food cabinet holds various almost-goodies, including what look like custard tarts.

Despite all this paraphernalia, the ground floor of the Casa Santana is pretty spartan. It is certainly not the best place to go if, say, you are planning a small but discreet get-together with Sir Roy Strong, Barbara Cartland, Lady Antonia Fraser and Lord St John of Fawsley. Heaven knows what you would do with them if they expressed the urge to go to the loo, for the Gents was one of the dingiest I have ever been in, again placing it well in line with continental standards. Nevertheless, beyond its realler-than-real rough-and-readiness, Casa Santana is extremely hospitable. The equivalent restaurant run by other nations, including the British, would have a standoffish air about it, the natives standing around the bar staring resentfully at you as you entered. But the Portuguese clustered around the bar seemed true gents, never for one moment making us feel unwanted and greeting each other with warmth.

The food is pretty damn rough, but as tasty as can be. My companion started with green cabbage soup, which was thick and comforting and would be just the thing, she thought, if you had a hangover. I had a flaming Portuguese sausage, which came lying on what looked like a hollowed-out piggy-bank, with flames leaping beneath it. It was very red and very spicy and absolutely delicious. My companion then moved on to dover sole, hardly the most ethnic choice, but she said it was perfectly cooked, though the accompanying veg was bland and overboiled. If my own main course, Feijoda, had been any more real it would have walked in carrying a carving knife in its trotters asking to be sliced. Described on the menu as 'black pudding' it was one of the most daunting dishes I have ever faced. I was on solid ground with the beans, which were kidney beans of some kind, and the black pudding was downhill all the way, but the sight of the pork and ham sent tremors shooting up and down my throat. Solid lumps of fat sweltered proudly on the plate, encased in yet more fat and rounded off with a fat layer of fat. I have nothing against fat, but I do like it singed a little, and with a good chunk of meat to eat alongside it. But this was macho fat, unsinged and defiant, with no need of namby-pamby meat. Occasionally out of the corner of my eye I would sight a string of meat sheltering in the belly of a piece of fat, but then I would look again and it would be gone, perhaps suffocated, perhaps even digested, for these lumps of fat looked to me very much like living organisms. But fat does have its firm fans, and all firm fat-fans should rush to Casa Santana, because even those who, like me, choose to leave the fat, will be bound to admit that the general taste of the remainder of the dish is rich and hearty.

Puddings were less distinct, with a so-so British Rail-style fruit salad and a cold baked apple served with a bare smattering of cream. The wine list, all Portuguese, is very good indeed, and I appreciated the way the wine the waiter recommended – a tip-top Bairrada – was also the cheapest.

On the way to the gruesome loo, I passed through the basement dining-room, which is, I imagine, only open in the evenings. Lit in nightclub-red and with no TV, it is a little more swish. Posters of bullfights and Portuguese matinée idols adorn the walls, along with flamenco shawls and fake guitars. The walls are decorated with wallpaper which looks like bricks, a sort of visual oxymoron. A couple of plastic crabs sit in a pot in an antique stove. This room gives off a feel of having witnessed a fair number of good times, and might be just the place for a party.

Casa Santana has no need of my recommendations: the people for whom it was intended are obviously already well aware of it and visit it regularly. But reasonably broad-minded outsiders too should find it fun, friendly, flavoursome, and, of course, frightfully fatty.

'Fuzzy Metaphors and Oily Prose'

Pepe and the Prose Stylists

Q: Over the past few weeks, I have come across the term 'prose stylist'. The late Bruce Chatwin, we are frequently told, was a 'great prose stylist'. What does a 'prose stylist' do, and how can I become one?

A: The job of prose stylist grew out of the old literary salons, where male and female writers would gather to have their prose 'seen to' by specialists. Few are better placed for an insight into the profession of prose styling than Pepe of Bond Street, prose stylist to three Booker Prize winners and one literary knight. Pepe started his career sweeping discarded adjectives off the floor in a literary salon on the outskirts of Barcelona, graduating to adding colour to lifeless characterisations, until he finally opened the first salon of his own in 1976.

Leading writer and politician Roy Hattersley drops in on Pepe when he feels that his prose is growing too ungainly. 'Just a trim, Pepe!' he says. 'And perhaps you would be so good as to snip off one or two childhood reminiscences. They are tending to get in the way.'

'Si, Senor Hattersley,' says Pepe, his delicate hands sifting through the greying strands of Mr Hattersley's soft and oily prose, 'and I take off the first and last line of each paragraph it is looking so untidy, no?'

Mr Hattersley looks a little discomforted. 'Oh,' he says, 'I rather like my curly intros. But as you say, Pepe, as you say!'

Brandishing his scissors with pride, the master prose stylist starts by cutting great clumps of prose off the first Hattersley paragraph, and, as the 'but-I-do-not-recalls' and the 'much-as-I-deplores' flutter to the floor, Mr Hattersley's prose begins to look almost manageable.

Next in the queue, quietly composing a major new opera for comb and loo paper ensemble, is leading author Anthony Burgess. 'I find that I have to visit a decent prose stylist at least once a week,' he admits. 'My prose seems to grow faster than anyone else's. Within days it has developed great big knots which only the experts can begin to unravel.'

Pepe tends to employ an electric power-cutter on Mr Burgess's prose, trimming whole paragraphs, even chapters, at a time. 'Mr Burgess, he has beautiful prose, but it need constant attention,' he explains. He laughs as he recalls some of the things nestling within it. 'Once, I cut a novel and I find six good short stories there, and I even find a whole polemic hidden beneath a book review.' It is sometimes rumoured that Mr Burgess uses artificial colouring on his autobiographies.

Many of Pepe's distinguished clientele suffer from thinning prose, including loss of meaning. Some discover an increasing number of subordinate clauses and even main arguments coming away when scratched. But Pepe finds that, with the application of a bit of hot air, even a few wisps of incoherent thought can be lent the impression of weight.

Take, for instance, the case of the next writer in the queue, Mr Melvyn Bragg. Seeing his lengthy novels on the shelves, plastered with shining reviews, a great many readers believe that there must be a lot to them. In fact, the illusion of depth is testament to the versatility of the aerosol, odd, derivative flecks of story gaining bounce from Pepe's Famous Prose Lacquer. Thus, many critics claim Bragg's prose 'lacqs for nothing'.

'At times like these,' says Pepe, as he sweeps up the assorted strands of fuzzy metaphors and split infinitives, 'society needs as many prose stylists as it can get.'

'Gee, That's Really Great'

Andy Warhol and Chairman Mao

A ndy Warhol died in February 1987, but none of his friends guessed that anything was amiss until February 1988. Some now believe that he had already died as early as March 1983, halfway through a conversation with Prince Albert of Monaco, but this seemed to have had little or no effect on his creative powers.

This month, London plays host to a huge variety of Warhol events, including a major retrospective of his minor movies and a minor retrospective of his major movies, 'The Unbegun Warhols', an exhibition of blank canvasses at the survivors of the Warhol Factory of the 1960s. This last event, a one-man show, can last for anything up to five minutes, depending upon how the performer's memory holds.

As a friend and confidante of the late Andy Warhol, I have been invited to share my thoughts on this restless, endlessly creative, enigmatic man. For the last 10 years of the artist's life, Andy and I had established a weekday morning routine of talking to each other on the phone. He made it a rule never to answer the phone until he had first heard it ringing. He would then signal that he had picked up the receiver by saying 'Hello', or, if he wished to conserve his creative energies, the shorter 'Hi'. I would then say 'Hello. Who's speaking, please?' And, if he could remember, our conversation would develop from there.

I assisted Andy with many of his movies, including my personal favourite *Lenscap*, his 15-hour epic shot entirely with the lenscap still on. To my mind, Andy will be remembered as one of the greatest lenscap artists of all time.

He followed *Lenscap* (1969) with *Blur*, the very first six-hour movie of an undecorated wall shot entirely out of focus. This was acknowledged as a masterpiece of the genre by the avant-garde, including Hiram V. Holtz, the famous blind art critic. Of Warhol's next movie, *Blank*, shot entirely without any film whatsoever in the camera, he wrote: 'Warhol is fascinated by the apparent paradox of watching nothing at all. Without film in the camera, the movie has no beginning and no end. In a curious way, it was both always there, and yet never there at all. The language of film is reduced to an essence of nothingness. Out of vacuity springs fascination.'

As Associate Editor of Warhol's *Interview* magazine, I would oversee

Andy's brilliant probing of celebrities, often helping him to press the record button on his tape recorder, checking that the subject was there before Andy started asking questions, and so on. As a result, we were able to print fascinating transcripts of Warhol's interviews with the famous, including this revealing excerpt from Andy's exclusive interview with Chairman Mao in a New York Bagel Parlour in 1972:

Andy (looking at teaspoon): Gee, isn't that really great.

Mao (grunts).

Andy: I'm really into teaspoons this year. Are you into teaspoons at all?

Mao (after some thought): No.

Andy: Hey, isn't that really great, he's not into teaspoons. That's just amazing. You're Chinese, right?

Mao: That is correct.

Andy: That's really great. Chinese! Wow!

Mao: (takes bite of bagel).

Andy: Have you ever met Liza Minnelli?

Warhol would constantly hone his aphorisms until they shone with a prophetic wisdom, and only then would I put them into my notebook. 'In the future,' he once said, 'everyone will be farmers for 15 minutes.' Due to a printing error, this became more widely known as 'In the future, everyone will be famous for 15 minutes', but happily with no consequent loss of meaning.

'A Gob of Phlot-Snegm'

Martin Amis's Diary

The possibility that Iraq will soon have nuclear weapons could have chilling consequences for the world. It is up to writers who have the power to articulate the unimaginable to stress the urgency of the situation, to pick words of sufficient terror to show that nuclear weapons are the exploding turds of our age, that a nuke-turd is like a liquified-biro in the top pocket of a beige suit, probably three-piece, that the aftermath of nuclear collar-hoist will be more serious than anything we have so far encountered, like a gob of snot-plegm – phlot? snegm? – on a shiny kitchen surface, or an ear-glob in a plate of vichyssoise, which is chilling; chilling at the moment in fact: I'm having it for lunch with croutons after tennis with Barnesy.

Tennis with Barnesy is, as you know, a regular fixture of my afternoons. Here's a rundown of my morning:

8.00: Have breakfast with my kids. Worry about them being nuked before lunch. At least they weren't in the Holocaust. Or were they? Play with the concept. Walk them to school for a photographer from *Time Out*. Taxi back.

8.45: Arrive at my work sock. 'Sock' has become famous as one of the brilliant new words I have invented. It means 'flat', but I don't say 'flat', I say 'sock'. I like to think of myself as primarily a comical writer, you see. Arrive at my work 'sock' (!) and write three sentences. Ring my agent to tell her that I have written three sentences, immediately. Quickly stick up the dartboard and push the pinball-machine centre-stage in preparation.

9.00: Journalist arrives to cross-question me about the three sentences. As he walks in, he notices the pinball-machine and the dartboard, thank God. I say the three sentences have gone pretty well. He wonders if he can ask me what they're about. I say writing three sentences is a bit like dropping a nuke, you never know whether you've hit the target or not, so I'd rather not say.

11.45: Still talking about the three sentences, and about death, which I don't call death in the middle sentence, I call eadth. This is because it's the duty of every novelist living now, in the first half of the 20th Century, to re-invent the language. By writing 'eadth', I am forcing the reader to confront what it really means.

Suddenly realise that I haven't shown the journalist my snooker cue. Say:

'Sorry, lad, time's up. I've got to play a game of snooker with an ordinary person.' Journalist obviously impressed, never heard of a writer playing snooker with an ordinary person before. I demonstrate my ear for language 'Ordinary person says "innit" and "as such" all the time.' I tell him. 'Very acute,' he says, and I give him time to write it all down with his pus-pen in a scum-pad before showing him the front hole of the – (!) – sock.

Death is the snare in God's drum-set, the pot-noodle in the scabby puddle, the dandruff in the bouffant, the zit in the plug-hole, the mouldy slice of pig in the two-door saloon fridge.

To lunch at the Caprice nosebag with my mates McEwan and Raine. McEwan is writing a new novel about a man who has sado-masochistic sexual intercourse with a koala and ends it all by biting its head off and hiding it under his hat but he is found out when he goes to somewhere un-named but which seems very like Buckingham Palace and he is asked to remove all headgear before greeting the Head of State. It's about the psycho/political male/female relationship, and it's very 20th century.

Raine is working on a new poem in which he voices his fears about death today. In one of his most haunting images in 20th-Century Literature, he compares death to a 'can of Australian peaches in heavy syrup'. Over lunch, we discuss this haunting image. 'I remember when I saw the corpse of my great-granny,' says Raine, tear-pustules bursting through his head-sockets. 'I had two vivid impressions. First, that she looked like an Australian canned peach in heavy syrup. Second, that there was snot still in her nose, *even though she was dead*.'

'Says one helluva lot about the 20th Century,' says McEwan, dabbing his eyes.

'Utterly memorable,' I choke.

'Who's for the Creme Caramel?' says the waiter.

Silently, with no conferring, each of us jots down 'Creme Caramel' as a suitable shattering image, probably of AIDS.

Choosing names for characters is a complex job for any novelist living in the here and now, the vying demands of swirling realities encroaching on a detumescent actuality to be crystallised in specific codes and propagated in words at once formal and meaningless. For example, probably my most closely realised character was Kevin Gobfart.

Let me, the author-figure, explain. I had spent weeks trying to create a combination of names that would echo the character's almost apocalyptic obsession with cultural detritus. I had first heard the name 'Kevin' about three years ago while watching football on television at the Pinters' in Campden Hill Square, and I had been storing it up for possible use in the future. Then, beating around for a surname, I combined 'gob' with 'fart' to form 'Gobfart', so that the subliminal message to some form of bodily excess might find its way into the intelligent reader's consciousness without detracting from the moment-to-moment realism of the novel.

In my new novel, I have an entirely different main character – more sophisticated, more essentially *humane*, some would argue – and so I have had to think of an entirely different name for him. After hard thought and creative interplay, the name I have come up with is: Trev Belchwilly.

Raine has already faxed to say he considers it my most ingenious yet, well up to Nabokov at his best.

I have been called the poet of the nuclear under-class. Though my own background was 'privileged', I have tramped the low-life of Notting Hill and South Kensington in my 'foot-socks' (shoes!) for minutes on end, even dropping into pubs and coffee-bars and 'rug-rethink-parlours (that's barbers to you!!!) with a mission to capture that authentic jungle-language of urban decay. So when the gourmandising Jeff T. Fatface eats a Farty-Wankburger in the Shag'n'Piss Diner in the third chapter of my last novel but one, *A Concerned Warning to the Planet* (1983), then burps and says: 'Crikey, mate, jolly tasty, 'ave one on me, me old hearty, innit as such, gor bless yer guv', you can be sure that this is the dialogue of today, visionary, disturbing, and chillingly true.

'Good and Soggy'

Hugh Montgomery-Massingberd and The Full English Breakfast (Table Talk 3)

Surveys showing the startling truth that the traditional full English breakfast is a thing of the past are now a recurrent news item on dull days for newspapers, along with articles by or about Michael Heseltine's future chances and think pieces about whether you can be both a successful career woman and an award-winning mother. These surveys tend to suggest that only the mentally deficient still bother with the traditional English breakfast, whilst all the real achievers in our society are satisfied with a bowl of Swiss-style chalet-packed muesli combined with the merest sprinkling of fully-pasteurised, fat-free milk, electronically skimmed to remove all taste and impurities.

But, I'm glad to say, there are still a few standard bearers for high cholesterol, prominent among them my old friend, the leading obituarist of our age – or any age – Mr Hugh Montgomery-Massingberd. As he was tucking into a large breakfast at the Connaught Hotel back in 1972, his waitress marched up to him to tell him that it was the largest breakfast they had ever served, beating the previous record-holder, King Farouk I of Egypt. Who better, then, to take along to review breakfast at Claridge's?

Claridge's is, I think, my favourite hotel in London. The Connaught is too smart, the Ritz too common, the Savoy too busy, Trusthouse Forte hotels too Trusthouse Forte, but Claridge's combines grandeur with *laissez-faire*, meaning that the Claridge's staff seems happy to allow someone as unkempt as me to loiter in the hotel's beautiful public rooms without raising so much as an eyebrow.

I had never before eaten breakfast at Claridge's, and was a little worried that it might be a let-down. I have stayed in hotels that seem tip-top until the hour of breakfast looms, when all standards leap out of the window and a single Wall's sausage arrives beside a hard fried egg transported by a surly waiter who tells you proudly that they don't do bacon any more, sorry. One look at Claridge's breakfast menu makes it clear that they don't regard breakfast as the poor relation of other meals: the set menu has everything one might expect – sausages, bacon, cereals, eggs – while the *à la carte* is full of things of such extravagance that they look as if they are on holiday from the full dinner menu.

Mr Montgomery-Massingberd arrived looking almost svelte, a change he put down to dropping any evening meal in favour of yoghurt. But if the end of the day spelled austerity, the beginning of the day seemed to more than make up for it, as I discovered when the waiter came to take our order.

The waiter seemed bored stiff as he took down my own boring order of poached egg, ham and sausage, looking around the room impatiently as I debated with myself whether to have tomatoes or not. Having written my order down on his little pad, he turned to my guest, 'Do you think it permissible to have both the fish *and* the meat courses? It's so hard to make the choice this early in the morning, don't you find?' Mr Montgomery-Massingberd asked me, politely. 'Oh, quite,' I said, and Mr Montgomery-Massingberd went full steam ahead.

'Well,' he said to the waiter, who was still looking bored, 'I think I'll have some croissants and toast . . . and then, if I may, I'll have the porridge, yes, the porridge . . . and then I think a couple of kippers might be a good idea . . .' Around this point, the waiter's interest began to be aroused . . . 'And then I'll have a couple of fried eggs, please, and some bacon, and some field mushrooms, oh, and some tomatoes and some sausages of course . . .' The waiter turned over the page of his little pad and I saw him struggle to suppress a smile. '. . . and then perhaps a few kidneys might do the trick. How many would you say I should have? Four, perhaps?' The waiter said, yes, he thought four might be advisable. '. . . and then that minute steak looks jolly good, yes, I think I'll have the minute steak – oh, and a jug of orange-juice, if I may.'

By this time, the waiter was beaming broadly while I too was chuckling. I watched delightedly as he ran off to a huddle of other waiters and showed them the staggering length of the Montgomery-Massingberd order, at which they all gasped in astonishment and admiration.

Tucking into his porridge, Mr Montgomery-Massingberd told me that his late friend Sir Ian Moncrieff of that Ilk had always eaten his porridge standing up, holding it in the left hand, so that he was ready to draw his sword if attacked. Personally, I would guess that the mere sight of porridge would be enough to fend off any assailant, but then I have always disliked it.

Next on were two very generous kippers. 'Very good for you,' said Mr Montgomery-Massingberd. At the Ritz, he thought, they served them too dry, but these were just right: moist and juicy. Meanwhile, I tucked into my relatively modest cooked breakfast, and found it to be one of the best I have ever eaten, with proper, meaty sausages, excellent ham, and eggs poached just right, still runny but not all over the place.

Our fellow breakfasters were plentiful and various, with a good many oddly-shaped Americans – square, oblong, pear-shaped and so on – one or two captains, or at least lieutenants, of industry talking trade, a smattering of hungover young rakes and some tweedies reading the newspapers in solitary pleasure. The dining-room itself, with shiny art deco mirrored walls, is a joy to be in, with enough layers and alcoves to afford everyone a feeling of privacy while still retaining a unified magnificence. Here and there are nice little art deco touches, such as the silver ashtrays with incorporated matchbox-holders on every table.

By now, the kippers had been cleared away, and I was just congratulating my guest on his acute obituary of the actress who played Miss Amy Turtle on *Crossroads* (I had been especially impressed by his ability to remember that she was once suspected of being Amelia Turtolovski, a Soviet spy, a charge that was later refuted, and rightly so) when the waiter, smiling fit to bust, brought him his main course, and I found myself struck dumb.

I would describe what I saw as a mountain if ever I had seen a mountain big enough. Kidneys were piled upon kidneys, sausages on sausages, rashers upon rashers and, beneath it all, sat a minute steak of quite extraordinary length. Perhaps out of decorum, Mr Montgomery-Massingberd feigned astonishment. 'I say!' he said.

His enjoyment was a thing to behold, marred only by the propensity of each kidney to spurt a little blood over his smart check suit each time it was pronged. 'Alas,' he said, pulling his napkin higher and higher towards his collar, 'my suit now resembles a butcher's apron.' This mishap aside, he adored every mouthful, singling out the kidneys and the steak for particular praise. He also liked the toast which was, he declared, 'good and soggy. I hate spreading butter on toast that's too crisp, don't you?'

When he had finished what was on his plate, I asked him, half-jokingly, whether he would like anything else. He had noticed, he replied, that there was fruit salad on the menu, and he thought that might be a healthy way to finish up. I joined him with a yoghurt, as real as can be, with a pleasantly tart taste.

At the end of our breakfast, I asked Mr Montgomery-Massingberd if he felt full. 'I do actually feel very full,' he replied.

'Indeed,' he added, 'I might be a bit pushed to swallow the grouse that I'm having at lunchtime.'

'The Great Adventure'

David, John and Rosie (Political Sketch 3)

The SDP votes on merger

'Let me ask you to rise with me and welcome David Owen.' Mr John Cartwright, ever the greeter in a prosperous firm of undertakers, had been judged the man most fitted to make the speech of welcome.

In marched Dr Owen, waving his assured and manly wave. Taking to the rostrum – a set in front of the official set, strangely reminiscent of a Punch and Judy box plopped into the middle of the Royal Opera House – he held raised hands with John and Rosie, his crocodile smile snapping around in search of babies to eat.

'I think that says it all,' he said, as the applause died down. He stood erect and immobile, his hands on the edge of the dais, black hair, white cuffs, dark suit, red eyes. Rosie, dressed in prim black and beaming away like Mary Poppins gone loopy, stared wide-eyed up at the Doctor from her seat. This is a man, she seemed to be thinking, for whom I would gladly be Chancellor of the Exchequer.

'Remember how they used to write about us – that we were a rump, a faction, a fan-club,' continued Dr Owen to his rump, his faction, his fan-club. Mary Poppins's eyes seemed to mist over at the memory. If need be, she would be his Foreign Secretary and his Minister of Trade as well.

The Doctor praised the courage and conviction, the tremendous clarity and consistency, of those who still agreed with him. 'We all sustained each other,' he declared. 'We who love this party – and there are many in this room who love this party,' he went on, and Mary Poppins continued to beam upwards, now sure in the knowledge that she would, if called upon, take on the portfolios of Health, Employment and Northern Ireland. 'We who *love* this party – we will not be forced into a loveless marriage.'

This was a sombre Doctor, barely raising his voice, his once-dangling forelock now cut and trimmed and neatly swept back. Many of his old gestures had been abandoned: no more the 'when I was foreign Secretary', no more the uplift on the end of each paragraph to indicate a suitable period for applause, no more the purposeful gesticulations or the shrewd half-smiles.

This was the International Statesman, above all that. 'There's no need to cut each others' throats as we go our separate ways,' he stated, the director of the abattoir espousing the noble cause of lifelong vegetarianism.

Perhaps quoting from Peter Pan, he began to talk of the 'Great Adventure' on which they had embarked. 'You've got to know what you love and fight for what you love.'

Oh, yes! Oh, yes! Her smile all a-quiver, Mary Poppins seemed about to burst into song. *Chim-chimanee, chim-chimanee, chim-chim-cheroo. Good luck will rub off when I shake hands with you.* Those joyous words kept flooding back.

For Mr Maclennan's speech the next day, Mary Poppins stood at one side, her side smile now absent. At the last SDP conference, Poor Bob's freshly-choreographed gesticulations lent him the appearance of a well-to-do Catherine Wheel, but now he, too, was sombre, his curious twitchings more appropriate to a confrontation with a lackadaisical flea than with a mass rally of over-heating Social Democrats.

In moments of great seriousness, he bears a strong physical resemblance to a ventriloquist's dummy, his eyebrows leaping up and down on his forehead, his hair so carefully coiffed that it might be sculpted in plasticine, the words he enunciates sounding as if thrown from a little man – or possibly woman – crouched in the dais beneath him. He pronounces the word 'found' to rhyme with 'rind' and the 'u' in 'illusion' is borrowed from the word 'Tuesday'.

'I commend it to you: your vote must be yes.' Mr Maclennan sat down and, rightly guessing that his speech must now be over, the audience stood up. Waving like a man who had only recently learnt how, Poor Bob issued a mouthy smile. The beams on the faces of the pro- and anti-mergerites as they left the hall made it clear that for them all, bliss was it in that dusk to be alive.

1 February 1988
Postscript: The SDP gradually petered out, eventually disappearing in 1992. David Owen was made a peer in 1992. Both Rosie Barnes and John Cartwright lost their seats in the same year.

'Harold Who?'

Central Lobby Dawdling

Quite the most interesting place to pass the time of day in London is the Central Lobby of the Houses of Parliament. A decorative octagon with a towering, vaulted ceiling, it presents a 24-hour, ever-changing drama, with a tendency towards high comedy, but with a little pomp and pathos thrown in. In many ways, it offers a Walt Disney version of an Olde Englande, before motorways and computers, before nationalisation or privatisation, before lager louts or Lord Young. On one side, there is an ornate little Post Office plus elderly post box, without the weird mazes of ropes and arrows and video advertisements now rife in the world outside. One half expects to see Dr Finlay queuing there, with Janet in attendance, and perhaps Will Hay in appropriate uniform behind the tiny counter. On another side, jovial British bobbies, of a type not seen since Sergeant Dixon, survey the comings and goings with a benevolent air, occasionally swapping pleasantries with be-tailed clerks, as spruce as can be.

Through the doorway leading to St Stephen's Entrance, the public shuffle in, some with grievances, some to hob-nob, others just to take a peek. A lot of waiting goes on in the Central Lobby, for this is where people without passes must wait for those with. But it is also a natural corridor, linking three routes into the Palace of Westminster, and the dawdler can spend many a happy minute observing politicians as they scoot and swagger to and fro. During the year I spent as *The Times's* parliamentary sketch-writer, I came to feel that to catch sight of the politician at his most content it was necessary to wait awhile in the Central Lobby. In the Chamber of the House of Commons, the politician's claims to grandeur suffer greatly from his proximity to six hundred or so others, each with similar claims, but the Central Lobby is a far kinder stage, a setting infinitely more conducive to the swelling of the chest. I used to enjoy watching Members of little significance within the Chamber increase the strut in their step as they strode, in worldly, proprietorial fashion, across the Central Lobby to meet a small band of awe-struck constituents. Elsewhere in the Palace of Westminster, these same Members would face drudgery, conspiracy and aggression, but here they could act the cock of the walk, with all the little chicks clucking appreciatively at their every crow. In Central Lobby, MPs could stand a-grinning, jangling loose change in their pockets, buttoning and unbuttoning their double-breasted jackets, listening blissfully to the reverential queries of strangers, occasionally nodding in a knowing, supportive way as a Minister strode by.

And yet how often must intimations of political mortality intrude upon such bliss! I well remember first setting eyes upon Lord Wilson of Rievaulx, small and unaccompanied, as he pottered from one side of the lobby to the other, unnoticed by all tourists and most Britons, recognised only, I suspect, by those politicians for whom he was once the arch-enemy or arch-hero, the all-powerful and ever-present, the personification of a decade, the cunning, the wily Harold Wilson. Yet now he resembles nothing so much as a neglected Chinese doll, cracked and dusty, an actor whose soap-opera was shelved long ago, an old man whose face probably means less to most people than the face of Kylie Minogue.

Even a year in Parliament is quite long enough to note the transience of political fame. Some, like Peter Bruinvels, frittered away into nothingness upon losing their seats in the election while others, like Denzil Davies, became famous only on waving farewell. Within that year, Robert Maclennan rose from obscurity to national fame, returning to obscurity by the next bus out. The Alliance came and went. I still find it odd, upon seeing a group photograph of all living former Prime Ministers, to see James Callaghan's cosy, bespectacled head popping into the frame, so rapidly has he evaporated. And even some of Mrs Thatcher's own Cabinet seem to have disappeared without trace. Who, for instance, was Mark Carlisle? No one seems to know.

Perhaps these ghostly figures might be encouraged to burrow underground rather than parade so unashamedly through Central Lobby, to the consternation of their colleagues. One of my earliest visits to the House of Commons was in 1977, to interview John Stonehouse for a play I was writing about him. At the time, he was about to face trial, but was still a sitting MP. We met, and, as we walked along the corridors of Westminster together, Stonehouse would greet each passing colleague with an ostentatious 'Hello', or 'How are you?', and each passing colleague would look the other way, say nothing, and bustle ever onwards. It was like walking with a noisy, gregarious ghost, whom only I could see or hear. After a year inside Parliament, this still remains my strongest impression of MPs: ghostly figures, waving their arms and raising points in an endless bid to see themselves as real and wanted. And parliamentary journalists are riders on the ghost train, occasionally enervated or amused to be brushed by these spooky apparitions, but grateful, none the less, to return to fresh air after their daily spin.

Since abandoning my sketch-writing post, I have read an essay by Max Beerbohm published in 1909, in which he contrasts the newspaper image of the House of Commons, a place where 'nowhere is the human comedy so fast and furious, nowhere played with such skill and brio', with the drab temple of inconsequence he could see for himself. 'Look at them, hark at them, poor dears!' he wrote. 'See them clutching at their coats, and shuffling from foot to foot in travail, while their ideas, ridiculous mice, for the most part get jerked painfully out somehow and anyhow.'

Beerbohm blamed the gross disparity between report and reality on the gradual lowering of a reporter's standards: 'If a man criticises one kind of ill-done thing exclusively, he cannot but, in course of time, lower his standard. Seeing nothing good, he will gradually forget what goodness is; and will accept as good that which is least bad.'

To maintain any interest – his own and his readers' – the journalist has to exaggerate the difference between MPs, caricaturing their human characteristics, portraying the grumpy as furious, the fidgety as rebellious, the dull as dignified, the mistaken as brave, and so on. But, in reality, it is the homogeneity of politicians that is most outstanding. MPs left, right or centre are a breed apart, a breed prepared to undergo the processes of selection and election, a breed which feels itself able to determine the needs and motives of vast numbers of people it will never meet, a bossy, determined, public-speaking breed to whom hesitation and apathy are strangers. If there is one thing that I learnt, it is that Neil Kinnock and Mrs Thatcher have far more in common with each other than they have with their milkmen.

'Hawaay The Lads'

J. C. and The Sunshine Band

Whenever there is a war or a world cup, the air rings with the sound of one grim word: 'Lads'. No-one quite knows where 'lad' came from (though some claim it is a variant on the past participle of 'lead') but of one thing we can be sure: for as long as we are threatened by bombs and by footballs, lads will never go away.

Why should the word arouse such irritation in me? It reminds me of the heartiness that pursued me so relentlessly during my time in the Boy Scouts ('c'mon, lads, one more verse of 'Gin Gan Goolie', then last one in the lake's a cissy') and of the lack of Team Spirit with which I was always charged as I cowered at an unobtrusive corner of the Rugger Pitch ('let's see you muddy those knees, Brown!'). But my aversion to the word is not solely based upon the horrors of personal experience. It is a word that pretends to be chummy but which is jam-packed with condescension, a word given to wearing the fancy dress of rugged matiness in order to disguise something prissy, smug and rather bossy.

Cyril Connolly noted that A. E. Housman used the word 'lad' 67 times in the 63 poems in his *A Shropshire Lad* volume. Yet the laddishness of his poetry never transferred to his private life. 'Dry, shy, soft, prickly, smooth, conventional, silent, feminine, fussy, pernickety, sensitive, tidy, greedy' were just some of the adjectives used to describe him by Harold Nicolson. Interestingly, two other writers who delighted in using 'lad' were equally aloof and unclubbable, and would have blanched at the arms-round-shoulders bawdy singalongs the word suggest. Both T. E. Lawrence ('Rehail was quite a lad: a free-built sturdy fellow, too fleshy for the life we were to lead' and John Ruskin ('all handsome lads and pretty lasses') scattered 'lads' in their prose in a bid to leaven into normality their own peculiar, repressed feelings towards men. The effect is artificial and not a little ridiculous.

In our own time, 'lads' is no less bogus, particularly when delivered through the mouths of the middle-classes. For those on top, it forms a one-way bridge between matiness and condescension. There is an unintentionally funny passage in Jim Callaghan's autobiography in which he describes escorting President Jimmy Carter on a trip to Newcastle, where the Carter family was believed to have had its roots. '. . . his most tumultuous reception came when he stood on the steps of Newcastle Town Hall', writes Callaghan, 'and began his reply to the Lord Mayor's speech of welcome with the famous local rallying cry, "Hawaay the lads!" The phrase was of course unfamiliar to Jimmy Carter, and he was doubtful about using it, but I coached him during the motorcade procession and as soon as he uttered it, a tremendous cheer went up.' In all likelihood, Callaghan, a Portsmouth man for whom the phrase 'Hawaay the lads' would have been as alien as 'Och the Noo' or 'Call me Bwana', himself required a coach before coaching the President.

Politicians chirrup the word 'lads' at their peril. For a middle-class politician, it betrays a strong drive to patronise, for a working-class politician, naivety. In all his lengthy diaries, full of meetings with workers and unionists, Tony Benn is careful not to use the word once. Eric Heffer, on the other hand, has always made free with his 'lads'. After he had walked out of the 1985 Labour Party Conference in Bournemouth in protest at Neil Kinnock's rejection of Militant, Heffer was pictured on his hotel balcony declaring that Militant were 'decent working-class lads' whom Kinnock had no right to say such rude things about. As he watches Derek Hatton advertising wrist-watches on television, does Heffer still believe Hatton to be decent, working class or, indeed, a lad?

'His Little Thingy'

Jilly Cooper's Diary

en!! But, having said that, I can't help but feel just a mite boo-hoo-ish about poor old Radovan Karadzic. He must be hurting terribly. He looks such a sweetie but so utterly lost, poor love, with that simply *blissful* head of hair blowing this way and that across his poor old furrowed brow as if not quite knowing which way to turn. I know how he feels, because I went through the same sort of thing when Leo ran off with someone else, and deeply gloomy I was too, but that's meant to be jolly private and I literally never mention it, not even now. There I go again!

There's such a lot of unhappiness around at the moment, what with the recession and poor Fergie and Bosnia and that awful spell of rain we had last week and the beastly IRA and our lovely dog Josie having to go to our darling vet for fleas. This means that on top of everything else I simply can't bear to see Radovan looking so very, very miz.

'"Serbs" him jolly well right!' (!) some will say, but I can't help feeling the big softie could do with a bit of a cuddle, a jolly good night's sleep and a rattling yarn, so let's hope the Red Cross reach Raddie with a copy of my latest book before those tears start plopping on his pillow, poor love.

Rushed off my feet with this book, I've already got going on my next, which is going to be completely different and awfully artistic, set in lovely snowy Norway at the turn of the century, with lots of friendly huskies and really smashing reindeer and super cuddly polar bears.

The plot is going to be very, very Norwegian – 'Nor-way' to treat a lady, you might say! – with our hero, Sven Lloyd-Johnson, impossibly handsome, chasing after all the married women in the little Norwegian community of Cosytown-on-Fjord, but eventually falling absolutely madly in love with the lovely heroine, Brigitte, or Brigie for short, who's always a bit of a mess and can't stop bursting into absolute fits of giggles at all the wrong moments but has an insatiable passion for mongrels and a pet moose called 'Moose at Ten' (!) and is blessed with an utterly blissful heart of gold.

Of course, there's simply oodles of the most super sex in the book, very passionate and deliciously steamy and very, very Norwegian. In this opening passage, Sven has it off with Hedda, or Heddie, on the tundra he has just had laid – at the most frightful expense – outside his £2,000,000 mansion. Quite a turn-on – or 'tundra-on' (!) – I think you'll agree!':

'Sven was like the most amazingly bouncy energetic dog when it came to sex. He insisted on eating minced morsels out of a bowl on the floor before leaping on to his latest love.

'When he leapt at last, Heddie, super, adorable, kind-hearted Heddie, who looked rather like the lovely, brilliant Anne Diamond when she became a TV superstar in Britain a full eight years later, lovely Heddie was waiting for him like an obedient Spaniel, her ears flapping over the sides of the pillows.

'There followed three hours of deliriously passionate love-making, absolutely super and hardly messy at all. For Heddie, it was like nothing she had ever imagined before: like winning all the rosettes at the very best gymkhana and seeing the most fabulous film and being awfully naughty and stealing some chocolate mousse from the fridge and having a jolly good giggle – and all at the same time! It was super to be a sexy girl in Norway at the turn of the century, she thought.

'When it was all over, Sven picked up his 19th-century Norwegian mobile phone and forcefully tapped out a number with his wildly masculine forefinger. "Hello!" he barked, setting the scene. "This is ruthless but irresistible Sven calling from Norway. The time is 1901, just one year into the new century."

'Suddenly, Sven felt the utterly over-whelming urge to make a Norwegian pun. "Let me inform you that there hasn't been much sunshine here. Also, thank goodness I'm not a soldier outside Buckingham Palace," he said, a smile lighting up his heart-stoppingly fanciable face, "or otherwise it wouldn't be so much 'the turn of the century' as 'the tan of the sentry'!!!" From the other end came simply gales of merriment. No-one in Norway had ever made a joke before, and this was simply the best ever.'

I'm sorry, but I really and absolutely don't, don't, DON'T want to say anything about that awful business a couple of years ago when lovely, kind Leo had his little thingy with that poor sweet love of a woman – let's not name her for her own good – who must be hurting dreadfully, poor thing. It was just one of those simply dreadful damp-hankie-ish sobby sort of things, and I have vowed not to talk about it in public, but to let bygones be bygones, and it would be just so frightfully unfair on her, poor poppet, to rake over it all again in print, going on about all the ghastly unhappiness she caused, poor love, and all the simply horrid hurt she brought onto us all by being so very, very public about it, poor lamb, so I'd like to make it quite clear that in my new book the character of Grizelda Garst-Leigh, the hideous, fat-thighed, semi-alcoholic, fifteen-times-married utter tart, poor love, and the character of the internationally successful overweight publisher Leo Olde-Lecher, married to lovely, bubbly, tremendously sexy yet discreet and utterly loyal media superstar Gillie, are all entirely fictitious, and have nothing to do with the true-life characters they're completely based on, poor loves.

Today I felt like strolling out into the country so I went for a lovely long country walk in the tremendously jolly countryside around our country house which is right bang in the middle of the country, completely surrounded on all sides by country, and I was walking towards a country wood – best foot 'for-wood'!! – I thought, 'Golly, how lucky I am to live here, right in the middle of the countryside, full of country air and country people and countri-ish things to do'. But then I thought, 'But golly, I love London too, with all my chums and jaunts and giggles and flirts and shops and devastatingly good-looking men and cars and buses and Londony things!' In an ideal world, I thought, London would be in the very centre of the countryside and the countryside would be in the very centre of London, so then everyone would be happy and we wouldn't have this ghastly recession any more and Fergie would cheer up and Raddie would smile and everyone would begin to realise that Norman Lamont is a lovely, lovely man and a smashing host and they'd stop going at him in that beastly way. Poor love, he's hurting dreadfully. Hey-ho! Time for a drinkie with the lovely kind Leo, poor silly poppet! Men!!

'Hoots Mon'

Happy Days (Wallace Arnold 4)

A handy tip to my devoted readers, if I may: from time to time it can prove well worth reading the rest of *The Independent on Sunday* too, as it can often surprise one with other articles of real merit.

Let me explain. The Arnold Mansion is oft cheered through these long winter evenings with the lighting of a roaring log-fire. Needless to say, I insist upon 'laying' (dread word!) these fires myself, using the tried and tested Arnold method – newspaper at the bottom, then kindling, then coal, and finally logs, all set ablaze with a safety match. Who knows? You might care to try this patent method for yourselves in your own home this evening. But it was while embarking on this exercise last Tuesday that I chanced upon two pieces from a few weeks back, the first by a Mr Jack, the second by Miss (Mssss!) Lynn Barber, that resolutely opinionated bird of the unfeathered variety.

The pair of 'em were recalling their magical memories of the 1950s. Though the name of Wallace Arnold was unaccountably absent from both accounts, it is considered by many to be synonymous with the 1950s, as it is with the four subsequent decades. But tempting though it may be to recall some of my own Arnoldian highlights from that golden age of commonsense, I prefer to offer a more detached, statistical view, plucked from the Arnold archives.

In the 1950s, most ordinary, decent people had never heard of 'television' (87%), 'America' (92%), the 'super-market' (77%) or – dread word indeed! – 'sex' (83%). Instead, they contented themselves with simple pleasures. Every Friday evening, they would down-tools for 'Friday Night Is Music Night' compèred by 'Mr Wireless' himself, Wallace Arnold, and these tunes would be whistled in the streets by the paperboys throughout the next seven days.

Research now confirms that, in the 1950s, 90% of males under the age of 18 were paperboys, and of these a clear 98% would spend their time whistling the latest 'hit tunes' from the wireless. 'How Much Is That Doggie In The Window?' was whistled by up to 73% of paperboys at any one time, with 'Hoots Mon' by Lord Rockingham's XI a clear second with only 15%. As it is now widely known, working-class males over the age of 18 tended to be either milkmen (30%) or postmen (30%) or policemen ('The Great British Bobby')

(30%). The remainder played football for England.

At that time, virtually all crime (approximately 96%) could be prevented by a quick clip around the ear, so The Great British Bobby spent most of his day bicycling and/or whistling, with an average of only half-an-hour a day devoted to administering quick clips around the ears to errant paperboys. The remaining 4% of crimes were straightforward domestic murders, usually of their nit-picking wives by thoroughly respectable doctors. The corpses of these wives tended to be discovered during the annual trawl through the left-luggage lockers at one of the major London Railway stations, with perhaps the odd finger or little toe popping up some time later at one of the main terminii such as Brighton (27%) or East Grinstead (34%).Of course, there were the usual young louts with more get-up-and-go than sense, but their japes were as nothing to the 'joy-riding' and 'grievous bodily harm' we are forced to endure today. If we take a typical year – 1955 – we see that most of these young tearaways were only playfully stabbing at one another's tummies with 'flick-knives' (62%) or having a marvellous time borrowing strangers' automobiles and driving them off – often at breakneck speeds! – along pleasant country lanes, usually taking the trouble to whistle a merry tune (37%).

Prostitutes barely existed, and those that did were unhappily married to doctors (68%) who later 'did away with them' in a discreet manner. Pornography was unheard of, and there was public outcry when it was discovered that Lassie, the wholly unpretentious canine star of the big screen, was a female: subsequently, she was to appear in all her movies clad in a full-length tartan dog-coat. The majority of those under the age of 18 read *The Boys Own Comic* (92%), thereafter switching to *David Copperfield* (87%) for the rest of their lives. Happy days, indeed, those Arnold Years.

'I'm All Right With Toffees'

Cyril Smith's Shopping Trip (Political Sketch 4)

'May I jump the queue for a couple of frankfurters, girls?'
'Have you got the sausages, Cyril?'
'Just getting them, mother.'
Cyril Smith was out shopping for his dinner before getting down to proper canvassing in the afternoon. He was striding in front through Rochdale market, while his younger brother Norman, up until last week the Lord Mayor of Rochdale, was pushing their 83-year-old mother in her wheelchair behind.

First stop was Billy Duff Cooked Meats. 'A bit of tongue, no, make that two bits, and not too thin. You've cut it thick have you? Good lad!' After buying half a pound of beef spread, the three moved to Collins' Biscuits Stall. 'Hiya girls!' 'Hello Cyril!' They all wanted Liberal stickers for their lapels.

Cyril ordered some Walkers Shortbread, Chocolate Chips, Almond Cookies, and 'mix us a pound of chocolate biscuits, love'.

'What you doin', Cyril?' said his mother from her wheelchair.

'Just getting the chocolate biscuits, mother.'

'Don't forget the chocolate biscuits!' replied his mother.

'And give me a pound of mixed creams.'

'What you doin'?'

'Getting a pound of mixed creams.'

'Are we all right for cream crackers?'

'Jacobs or Crawfords, mother?'

'Jacobs.'

Putting eight different packets of biscuits into his carrier bag, Cyril strode on. Everyone seemed to recognise him, and, more unusually for a politician, he recognised them. 'Aye! Aye!' he would say in passing to youngsters, and 'how are ye, old son?' to the older generation.

A woman came up and said that her daughter had got a job as registrar at the college. 'Ah, we went to tea there, mother,' said Cyril. 'I said, we went to tea there. D'y'remember?'

Like many old people, she told Cyril she'd be voting for him. 'That's kind of you, love,' he said. 'Tell you what, come half past ten Sunday to a great big rally if you want – David Steel, Shirley Williams, five other Liberals. Be smashin'.'

The procession came to a halt as mother chatted to a lady friend from her days when she cleaned the town hall. To one side, the friend's daughter asked Cyril how his mother was. 'She's proud of you. She's proud of both of you. And every reason to be!'

Cyril then got chatting to a young woman in a wheelchair about her disability allowance, saying cheerio with 'well done, love. Keep goin', kid.'

And on to the Bacon Stall. 'They never have trotters now, do they Norman?' Cyril shouted back to Norman. 'No, they never have trotters now,' agreed Norman. 'Do I usually have creamy or crumbly?' he asked the girl serving the cheese. 'Crumbly, Cyril.'

More cheese from Jill's Cheese Pantry. 'Some gorgonzola, please, love, D'ye'sell chutney? A jar of chutney, oh, and a jar of pickles, and one of your Stiltons.'

An elderly woman recalled her recent golden wedding anniversary party. 'It were all right, weren't it, kid?' said Cyril.

He stopped at Stocks sweet stall. 'What sort of toffees do you want, mother?'

'I'm all right with toffees.'

Cyril bought a quarter of chocolates for himself and squeezed them into one of the two carrier bags.

An old man came up and shook Cyril's hand. 'Last time I saw you was at Fred Kershaw's funeral,' he said. 'Aye,' said Cyril, holding him by the shoulder. 'Fred and I used to play together as kids.'

Two young women passed by eating their sticky buns. 'You'll finish up like me, girls!' said Cyril. They giggled and walked on.

Norman and mother had got chatting to someone else. 'Come on. I'm movin' now, Norman, or I won't get me dinner in time, so I shan't get out campaignin' this afternoon!' shouted Cyril.

On the way out, the smell of hot potatoes from Ye Olde Lancashire Oven was too much to bear. 'Tell you what,' said Cyril, 'we'll 'ave a bag of those for our dinner too.'

30 May 1987
Postscript: Mr Smith held his seat

'Is That Your Taxi?'

Patricia Highsmith

She lives alone with two cats in the village of Auregino in Switzerland. She likes it there because it is efficient and nothing happens. She moved there from France, and she moved to France from Suffolk. She has also lived in Florence, Munich and Massachusetts, among other places. Like the subjects of her strange and straightforward novels – she calls them 'my psychopath heroes' – she probably moves from country to country to avoid feeling attached, to avoid apprehension. Like them, she feels at home reading the anonymous pages of the *International Herald Tribune*.

I arrived in a snow storm. Hers was the house on the upper road with the green door. The green door was open, so I walked in. It was a very dark, stony entrance, rather like a barn. 'Hello,' I said, into the dark. 'You made it,' she said from up some stairs in her direct, nervous, American voice. 'Come up.'

'Coffee? Drink? I've got Campari if you want. Or beer.' She was wearing blue jeans, and a jean jacket. I didn't know whether to mention meeting her in France five years before. I decided not to. Then, when I had asked her about revenge, she had said she abhorred the idea: 'Mind you, the people I really detest seem to come to bad ends anyway. Car crashes and that sort of thing.' But she hadn't talked about her books, or much about herself, answering. 'That's true' or 'I wouldn't have thought so' when she could.

I chose to drink Campari, and we sat in the kitchen, two cats prowling about. For some reason, the subject of Peter Sutcliffe came up. 'I got a letter from Julian Symons about Sutcliffe this morning,' she said. 'I sent him a Christmas card with a note saying "So how come you think Sutcliffe was a repressed homosexual? It would explain a lot, but what's your evidence?" because he'd written in the *Sunday Times* that he was. His letter this morning said because Sutcliffe was always trimming his beard so neat, but he couldn't be completely sure.'

We got on to other murderers. 'Oh, Lord Lucan, he's a gem, isn't he? I've got rather fond of him. To think he's possibly still alive and living well!' She chuckled. And then we spoke of a book she had been asked to review called *At Mother's Request*, about a 17-year-old whose mother had willed him to murder his grandfather. 'I was reading that book when I had the flu. It was lovely to lie in bed reading this divine . . . this fascinating book. No, not divine, but fascinating.'

She behaved as one not naturally inclined towards being in a room with someone else: she liked doing something else all the time, like chopping up meat for the cats, or looking out of the window at the snow falling down and worrying about it, or ringing restaurants or taxis. So long as I didn't touch on her writing, she was quite chatty. 'My friend in NW8 has had three robberies and now all the silver's gone. I have *no* sympathy for the thieves. I wouldn't mind plugging them, the bastards, if I saw them. They're not starving in England, are they? You think I'm severe?'

I shrugged.

'You wanna see round the house maybe?'

It's an old, tall, stony house, very quiet. We saw her small study with a French desk and a typewriter, and a flat surface upon which she does her accounts. Up some spiral stairs, we came to her guest bedroom with shelves full of books, including one by the pathologist Dr Keith Simpson. 'Yes, I like the Simpson book. It's amusing.' Amusing is one of her words, but she uses it in strange ways.

Her favourite book as a child was *The Human Mind* by Karl Menninger. 'Out of print, now, I think, but my family had it. It's case histories of mental disturbances told very briefly, then below it tells you if the treatment was of any use or not. Full of anecdotes. All kinds of people – the paranoiac, the kleptomaniac, the everything. For a kid to know that this book is real, it isn't made up. Well!'

'Was it frightening?'

'Possibly. But it was much more . . . eye-opening. Eye-opening to the strangeness of the human mind. It would be hard to imagine some of those aberrations. It was always there, always on my parents shelf until I was 21 and moved out of the house.'

'How old were you when you began to read it?'

'About nine years old.'

'What other books did you read?'

'Bridgeman's *Anatomy*, which again is out of print. That was a drawing book. I loved anatomical books. Then Dickens. Dostoevsky, you know. And I loved to read of English public schools. My favourite was *Jeremy at Crale* by Hugh Walpole, also *Stalky and Co* and Tom Brown at Rugby. I remember being fascinated by the detail of them and consequently wanting to learn Latin.'

'But in those books Latin is a great chore the boys have to understand, isn't it?'

'That was why I liked it. It seemed to be essential.'

We went through to her room, again simple and straightforward. Two paintings she had done herself – of pretty Italian piazzas, with birds and colourful people – were on the walls. I like them a lot, I said: but they were very innocent and naive, and no one could say that of her books.

'True,' she said, and we went down the stairs, through the kitchen to the cellars.

'These are old cellars,' she said, shining a torch around. 'And this is the electrical system.' The torch flashed on an electrical system.

'What are those – spiders?' I said, pointing to white, leggy things dangling luminously off the ceiling.

'Just fungus,' she said, 'though they do look like spiders, I agree.' She chuckled again. We saw another cellar, dark and gloomy, and then went back upstairs.

She poured another Campari for me, and a beer for herself, and tried again to get through to the café in the village. 'I don't like them. Grumpy people. But it's the only place and it's not too bad.'

'Would you mind if I asked you about your childhood and your family?' I said. I thought her shyness would be enforced, but no. 'I was born in Fort Worth in Texas, and I lived mainly with my grandmother, so I have the fondest memories of my grandmother. My mother had married Highsmith when I was aged three. So aged six I was taken to New York and started school.'

'Highsmith was your father?'

'No, I didn't see my father till I was 12 when I met him for a few minutes. We got on quite well. My mother – she officially *told* me when I was about ten, but I knew long before that Highsmith wasn't my father.'

'She'd been telling you that Highsmith was your father?'

'Well, my mother's the type to leave the subject alone.'

'You'd already guessed?'

'Well, my mother's the blondish type. And my stepfather had greyish eyes.'

'And that's the first thing you noticed?'

'Well, no, because my mother had drawings in the house of my grandmother signed Mary C. Plangman, which was my father's name. I remember asking – why this name? I don't remember the answer I was given, but any child would have known. Not to mention the fact that my stepfather came on the scene when I was three. He hadn't been around before. When you're three years old, and this strange man comes on the scene, why should he be my father? I'd never seen him before.'

We talked about the diary she used to keep ('pretty boring') and of her writing notebooks. To my surprise, she brought out notebook number 36, a Columbia University Notebook, and placed it in front of me. This seemed very out of character with everything I had seen or heard of her before. She had once written: 'I cannot think of anything worse or more dangerous than to discuss my work with another writer.' And here it was! Her private notebook!

'There are what I call general ideas in the front and then toward the middle there's germs of ideas. Then the red stuff is the current book of short stories I'm writing called *Natural and Unnatural Catastrophes*. I'm working on number eight now. They're a bit fantastic.'

As she walked towards the phone to try again to get through to the café, I asked her if I could look inside. 'Sure,' she said.

I've always hated reading people's private letters or diaries. Even if they let me. I still think they will catch me. I flicked briskly and matter-of-factly through the pages of spidery writing, through the little cuttings from *International Herald Tribune* on nuclear disasters. While she was engaged in speaking Swiss on the phone, I brought my flicking to a halt at a page headed 'The Pocket Watch'. I felt it would be a bit naughty – or that I would be discovered – if I wrote any of it down, but it started off something like, 'At the age of 12, I agreed to mow the lawn for my grandfather, which was strange, as I had good cause to hate him at that time. For this he gave me a watch . . .'

During all our conversation about her family, Patricia Highsmith had not once mentioned a grandfather. She was now off the phone, coming back to the table.

'Your grandfather,' I said. 'What was his character?'

'Oh, he was a very nice, easy-going fellow. Six foot three, and if you wanted a nickel or a dime he'd give it to you. Lenient, I would think.'

It was time to go to the café.

We wrapped up well and made our way into the snow, Patricia Highsmith holding a large shovel to steady herself, me following. Her body is a bit crouched and tense, as if it is ready to pounce. She moves with an odd combination of confidence and nervousness. We walked about the silent snowy street corners, the odd couple.

People looked round as we came in, but not for long. The manageress, whose mood, it emerged, was less grumpy than usual, served us with a good stew and corn. I had wine: Miss Highsmith had beer. We talked generally, of Mrs Thatcher and the Westland Affair, of Reagan, of New York. I couldn't gauge her politics: at one moment, she would seem fiercely pro the underdog; at the next, quite certain that people could control their own destinies with a bit of effort. She was jocular, and occasionally vehement. We talked of Cyril Connolly, and, via him, of Truman Capote.

'I met him when he was 23 and he was already very fond of the social life, loved to meet the right people, to meet important people. There's nothing wrong with that except that he let it interfere with his work finally. He became obsessed with it. I remember I was working on a book in New York and he rang me up and invited me for tea. It was on a Sunday. Now at that tea party there was probably Irving Berlin and Bernstein, loads of people, but I said, I work on Sundays. I preferred to work. You can't do both.'

Some of her disciplined social life is conducted by post. She writes to

Graham Greene a bit, though they have never met, and she has occasional pen-pals. She once had a prisoner as a pen-pal, and he provided her with much of the horrific prison details in *The Glass Cell*, but they aren't still in touch. 'He let it drop. He was released. My last letter said watch out who you meet in the world outside. He's probably back. He was just in for breaking and entering. He wasn't sick mentally. Just badly educated. Got caught.' Now, she corresponds with a young librarian in East Berlin. Patricia Highsmith is popular in both East and West Germany. 'He writes me saying, "How I'd like to see Venice!" It's very touching. But I can't help him.'

We would have to get on to her books, so I thought I'd have a go. I was interested in her book *Edith's Diary*, about a woman whose family is falling apart, whose diary grows more and more idealised and fanciful. It's one of the most disturbing books I've read. 'It was quite a break having a woman as the main character in a novel,' I said.

'That's true,' she replied. I waited, but she said no more.

'Were you apprehensive about it?' I asked.

'No. No, not at all.'

'Was it more emotionally exhausting to write than other books?'

'No, I was able to work very well. No major interruptions.'

'If things are going well, do you find it easier to write about more depressing things?'

'There's no connection. What I aim at is concentration.'

'Erm, you've written, "Perhaps I have some severe and severely repressed criminal drive in myself."'

'Yes, but I can't elaborate on that. If I have, it doesn't bother me.'

'Do you know people who have murdered?'

'No. Not at all.'

'Have you ever suspected people of murdering?'

'No.'

Direct questions were no good: her books were her books were her books. She was something separate.

She began writing aged 15. She had thoughts of stealing a book from the school library. 'At the door of the library you had to pass between the eyes of two monitors who'd gaze at you to see if you were pinching something.' So she decided against stealing, but wrote a story in which the heroine steals. Her first published story was of two old ladies in the same bedroom. Frustrated with each other's presence, one cuts up the other's cardigan, and the other retaliates by cutting off her hair while she is sleeping.

It is called *The Cries of Love*.

After she had told me about it, I said, 'That's one of the themes of all your books, two people locked together, hating each other and needing each other.'

'That's true.'

'They hate each other and love each other.'

'I think life is full of that.'

Back at the house, she appeared fidgety. Polite, but fidgety. I thought it most tactful to call for a taxi. Once that was organised she seemed calmer. We talked about dreams. 'I've had two dreams, wildly separated, that I've actually killed somebody. In one of the dreams, it was a certain person whom I know, an older woman whom I specially dislike; she's an American but I dislike her because she's crooked. But the idea that you've done it! It's the most dreadful feeling to me. Then one dream, I was going in some place to buy a newspaper and I put some money down but I had the feeling that everyone could tell that I'd killed somebody. Dreadful, really dreadful.'

My mind had been lingering on the 36th notebook, and what I had read about her grandfather. 'What you read were the facts,' she said. 'It didn't belong to my grandfather. He got it from a negro. My mother was playing a cat and mouse game with it. I was livid. My grandfather had taken it from a negro instead of rent. My grandfather said I could buy the watch for 12 dollars if I cut the grass 24 times, so I bought it. I gave it to my stepfather with a French chain. He admired it. They were both in the house – watch and chain – until I was about 15 years old. Then they were lost, and my mother let it *get* lost. It was pilfered by a certain adolescent boy who was doing errands, oh, I know the boy, I know this light-fingered type, and it was my mother letting it slip out which annoyed me very much. She let everything slip out like that. She's unorganised. It's what annoys me. It's so unnecessary . . .'

'Your writing about women seems to be more sympathetic than it used to be. Are you conscious of that?'

'No. I hadn't thought about it. No.'

'For instance, the mother in *People who Knock on the Door* is sympathetic.'

'I'm glad you thought that. Some people might think she was weak, not observant.'

'Usually weakness is sympathetic in anybody.'

'Ha!' There was quite a lot of scorn in her laugh. 'No. Not to me. Basically. Because I think weakness can lead to trouble. In my opinion. It's better to have a strong person whom not everybody likes. In the long run, such people I like better. It's dangerous taking the easy course. If some problem's immediately in front of you it's easier to take the weaker course.'

I mentioned Vic, her psychopath-hero of *Deep Water*, a character who seems quite weak until he begins to murder his wife's lovers. 'He doesn't win,' she said. 'But he's not weak. He's mentally a bit odd, but at least finally he has a go. To impress on his wife that he's not taking any more he eliminates those boring lovers. At least he *has a go*, at least he *tries*.'

She paused and there was silence. The cat nibbled at the chopped-up meat. She looked at her watch. 'Is that your taxi?'

'It's Great To Hear The Bee Gees in The Philippines'

Tim Rice and The Snackeroo

Items in Tim Rice's office:
   One Le Gavroche ashtray.
   One secretary wearing T-shirt saying 'Chess'.
   Sundry other secretaries.
   One photograph of Tim Rice and Andrew Lloyd Webber shaking hands with the Queen Mother.
   One framed poster of the New York production of *Joseph and The Amazing Technicolour Dreamcoat* ('A Buoyant Musical' – *New York Times*).
   One large framed poster of *Chess* including autographs of Tim Rice and two Abba men in gold.
   One *Chess* notepaper holder.
   One photograph of Tim Rice, Mike Read, Jo Rice and Paul Gambaccini aping about after a game of cricket.
   One Tim Rice in bright pink 'casual' jacket.
   'Hi.'

'Great car, great car,' he says, pointing to a 1950s something or other as we walk down Shaftesbury Avenue, him in his sunglasses. At his suggestion, we are having lunch in the Groucho, which he is a member of.
   'Are you a life member or just a normal member?'
   'I don't know.'
   The difference is £850.
   The man who runs Tim Rice's publishing company is sitting at the bar when we enter. He breaks off his conversation and stands up. He chats amicably for a few minutes, until Tim says in a slightly satiric tone – similar to the tone men use when they say 'I'm just popping off to the little boys' room' – 'Sit down, please, sit down.' One of them is the boss but they are friends.
   At the bar, Tim gets into conversation about Robert Cushman. 'I mean, the man's admitted in print that he doesn't like Bill Haley or the Beatles. A guy like that shouldn't be allowed to write.' Someone asks him if he is just having a drink. 'No, I think we're going to have a snackeroo later,' he replies.

He is affable.

We talk about the record '19' which has topped the charts. He says it's a great record. I ask him what it means. He says: 'Well, the hook is that the average age of a soldier in Vietnam was 19. Now, if true, that's an interesting fact. But it's selling because it's a great sound.'

Tim has the top 100 albums and the top 75 singles on permanent order from a company called Quick Fast and In a Hurry. He keeps them in a converted barn in the country, with a secretary in the outer room. He had new shelves put up the other day which should keep him going for two years. He has long been interested in chronicling pop records because 'they're the most important art form of today.'

Why?

'Two reasons. One, more people buy records than buy books, or go to the theatre, or what have you – '

'But more people watch television than buy records.'

'That's arguably true, I suppose. But there's one helluva lot of people buying records these days.'

And what's the other reason?

'What?'

What's the other reason that pop is the most important art form?

'Well, mainly sheer numbers.'

He continues: 'You see, people all over the world have heard "One Night in Bangkok", but how many have seen *The Mousetrap*? You hear pop everywhere. It's great to hear the Bee Gees in the Philippines.'

The Rices are a busy family. His father ('my old man') is a head hunter in the Third World. His mother has written a book called *All About Clubs*. His brother Andy has an advertising company in South Africa and his brother Jo works for a company dealing in medical equipment ('things for shoving up the rear end of cows').

'Could I steal one of your fags? Oh, it's the last one. I almost feel guilty.'

He lights it. I take an ashtray from another table.

'What a man.'

The match continues to burn in the ashtray.

'My God, a fire's broken out.'

He was at Lancing from September '58 to December '62. Christopher Hampton ('smashing bloke') was a year below and David Hare two years below.

'David was the most successful at Lancing. He became second Head of the School, but then he was always the most organised.'

I say that this seems surprising giving the anti-authoritarian nature of Hare's plays.

'Plays have to be anti-authoritarian these days if they're going to be commercial. David earns a very good crust being anti-authoritarian.'

At Lancing, he was in a group called the Aardvarks. He is still in a pop group called Whang and the Chevietes. 'There's a bit of a dispute as to which one of us is Whang.' Later in the week, they were playing at a charity ball, 'in front of Princess Margaret, poor girl.'

After Lancing, he was a petrol pump attendant for four or five months ('really enjoyed it') and then a trainee solicitor for two and a half years. He left to join EMI records as a management trainee, making tea for Cliff Richard ('If I'd stayed on, I'd have stood a fighting chance of taking over producing Cliff') and trying to write songs. Someone who felt that his lyrics were better than his music put him in touch with Andrew Lloyd Webber. Their first musical together was based on the life of Dr Barnardo, the first in a short line of public figures who were to lend themselves to Rice/Lloyd Webber treatments, and the only one whose musical died before, rather than after reaching the theatre. Then came *Joseph and The Amazing Technicolour Dreamcoat* ('Joseph'), *Jesus Christ Superstar* ('basically just a great story'), *Evita* ('people criticised us for glamorising her, but she was one helluva glamorous woman') and *Blondel*.

Blondel?

Rice did *Blondel* without Lloyd Webber, but with Stephen Oliver ('smashing bloke'). He admits that it was not a success. 'Potentially it was *Joseph* Mark Two but we didn't get it quite right.' Now he has written *Chess* with the two bearded members of Abba. He plays Chess, the game, once a month or so with his friend Robin Cavendish ('great bloke, fantastic guy') so he knows a bit about it. If *Chess* is not a success, he thinks he will 'jack the whole thing in', but this now seems unlikely.

This is the way his sentences end when he speaks of Andrew Lloyd Webber:

a) 'and good luck to him'

b) 'and I admire him for it'

and this is the way they start:

a) 'Andrew's always been very single-minded'

b) 'Andrew's always been absolutely determined to get just what he wants'

We discuss his main failing, which he touchingly defines as 'a pathetic desire to be liked'. Like a psychiatrist, I ask him to tell me more. 'You can actually make most people like you if you set your mind to it. Mind you, it gets me into all sorts of trouble, like accepting lunch with people you don't like.'

I wonder if this is a reference to me, juggle with the idea, then decide it isn't. In a dither, I attempt to change the subject so hurriedly that I come unstuck.

'Do you find that people resent you?'

'Like who?'

'People who think that they could write lyrics better than you – you know, people who've never written lyrics in their life, ha ha.'

'You mean people who think I don't deserve my success?'

'Yes.'

'Do you think I don't deserve my success?'

I can't remember what I said, it all happened so fast; as far as I can manage to remember I argued that success provides its own justification. I kept the matter theoretical and general, without direct reference to Tim Rice, lyricist.

Our lunch together seems to be dribbling to an end. His enthusiasm suddenly regenerates itself. He tells me that he has been taken on as a disc jockey by Radio 1.

I pretend to look surprised, and enthusiastic.

'Jolly Good'

Willie Whitelaw and the Chocolate Factory
(Political Sketch 5)

'**P**leased to meet you very nice seeing you hello Willie Whitelaw how are you nice speaking to you hello Willie Whitelaw jolly good pleased to meet you.'

No time-and-motion expert could devise a means whereby Lord Whitelaw could shake more hands in a shorter time. He darted around Dewsbury market yesterday in five minutes, telling about 100 people how pleased he was to meet them.

His method brooks no appeal: the tone in which he says 'Pleased to meet you' signals a simultaneous goodbye. When he told a member of the public that he hoped they'd vote Conservative, and the man replied 'No', he answered 'Well, think about it, jolly good,' and then, to a new face, 'Hello, Willie Whitelaw, pleased to meet you.'

Similarly, when another person said, 'A lot of people are worried about education,' he replied genially, 'Quite right too, jolly good, hello, Willie Whitelaw, pleased to meet you.'

In his brown tweed suit, he speaks to passers-by with the air of a benevolent landowner wishing the staff a happy new year. His most frequent expressions are 'jolly good', 'gracious me' and 'but there we are' (as in 'I'm afraid we've never really managed to get the West Indian vote, but there we are').

When he talks of politics, he does so in the melodic stream of consciousness peculiar to the landed gentry. 'Of course people try and play tricks on you at these times, have scares and so on, but do people really want to go back to secondary picketing, do people really want to be ruled by all these left-wingers, because everybody can't have it, nobody can have it – is that really the way we want to carry on, for goodness sake, let's not throw all our achievements away or that would be a disaster.'

The width of his enthusiasm is boundless. As we scaled up a dark brick staircase in Batley he exclaimed, 'I say, this is rather marvellous, isn't it?' At the top of the stairs was a sweet factory. The owner explained that a combination of luck and initiative was responsible for their success.

'Fascinating performance, isn't it? Marvellous,' replied Willie. The owner explained that he was shortly going to Hemel Hempstead to view a hamburger machine with a view to adapting it to make truffles. 'Gracious me!' said Willie. He was then introduced to some of the female workforce. 'How long have you worked here?' 'Five months.' 'Jolly good! And you?' 'Eight years.' 'Have you really!' 'I was originally from Manchester.' 'Manchester! My goodness me!'

At times he is reminiscent of Alastair Sim. A photographer told him that he wouldn't fit into the picture because he was too tall. 'Too tall, am I? Deary me. Well, there we are. Jolly good.'

He had vowed twice 'I must not eat' but a photographer persuaded him to hold a nougat half way into his mouth. Could he move the position of his hand, asked the photographer. 'Well, I hold them like this usually, but there we are,' he replied, changing position. 'Just one more photograph,' said the photographer. 'It's always just one more, but there we are.' Realising the only escape, Willie popped the whole nougat into his mouth and swallowed it. 'There. Can't do any more now, can we?' he said, and then, to the owner, 'Mmmm, very good actually, terribly good, awfully good.'

And so to a warehouse packed with Masters of the Universe Jelly Coated Novelties, Strawberry-Flavoured Boot Laces, Slime Slurps, Rum-Flavoured Balls and many other varieties. 'Lovely goodies here, I must say,' he said.

There was a final demand for a photograph of him holding a bundle of gold and silver bubble-gum coins. The photographer poured too many into his hands, and they spilt. 'Oh, lord,' he said, as they tinkled on to the ground. 'Deary me. Oh, well. Jolly good.'

His sweet factory tour over, he looked ahead to the next few days. On Tuesday he visits Liverpool. 'Dead loss for us, I'm afraid,' he said, 'But there we are.'

6 June 1987

'Krantz's Pants and Cohen's Poems'

Clerihew Corner

The Rt. Hon. Peter Brooke
Favours the neater look.
He eschews the purple polo neck, the 26 inch flare and the platform boot
For sensible shoes and a pin-striped suit.

Jimmy Hoffa
Couldn't have been roffa
Though he might have looked kinda cute
In a concrete suit.

Salman Rushdie
Will not be hushed; he
Will go to any party for a chat, bar
The Annual Fund-Raising Disco for the Friends of the Fatwa.

Judith Krantz
'On Pants'
Might be worth a look
(Though I couldn't find any in her latest book).

John Cleese
Is the bee's knees
But I wish he wouldn't weary us
By becoming all serious.

J. Edgar Hoover
Was a bit of a groover:
The toughest guy on the planet –
Yet the 'J' stood for Janet.

Francis Ford Coppola
Has made another costly floppola:
Frankly, I don't like my Dracula
In the Transylvanian vernacular.

Zsa Zsa Gabor
Certainly knows how to score
She is currently doing fine
With husband number eight. (Or is it nine?)

Sir Norman Fowler
Is not one for the howler
You would have to search many nations
For 'Fowler's Humorous Quotations'

Vita Sackville-West
Wouldn't take second best:
She said 'The one I refuse is
Mr Violet Trefusis'

Doris Stokes
Was in touch with all folks
She spoke to anyone who'd let her,
The deader, the better.

Janet Street Porter
Was never taught to say 'water'
She pronounces it 'wor-er':
We are all the poor-er.

P.J.O'Rourke
Sure can talk
'I'm a hell of a guy'
Is his usual cry.

John Birt
Is a little too pert
I would have preferred a grandee
In the role of D.G.

Harold Pinter
Is a joy to his printer
So many blanks
Are a cause for much thanks.

Michael Heseltine
Would happily go down a mine
Providing his coiffure
Didn't suffure.

Leonard Cohen
Is a master of the poem
Which can sometimes nearly rhyme
In its last line.

Lucian Freud
Has little to heud
His 'Portrait of the Artist Naked with a Thistle Near His Backseud'.
I greatly enjeud.

Hailie Selassie
Was a lad, not a lassie.
Some think he was also God
Which is odd.

Marco Pierre White
Is an unnerving sight.
How much happier I'd be
If 'Le chef ne mange pas ici'

Ken Russell
Must solve one great puzzle:
How to cast Koo Stark
In The Mass in B Minor by Johann Sebastian Bach.

Malcolm X
Wore rather odd specs
But he couldn't have whipped up such frenzies
In contact lenses

David Bowie
Has become a bit showy:
Its not very mellow
To reply 'Yes' to 'Hello!'

Shirley Maclaine
Says, 'I simply can't explain!
I've lived so many times before
Yet I keep returning as a bore'.

Peter Carter-Ruck
Is down on his luck
For a digestive biscuit, a chat and a cup of tea
He can charge only £2986.55 + VAT.

Tony Slattery
Must run on a battery.
Viewers beware!
Slattery can get you everywhere

A.L.Rowse
Is a bit of a grouse.
Though he certainly didn't grumble
When Trevor Roper took a tumble.

'The Ladies in My Life'

Tony Blackburn and The Mood of Love (Table Talk 4)

A few weeks ago I sought in this column to raise the important question of where exactly Tony Blackburn takes the ladies in his life. 'I invite all the ladies in my life to the same Italian restaurant in west London where the waiters understand how to create the mood of love,' he writes in his autobiography, *The Living Legend*, adding, 'I have a special table and as I take a girl's hand in mine or look deep into her eyes the lighting is lowered by an attentive waiter to cast a seductive glow. I tell each girl that life is a journey and it is up to each of us to fill our time on this earth with as many wonderful events as possible . . . ' To cut a long story short, his technique is to then classify himself as a wonderful event and hope for the best.

A couple of years ago, I was in Il Portico, an Italian restaurant just near the Kensington Odeon, when I happened to hear a familiar voice coming from behind me. I looked round and it was none other than Tony Blackburn, escorting a foreign-looking lady. 'I have to be sexually attracted to a girl before I ask her for a date,' the words in his autobiography flooded back. 'If I am going to wake up with a stranger by my side, she may as well be beautiful. I prefer oriental girls because their English sisters seem to have such a lot of emotional problems.'

'It's Tony Blackburn!' I whispered excitedly to my father-in-law, who had a clear view of Blackburn's table. 'A black man? A black man? Where's the black man?' replied my father-in-law. Alas, it emerged that he had never even heard of Tony Blackburn, so my clear instructions to him to watch out for that moment when the lights dimmed and Blackburn's hand prowled its way across, or even under, the table, all went unheeded. The next time I turned round, Blackburn and his lady friend had disappeared into the night, all set, no doubt, for that wonderful event.

I have been back to Il Portico several times since. On each occasion, I think that I might catch another sight of Blackburn, but each time I am disappointed. Still in pursuit of this slightly offbeat Holy Grail, I went again to Il Portico a few weeks ago. Alas, he was not there.

But no restaurant should be criticised simply for the fact that Tony Blackburn is not in it, and Il Portico has a great many qualities deserving of praise, so let us forget Tony Blackburn for one minute and get on with reviewing the restaurant, which is, after all, the ostensible, if occasional, purpose of this column.

If ever there is a drama series or situation comedy set in a typical Italian restaurant, the BBC would be well advised to film it in Il Portico. In recent years, of course, there has been a trend for the Italian restaurant to forsake its pepperpots-cheery-proprietor-and-bottles-in-baskets image for something rather leaner, starker and more sophisticated. Cibo, The River Café and Orso are at the forefront of this trend, and very nice they are too, but I hope that there is still room for the old-style Italian restaurant, where neither the décor nor the food are much to write home about, but where an air of inexpensive jollity prevails.

Outside, baskets of flowers hang from moulded archways, and inside is also proudly Italian. On the walls are pleasant paintings of Italian peasant life. Bottles in baskets hang from ironwork, and breadsticks await the diner on every table. There is also a Swiss tinge to be detected in the décor, with the light wood and beams one might expect to find in a mountain chalet. A stuffed pheasant sits above the door, in memory of some Italian shooting season of years gone by.

On the evening of my last visit, Italy was playing someone-or-other in the World Cup, and so service from all the waiters tended to be punctuated by swift glances to the television in the corner, making them appear as if they were the victims of severe nervous twitches. Nevertheless, they were as merry and charming as only Italian waiters can be, never forgetting that a smidgin of theatricality more than makes up for a dawdle by the telly.

Rather as Kafka's unhappy man found himself turning into an insect, I have, over the past few weeks, suffered grave intimations that I am turning into Terry Scott, or someone very much like him. First of all, I found myself at a Garden Centre, and then, while standing in that Garden Centre, I found myself buying a barbecue set. As if this were not proof enough, when the waiter came to take our orders at Il Portico I noticed that when my mouth opened, the words, 'I think I'll start with the Prawn Cocktail' came out. Whatever next? A boxed set of James Last via a form in *Reader's Digest*? A dinner-dance at the Golf Club? The new Melvyn Bragg book on the beach at Alicante?

Who knows, I may well be the very first food critic ever to review a Prawn Cocktail. For some reason, Prawn Cocktails are ignored by food critics, just as The Carpenters are ignored by music critics and Catherine Cookson is ignored by book critics. Well, here, in what will undoubtedly come to be regarded as something of an historic occasion, are extracts from this, the first ever review of a Prawn Cocktail in the British Press:

'Quite nice'

'Not at all bad'

'I rather enjoyed that'

This may well be worth cutting out and keeping, so that in years to come your children and your children's children can understand the excitement when members of the older generation are reminiscing about where they were and what they were doing when the Prawn Cocktail was first reviewed. Let us hope my pioneering role prompts food critics on lesser newspapers to follow suit.

And so to the other dishes. One of our companions, an editor on a rival Sunday newspaper, kicked off with a seafood pancake, which, he reported, looked horrible, 'as if a tin of diced vegetables has been slightly mashed,' but tasted very good. His wife had the melon and Parma ham which tasted exactly like melon and Parma ham, and my own wife had the *tonno i fagioli* which she said was 'greasy and full of onions, but I quite like it like that'.

So far, so good. Looking around, I clocked a high level of enjoyment on the faces of our fellow diners. I have noticed that there is some sort of correlation between the cheapness of a restaurant and the frequency of smiles on diners' faces, as there is between the expense of a restaurant and the frequency of scowls, rows, tears and walk-outs.

My main course was pleasantly stodgy veal with ample spinach. My wife had the cannelloni which she suspected had been warmed up from lunchtime, or even the day before, and the top did seem suspiciously crispy. Our editor friend had calves' liver with sage which he said was very good, very thin and not stringy. 'But then it was a safe choice,' he added. I didn't agree: liver can be a disaster in restaurants, a great slab of grey toughness like a dull table-mat. His wife ordered the *crespoline* pancake with spinach and ricotta, her constant choice at Italian restaurants, and awarded it full marks.

I think Italy must have just lost, because a subdued air seemed to overtake the staff towards the end of our meal. Nevertheless, they managed to smile briefly through the tears as they bade us farewell. After all, tomorrow was another day, and – who could tell – Tony Blackburn might be putting his head round the door.

'Lateral Thinking'

Edward de Bono's Diary

Allow me to introduce myself within a self-introductory mode-allow-ance framework. Not only am I the Director, Supervisor, Attention-Flow Administrator and Founder of the newly-formed organisation for Cognitive Research Approach Precepts (CRAP), currently advising representatives from many different international countries, including Indonesia and Finland. But I am also world-renowned on a stratal-design-outcome-mode basis as the originator of both Lateral Thinking – of which more later – and, more recently, Triangular Thinking.

WHAT IS TRIANGULAR THINKING?

This is a triangle (supra-diagram A):

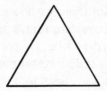

Supra-diagram A: a 'triangle'

It can be recognised by its three sides, all joined together. It is similar to a square. But with one less side. With two less sides, it would just be a straight line. But it has three sides. So it is a triangle. Not a circle, which arguably has no straight lines. But a triangle.

SO WHAT EXACTLY IS TRIANGULAR THINKING?

Take an example.

A person – let us say YOU – has a bank account. There is money in that bank account.

Another person – let us say ME – has another bank account. Or a variety of bank accounts in places where he is recognised as one of the great original philosophers and thinkers of our time and whose governments beseech him to educate their people.

Let us recap.

For the sake of this dialogue-mode-perception-design-conflict-paradigm, there are two major bank accounts. MINE and YOURS. These are two sides of the triangle.

But a triangle has three sides.

SO WHAT IS THE THIRD SIDE?

The third side represents the flow of money from one bank account (YOURS) to the other bank account (MINE). And what I offer you in return is any of my thirty different books, translated into twenty-four languages, read by a great many people who occupy senior positions in such countries as Finland or Indonesia. The sooner all the people of all the countries in the world adapt to

TRIANGULAR THINKING

the sooner that the Strata-Happiness-Intercognitive-Therapy (SHIT) I have been preaching will come to fruition.

* Nothing can happen until something happens. Something happening cannot be nothing. But when something happens, nothing cannot happen. The happening is nothing if not something, yet nothing is not happening. Or something.

* For the past two thousand years, Western civilisation has foundered on the outdated thought-conflict-mode based on the I-am-right-you-are-wrong syndrome.

The time has come for a radical reappraisal of the very way in which we think.

This is why I have set up the Union of Taskforces Teaching Educative Re-thinking of Corporate and Rational Appraisal Paradigms (UTTERCRAP) which has already attracted widespread international interest from such countries as Indonesia and also Finland.

Supra-diagram 'B': Two men locked in an arm-wrestle

Some concepts are so simple and beautiful that they appear complex. One such concept is UTTERCRAP.

Imagine two men locked in an arm-wrestle (supra-diagram 'B'):

Each is struggling with all his collective strength to beat the other, but really there is a no-win situation in which victory will only come to the man who is not beaten, and that is no victory at all.

The concept of UTTERCRAP would teach them a radical reappraisal of the situation in which they found themselves.

Instead of arm-wrestling, they could use their arms for a productive, progressive, forward-looking-mode-opportunity design idiom.

As you can see from Supra-diagram 'C': SOLUTION, these two men would be exerting less negative energy-mode clash-units were they to instead employ the UTTERCRAP design-virtue process.

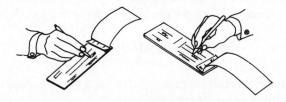

Supra-diagram 'C': solution: Two men writing out cheques crossed to 'Citizen of the World E. de Bono'

★ Simple everyday problems can be solved by unlocking the side of our brain which houses what I have termed the Basic Attitude Lateral Logic Sequence (BALLS). For instance, how to brush your hair without releasing valuable energy via use of the hand: simply place your hairbrush in a carpenter's vice, then turn your head upside down and move it back and forth across the hairbrush. This is now the accepted method for brushing your hair in countries as diverse as Finland on the one hand and Indonesia on the other.

★ You are wrong, I am right. I am right you are wrong. You are Ron, I am Reg. But who is he?

★ A true story. Earlier this year, the highly successful Swedish Prime Minister, Olaf Palme, telephoned me at my recently-formed Institute of Interstrata-Fulfilment Bureau. 'You are not only the author of twenty-eight books translated into thirty-nine world-famous languages,' he confided, 'But you are internationally renowned as the creator of new words for new situations.' This is a view shared by many top figures in the world today, including leading representatives of the governments of many prominent countries, including Finland and Indonesia.

New words for new situations have never been more important than they are now, when I have a new book to sell. Among these new words for new situations are:

Attitude-deconflict: The only solution to strategy-attitude.

Deconflict-perceptualisation: Greater perceptualisation of a deconflict situation will give rise to the right attitude.

Perceptualisation-strategy: A strategy for greater perceptualisation will result in an adjustable attitude-deconflict.

High-strategy-yield-attitude: The only solution to attitude deconflict.

High-yield-deposit-account: The right environment for the end product of Gullible Response Syndrome.

'The Least Weird Man I've Ever Known'

Michael Jackson

By far the oddest thing on television all week was *The Michael Jackson Interview* with Oprah Winfrey, beamed live across America a few days before. With his womanly voice, stark white skin and Medusa hair, his gash of red lipstick, heavy eyeliner, almost non-existent nose and lopsided face, Jackson was making this appearance in order to scotch all rumours that he is not quite normal.

The whole event was strangely reminiscent of a gothic movie. It opened with Oprah Winfrey standing alone in the high-ceilinged hall of Jackula's mansion, pointing out how eerily normal everything was, including 'a library filled with leather-bound classics and artwork on the walls'. Then in stepped Jackson wearing semi-military uniform – kiss, kiss – and they sat alongside one another in mock-Victorian chairs.

Never have the bland and the bizarre been more closely allied than in this most curious of creatures. The most frequent adjective he used throughout the interview was 'sad', the most frequent verb 'cry'. As a child performer, he saw being onstage as home and 'when I got offstage, I was, like, very sad'. His early teens were 'sad, sad years for me'. His skin disorder 'makes me very sad'. After a performance, 'I was sad.' As an adolescent, his pimples were so bad, 'I cried every day.' The story of the Elephant Man 'made me cry'. Entertaining children with cancer 'makes me cry happy tears'. 'I was sad for years and years and years,' he told Oprah towards the end, adding unconvincingly, 'but now I'm very happy.'

Jackson chose this, his first television interview in ten years, to announce live to his father that there were times he had been sick with fear of him. 'He's never heard me say this,' he said. He then looked to camera and said to his father, watching somewhere out there: 'Please don't be mad at me!' Turning to Oprah, he added, 'But I still love him.'

Shortly afterwards, Oprah Winfrey called in Elizabeth Taylor as a character witness. Michael stood up to greet her and she sat in his chair. 'Michael is the least weird man I've ever known,' she purred. ' . . . What a wonderful, giving, caring, generous man he is.' Cut to Michael, looking oddly to the side, awkwardly hiding his right profile from the camera, as he continued to do throughout the rest of the show. When Michael began chatting to Elizabeth, I realised that if I shut my eyes I really couldn't tell which of them was talking.

Throughout, it was as if Jackson had learnt to speak solely from watching old Disney cartoons, so ill-suited was his language to either the communication or the camouflage of the obscure hurt that seems to beat within him. Only when he sang accappella for Oprah, and danced all alone on his own private stage, did he seem to regain a link with himself. One of the last shots was of his own personal fairground, lit up and spinning and turning against the dark sky, as empty as can be.

Back in Britain, *The Brit Awards 1993* took the form of a thanksgiving service to the memory of British rock, which died peacefully in its sleep about ten years ago. The elderly mourners – immobile, silent and dignified in their grief – were gathered in Alexandra Palace, portly and balding in their black ties and dinner jackets, to hear a business associate of the deceased, Mr Richard O'Brien, read a roll-call of Those We Shall Never Forget, some of whom, it emerged, were still struggling on, keen for one last stagger down memory lane.

The Brit Awards was embalmed in a gooey mixture of commerce stippled with irony. Never have I seen so many rock stars in suits and ties, beady little businessmen attempting to excuse their presence at such an un-hip marketing exercise by leaving a false trail of offhanded mumbles behind them. 'You are watching the music business event of the year,' announced Simon Bates at the beginning, and the key word the whole way through was 'business', with virtually every 'artist' (ho, ho) reeling through a long list of business associates in their record and management companies as they accepted their awards.

When a list containing Joe Cocker, Eric Clapton, Phil Collins and Elton John was read out, I imagined that this was a new award for Oldest Male Artist, or even a special Still With Us Award. In fact, they were all in line for Best Male Artist, and at the end a Long Service Medal was presented to Rod Stewart, a sort of wiggly-bottomed Mike Baldwin. As Rod and The Faces chugged their way through some awful old Faces 'classic', like members of Dad's Army on an April Fool, I couldn't help feeling that at their age they ought to know better. Heaven knows what a 16-year-old would have thought of it all. Once upon a time, rock music was sung by the young to disgust the old. Now, it seems, it is sung by the old to embarrass the young.

On Tuesday, *Without Walls* made a welcome return, with its J'Accuse slot given over to a fierce attack by Rory Bremner on Barry Humphries' Dame Edna Everage. Dame Edna was a brave target for Bremner to choose, as she seems adored and revered by one and all, and her smallest grimace sends millions of people, including me, into howls of laughter. Bremner's attack was deftly executed, with apt extracts and a nimble commentary, but it amounted to nothing, possibly because its argument was almost entirely bogus.

The thesis went like this. Dame Edna was once a charming Alan-Bennett-style timid Melbourne housewife; unable to find success in Britain, Humphries sold out, 'began to shed the reality of the original character', and now sucks up to audiences with 'coarse double entendre and audience exploitation'. Two *Guardian* journalists and a sensitive comedian, Sean Hardie (looking spookily like Madge Allsop), were at hand to complain of politically incorrect ('grotesque and disturbing') jokes.

Alas, anyone who has read either Humphries' brilliant autobiography, or the original scripts for Edna's earliest appearances, will know that Edna has always been a monster, and that one of Humphries' main aims in life has always been to disconcert the priggish, be they drawn from the bourgeoisie or the liberal intelligentsia. Over the years, Dame Edna has grown more affluent, more self-confident, more cosmopolitan and more celebrated, but neither her opinions, nor her audience's fathomless love/hate complicity in them, have altered one jot. I have in front of me a Barry Humphries script in which Edna is bartering for lodgers for the Olympic Games. There are jokes against Swedes, Red Indians and Africans ('Merv – that's my son-in-law – said he wasn't too keen on the idea of Mau Maus'), against the elderly, the young, housewives and home furnishings ('We pushed back the Genoa velvet couch and rolled back the burgundy Axminster squares for Valmai's 21st and the young people had the time of their lives'). This script was performed by Mrs Norm Everage, as she then was, 37 years ago, in 1955.

True comedy – that is funny comedy – is borne of its creator's ambivalence towards its target. Humphries' target is, I suspect, his mother, whom he loved and loathed in roughly equal measure. Such deep-seated inspiration cannot be subjected to the laws of propriety. Sometimes, Dame Edna might go too far, offending prudes on all sides of the political and social spectrum. But what is comedy – what is life – if it cannot go too far?

'Letters to the Editor'

Pot Noodle and The Poll Tax

From Letters to the Editor of The Times

July 24th 2020:

Dear Sir,

May I add my voice to those of your many readers who have lamented the recent passing of the well-loved Poll Tax? Since its inception 30 years ago, it has, as your correspondents have pointed out, carved itself a special nook in the hearts of the British people. To change it now for some new-fangled tax is tantamount to killing off a very dear and venerable old companion. I feel sure that your readers can think of many other examples of beloved institutions that have been destroyed in recent years by the insensitive actions of the so-called 'reformers'.
Yours faithfully,
Paul Wheatcroft (Major)

July 26th 2020

Dear Sir,

Further to the letter from Major Wheatcroft of the 24th, might I beg leave to condemn the wanton destruction of many of our finest old National Car Parks? These noble and delightful buildings have, for the past 50 years or more, greatly enhanced the character of many of our city centres. The simple beauty of their clear horizontal lines, manufactured in some of the finest grey concrete, lends a sense of cohesion to their surroundings. Members of our organisation are fighting to preserve these vital parts of our national heritage. For just £10,000 a year – no more, after all, than the price of a couple of gin and tonics – members are taken on guided tours of early National Car Parks (this year's expeditions include NCPs in Birmingham and Wolverhampton) as well as receiving a complimentary booklet, *Remove Ticket Now: The Magic of the NCP*.
Yours faithfully,
Peregrine Stamp (Miss)
Secretary, The NCP Heritage League

July 27th 2020

Dear Sir,

It is, alas, not only such magnificent old institutions as the Poll Tax and the NCPs that are disappearing under the iron heels of the progressives. Our leadership itself is in decline. Take, for instance, the National Union of Mineworkers. There are those of us who still remember with affection those balmy days when Arthur Scargill was its President. A charming man, a cheery quip ever playing on his lips, he would always be ready with handy advice to one and all, delivered in those gentle tones once memorably compared to the chirruping of a lark. These days, alas, the NUM Leadership is ruled by the politically motivated, an idea which would have left dear old Arthur, loved as he was by employers, workers and the general public alike, quite bemused.
Yours faithfully,
George Johnson

July 29th 2020

Dear Sir,

Am I alone in lamenting the decline of the Pot Noodle? This hallowed national dish, for so long the staple fayre of millions of ordinary, working people, is, I understand, to be phased out. Soon the beleagued consumer will be forced to purchase 'raw' meat, to be 'cooked' at home – a potential health-hazard and a slap in the face for all those who value the great culinary traditions of the British way of life.
Yours faithfully,
Geoffrey Gale

July 31st 2020

Sir,

I feel most strongly that the old M25 should not be allowed to disappear without tribute. As dear to the heart of every Londoner as the River Thames, the M25 has gained a unique position in our national life by preserving the more leisurely pace of happier times. The Sunday afternoon picnic on the M25, with hundreds of thousands of families laying out their rugs on the tarmac surrounded by stationary cars, has become a vital part of the fabric of the British lifestyle, and to see this time-honoured tradition destroyed will be deplored by parents and children alike.
Yours faithfully,
W.F.Kenny

August 2nd 2020

Dear Sir,
   Might I bemoan the demise of the much-cherished 'Video Nasty'? At the turn of the century, it would have been unthinkable for a family of four to eat their dinner without first sitting down to enjoy an example of this, the finest flowering of the cinematic art. Personally, I blame it all on the decline of the Pot Noodle, the phasing-out of the Poll Tax and the wilful destruction of the National Car Park. This would never have happened in Arthur Scargill's day.
Yours faithfully,
Gavin Deedes

'Little Robin Redbreast'

Our Feathered Friend

A month ago, a little robin flew into our house through the window. 'Ahh!' I exclaimed, 'Look at that sweet little robin.' He hopped from one room to another, hopped back again and then chirruped a little. We all agreed how sweet he was. Other birds have occasionally dropped in – one even came through an open letterbox – but they have then panicked, flapping around in a frantic fluster, desperate to get out and yet, through sheer stupidity, quite unable to do so. But not our little robin. He seemed quite at home, as happy as Larry, and, when he had had his fun, he chirruped away, back out through the window.

The next day, our robin came again. I had my camera, and thought that it would be amusing to take a couple of photographs of him as he perched on an armchair. In years to come, I thought, these photographs will afford us hours of amusement, and might well foster in our child a burgeoning love of nature.

The next day, our robin came again, only this time he arrived through our bedroom window at six o'clock in the morning. I just managed a 'how sweet!' before growing slightly irritated that one so small could make a chirrup so loud. It was still chirruping in our room at 6.45 so I decided to shoo it through an inner doorway, out into the corridor and into our child's room where its chirrups woke our child, who also began to chirrup.

The next day, our robin came again, at dawn, in the afternoon, and again in early evening. By this time, I had stopped thinking of him as a jolly little fellow. I was fed up with his silly, mindless chirruping, sick of his complete lack of tact and basic good manners, bored stiff by his pathetic attempts to ingratiate himself into the household. 'GO AWAY!' I would scream whenever he came in, but his pushiness knew no bounds. Armed with a few copies of *The Watchtower* magazine, he might have made an effective Jehovah's Witness, but he appeared to be quite content simply wasting the time of himself and others.

The next day, our robin came again, and the next day, and the next day, and the next day. All day and every day, he would be either inside or nipping outside for a quick breather before coming inside again. If we shut all the doors and windows while he was out, he would – this might sound odd, but it is true – sit on the outside handle of the front door, ready to zoom in the minute we opened it.

Better-mannered friends told us that a recurrent robin was a sign of love, while more brutal friends told us that it was undoubtedly a sign of death. The death supporters seemed to have literature on their side, citing these four lines from Webster's *The White Devil*:

> Call for the robin redbreast and the wren,
> Since o'er shady groves they hover,
> And with leaves and flowers do cover,
> The friendless bodies of unburied men.

The champions of a cheery robin in literature seem few and far between.

'Come in robin, do not fear us/Thy bright eye and chirping cheer us' runs a traditional Welsh folk song, getting it all wrong, as traditional Welsh folk songs so often do. 'Push off robin, and take your chor-us/Your presumption and your chirping bore-us' might have struck a truer note.

He was in again this morning, chirruping away in that smug, conceited way of his. I managed to get him out – he seemed a little scared of my impersonation of a sparrowhawk – but when I went down to the kitchen he was already there, having a quiet giggle to himself. The armchair on which he likes to pose is now covered in a greyish white, and even purple, for he has taken to eating blackberries.

We now sleep with our bedroom window shut, but he generally finds his way in. He is like the entire cast of Hitchcock's *The Birds* rolled into one. 'Who killed cock robin?' is one of the great mysteries of English verse. I think that I am now in a position to solve it. It was not only the sparrow: they all did it. It was probably the only way to stop him carrying on with all that hopping and chirruping. If I were the judge I would grant them all a full pardon, and no questions asked.

'Liver and Kidneys'

Roy Hattersley Incorporating Giant Haystacks (Table Talk 5)

I tend to think of Smithfield Market as one of the few places in London where time really has stood still. It is reassuringly decrepit, and its alternate time-scale – just finishing when most people elsewhere are beginning to think of getting up – gives the impression of a secret city within the heart of London, a city where past ages still congregate nightly to sing and dance.

In fact, nothing could be further from the truth. Though it may seem rough and ready to our namby-pamby eyes, Smithfield is still a very poncified version of what it once was. For 400 years it was the key place for public executions: in the four years between 1554 and 1558, a good 200 martyrs were burned there. When it became a cattle market in the 17th century, the gore did not let up. Live cattle were driven through the streets, sometimes taking refuge in shops (hence the expression 'bull in a china shop') and were then slaughtered, their blood flowing through the streets. 'The ground was covered nearly ankle-deep, with filth and mire; a thick steam perpetually rising from the reeking bodies of the cattle . . . ' wrote Charles Dickens in *Oliver Twist*.

Not the most deluxe location for a full English breakfast in Dickens' time, maybe, but in these somewhat sprucer days it could well be that the best breakfast in town is to be enjoyed at the Sir Loin Restaurant, above the Hope and Sir Loin pub.

I arrived at the Hope and Sir Loin at around 10 a.m. on a drizzly Friday. Pushing the wrong door, I entered the pub itself, to be struck by a scene of almost Buñuelian surrealism. Every single person except for me in this crowded bar was a postman, all of them standing in circles, downing pints of beer. Thinking that the Sir Loin restaurant was through a door at the far end just visible through the crowds and the smoke, I squeezed my way through the postmanly circles with plentiful 'excuse mes' and 'sorrys'. Alas, the door was for the toilets only. I then had to squeeze all the way out again, hoping that I would look to the macho postmen as if I had planned this route all along. But postmen are a canny bunch, and their looks made it quite clear that they knew full well there was a wally in their midst.

Back out on the street, I went through the correct door and up a flight of stairs to a smallish room of unforced antiquity. It has about it a pleasant air of shabbiness: its Olde Englande quality owes less to Colefax & Fowler than to Capstan Full Strength. Its red and green carpeting is as worn as you would expect in the upper room of a busy pub. The peach tablecloths are blotched with the odd stain. Great clouds of smoke hang in the air and one's fellow breakfasters look much like Fred Flintstone.

The Hope and Sir Loin (this is, by the way, the correct way to write sirloin, for it got its name when King James I, enraptured by a cut of meat served to him at Houghton Hall, decided to knight it) is also very close to Bart's hospital. I am told that doctors who have just come off night shifts are often to be seen polishing off full English breakfasts. To be tucking into dead liver and kidneys so soon after operating on live liver and kidneys must be a bizarre experience: one only hopes that it never results in an awful muddle-up in the operating theatre should the doctors become peckish too soon.

Could any speculation be less suited to a pleasant little restaurant column on a Sunday morning? I think not, and so I will pass on swiftly to a proper description of the breakfast itself. There is no menu, nor any of the fripperies to which one has grown accustomed with breakfasts in hotels: no baguettes or croissants, no porridge, no fruit compote, nor even any cereal. The waiter comes along, asks you whether you want tea or coffee, and then tells you that they serve a full English breakfast, and that that is what you are getting.

Full! The most jam-packed Tokyo tube train could hardly be fuller. Years of diets and health-plans on television and in magazines have passed the Hope and Sir Loin by; here, Desperate Dan, Billy Bunter, Giant Haystacks and even Roy Hattersley himself could all take to their chairs content in the knowledge that the grim spectre of Ryvita is far afield.

Here is what was on our plates (arranged, my companion enthused, 'like a still life, yet without any trace of self-consciousness'): two perfect fried eggs; proper grilled tomatoes (even relatively posh hotels nowadays palm breakfasters off with tinned tomatoes); vintage Heinz baked beans in a generous portion (approx one small tin); two thinly-sliced pieces of liver done to a turn; kidneys (ah, kidneys!) with just a tiny bit of blood cowering somewhere towards the middle; two big fat sausages; a quantity of bacon; two slices of square-shaped black pudding, thinly cut; and, beneath it all, that most necessary ingredient of a cooked breakfast, a generous slice of fried bread, one half slightly crisp, the other slightly soggy. There will now be a short intermission so that readers of this column may take a breather and recover their digestions. During this intermission – believed to be the first supplied completely free with a restaurant column – you might care to hum the chorus of 'Love Grows Where My Rosemary Goes' by Edison Lighthouse (words supplied):

Love grows where my
Rosemary goes
And nobody knows
Like me
La la la la la la la la la la
la la la la la

Nice to have you back with us. Now that your stomachs have settled, I feel I should add that each individual ingredient was cooked just so, with none of the prissiness or stinginess of smarter places, and none of the lard 'n' muck of a greasy spoon. Another great advantage of the Hope and Sir Loin is that, being next to Smithfield, it enjoys particularly liberal licensing hours, so that we could drink bucks fizz at 10.15 a.m. without anyone batting an eyelid. I should add that the bucks fizz was served in chilled glasses, a service you would be hard-pressed to find at any Park Lane hotel.

Our bill for two vast breakfasts – each one about three times the size of a normal lunchtime main course – plus a bottle of champagne, a seemingly infinite supply of orange juice and (poorish) coffee came to just £33. When lunch came around, I was still full up, and I could only manage a couple of fish-fingers for supper. Beat the recession! Breakfast at the Hope and Sir Loin! Mourning for the passing of nouvelle cuisine may now commence, and no giggling at the back.

'Lovely Lady'

Madonna and The Boys (Wallace Arnold 5)

My eyes positively lit up. The editor of *The Independent on Sunday* newspaper had asked me if I would write an essay about my dinner. My friends invariably accuse me of being the veritable *doyenne* of food writers so I found myself agreeing forthwith. It was only some minutes later that I discovered, with no little disappointment, that he wished me to write not about my dinner but *Madonna*.

It emerged that *The Independent on Sunday*, responsible, 'up-to-the-minute' (!) newspaper that it is, had spent a great deal of money in securing the rights to a small portion of the aforesaid Madonna's latest *oeuvre*, *Sex* (dread word!). For the full 5,000 pounds, 17 shillings and sixpence, we are now legally entitled to reproduce:

(a) three (3) buttocks, fully naked
(b) one (1) bosom, partially bared, and
(c) one (1) head-shot of Sir Norman Fowler with spectacles.

(The last-named item being acquired as a tie-in with the publishers, who are also responsible for Sir Norman Fowler's forthcoming *A Vision of Britain*, thus accounting for the additional 17 shillings and sixpence).

For an extra £3,000, the newspaper was entitled to send a leading representative to New York, there to peruse the aforementioned tome in conditions of strictest privacy. The editor had lined up a short-list of intellectuals for the task, the first being the great Argentinian scrivener Jorge Luis Borges. Alas, it had emerged that not only was there, as yet, no braille edition of the book available, but also that poor Borges had died a full three years ago.

The third choice was Dame Iris Murdoch, but she was 'pipped at the post' by the second choice – yours truly. My commission was to write an accompanying text of 2,000 or so words emphasising the deep seriousness of the project, showing how the publication of three buttocks and one half-bosom was indeed a worthwhile and thought-provoking exploration of the nature of contemporary celebrity.

I arrived at the New York headquarters of Madonna's publishers, to be ushered with a copy of the tome into a gentleman's lavatory and directed to the cubicle bearing my own name. As I passed along the row of cubicles I noted the full range of well-respected authors and thinkers whose illustrious names were posted on the adjoining doors.

In the first cubicle, grunting learnedly, sat Mr Norman Mailer, reporting for that once-doughty journal, *The New Yorker*. The next cubicle betrayed odd swishing sounds which I can only imagine emanated from the inhabitant, Mr Martin Amis, in his struggle to pull the top off his felt-tip. In the third cubicle, my old friend and quaffing partner Mr Andrew Neil could be heard getting in trim for his forthcoming in-depth interview with the 'lovely lady'. In the fourth cubicle sat Mr Melvyn Bragg, reciting over and over again in his sonorous Cumbrian voice a freshly-composed extract from his new book, in which the hero, Martin Bagg, a highly successful Northern television producer and Booker Prize-winning novelist, finds himself in bed with the world-famous pop-singer 'Gadonna', only to find himself questioning the very nature of his existence as he grapples with her suspender belt. Finally, there in the fifth cubicle was my dear mentor Lord Rees-Mogg, meticulously studying the work with high-powered binoculars in search of any stray sightings of artistically invalid flesh.

Taking my place in the sixth cubicle and carefully locking the door behind me, I opened the book with an intellectual excitement unequalled since my first reading of Proust. For the next hour, I studied those extraordinary photographs with a fierce intensity, breathlessly decoding the semiotics of celebrity, time and time again deconstructing the resonances of such polymorphous cultural weaponry, and urging myself on and on in my quest to ponder the palpable otherness of fame. I emerged from that cubicle breathless, yes, exhausted, yes, but also strangely elated. Next week, our magazine will proudly publish my definitive essay on the work, alongside full colour photos of the three buttocks and half a breast. Incidentally, reports on the recession, the cutbacks in the mining industry and news from abroad have now been re-scheduled for February, 1993.

'Mainly Grey'

John Major and The Massed Bands of The Coldstream Guards (Political Sketch 6)

I t was a day like any other, but it seemed to last several weeks. Jeremy Corbyn (Lab, Islington North) wasn't wearing a jacket or tie, a state of undress that once again unduly upset Mr Anthony Marlow (Con, Northampton North).

Mr Tam Dalyell was perplexed about the amount of blowpipes in Afghanistan. Mr Andrew MacKay (Con, Berkshire East), who bears some resemblance to the type of fresh-faced god-fearing youth so often found with the gun in his hands after a presidential assassination, asked Opposition members to 'stop whingeing'.

The bearded Mr Martin Flannery (Lab, Sheffield, Hillsborough) complained that he was only getting 'small tinkles' from his British Telecom telephone, and was it not a disgrace? Miss Clare Short (Lab, Ladywood) said that there was no reason for the House to imitate a boy's public school and that dress regulations were ridiculous.

These are all events that seem to happen every day, like the coming up of the sun and the going down of the moon. But one doesn't hear a speech from Mr John Major, Chief Secretary at the Treasury, on finance every day. Were such a prospect to be included in the Commons procedure on a regular basis, the sun might well decide not to come up; and the moon would simply switch itself off.

Mr Major is grey and tall, but mainly grey. His prose style suggests that he has yet to read the works of Ronald Firbank; his delivery is that of a doctor with indifferent news for a patient for whom he has no particular feelings.

By the end of his Opening Speech for the Second Reading of the Finance Bill, the sparse chamber was so thoroughly somnolent that the massed bands of the Coldstream Guards could have heralded the entry of the entire cast of *Ben Hur* and not even the most energetic member would have managed to bat an eyelid.

'Essentially, however, these proposals are the same and they represent a significant initiative. They form an important and imaginative element in our strategy to improve the supply performance of the economy . . .'

149

This came towards the beginning of Mr Major's speech, when the world still seemed fresh and bright-eyed. By the end, the chamber looked as if an alien force had preyed hideously upon all members: the lucky ones had disappeared entirely, and the few who remained, their faces horribly swollen, their bodies immobile, were mute and dispossessed.

'There is no quick and easy solution . . . ' At this, Mr John Wakeham, the new Leader of the House, appeared to slump forward, while the Chancellor of the Exchequer began chatting to a backbencher behind him.

It might have been the Annual Summer Ball of the Tired Phrases. Other members were opening buff envelopes, sauntering through *A La Recherche du Temps Perdu*, planning and creating a family, or whatever they could fit in during the time available.

'Finally,' Mr Major said, and triumphant cherubims seemed to fly through the upper windows trumpeting messages of goodwill to all men on earth, 'there are a few fairly minor changes to the Bill which I should mention briefly'.

At this point, Mr Nicholas Soames (Con, Crawley) came in, a big bundle of envelopes under his arm, hardly a cherubim, but nonetheless a welcome diversion. ' . . . There are also a couple of amendments to the Finance Act passed before the election . . . ' Mr Major continued, and Mr Soames' left shoe began to slip from his left foot, revealing a bright yellow sock.

'A measure of counter arrangements to circumvent . . . ' Mr Major said. Would the shoe fall or would Mr Soames notice in time? Sometimes these apparently trivial details assume a position of such importance that they command the whole of one's attention.

9 July 1987

'Me and You and a Dog Named Boo'

King's Road Jam (Table Talk 6)

By the way everyone goes on about how miserable the 1970s were, you would imagine that every house in England had its own President Nixon covering up robberies from the local hotel, that Jimmy Carter was jogging sweatily through everybody's front room, and that the whole world was in mourning throughout the decade, their platform boots draped in glittery black. Of course, I would never deny that there were one or two things that went wrong in the Seventies – that haircut of Slade's Dave Hill was, to my mind, a big mistake – but one or two things went right, too. NAME THEM! Well, erm, erm, I quite liked that Christmas number by The Wombles, and I never thought that Edward Heath was quite as bad as he was cracked up to be and . . . and . . . there's the King's Road Jam. *Touché!*

The King's Road Jam, like Alvin Stardust, has changed its name a number of times, but it's still the same old place, the Chelsea Pensioner of trendiness, the Alan Freeman of the restaurant world. It is situated quite a way up the King's Road, beyond the fire station and on the left and, though it is mentioned in not a single restaurant guide, it has been there for ages.

Chelsea restaurant years are a bit like doggie years, with one doggie year equalling about ten Chelsea restaurant years. On this reckoning, the King's Road Jam is roughly five hundred years old, its origins lost in the mists of time. Some say it began in the late Sixties, others in the early Seventies, still others in the mid-Seventies, but written records of Chelsea life do not go back that far. Let's just say that it began some time after Lobo's 'Me and You and a Dog Named Boo' and some time before Mud's 'Dyna-Mite.'

Enough history for the time being, I think. What I like about the King's Road Jam is not so much its pedigree as its design. On the ground of this small restaurant are wooden cubicles, three or four on each side of the gangway. Nothing odd about that, you might think, but above them, reached only by step-ladder, are three or four more cubicles on each side, six foot from the ground, giving the adventurous diner the impression that he is in a treehouse, at one with the apes. Cra-zee! as Mud might have put it.

There is little point in sitting downstairs, to my mind, unless you feel like yet another boring old meal in yet another boring old restaurant, but up the step-ladder is a world of its own, something akin to Kenya's Treetops, a place to view the Chelsea wildlife without having to get involved. Each cubicle – vaguely reminiscent of a second-class sleeping compartment on British Rail – comes with its own dimmer-switch and a volume-control for the piped Motown music. There is a cosy, Wendy-House-style privacy to it all: you are separated from the table opposite by a great ravine, and you are cut off entirely from the tables on either side of you. If you like, you can observe two or three of the downstairs tables without being observed yourself. I'm told David Bowie used to eat at the Jam when he lived in Oakley Street, so keen was he on not being seen, and – who knows? – perhaps other 1970s figures, among them Lord Lucan, are eating there still.

Up the ladder, and into our seats, we were just about as close to the ceiling as human beings have ever managed to get. Fittingly, the ceiling is painted in black-and-green psychedelia. Stare for too long at it and you begin to think that you are a prawn in the centre of a mass of Chinese seaweed, the type of hallucination that formed the basis of many a lyric on Seventies concept triple albums.

The waitresses – recruited, I suspect, from the Royal Marines Catering Corps – hang on to the bar of the ladder while distributing the knives and forks and delivering the menus. Given the hazardous nature of their profession, they seem remarkably even-tempered. The menu itself is reasonably varied and reasonably unexciting, one up from a pub menu and one down from the normal restaurant menu.

On the night in question, I chose whitebait and my friend Mr Miles, feeling almost as genocidal, chose the *escargots*. My wife, perhaps shocked by the prospect of a table laden with over 30 dead bodies, plumped for strictly vegetarian mushrooms in breadcrumbs.

Like hundreds of Unlaughing Cavaliers, the eyes of all those little whitebait seem to follow one around the room until, that is, one swallows them. Whitebait never seem to deliver in quality what they offer in quantity, and these were no exception. Mr Miles's *escargots* were, he thought, 'perfectly reasonable, actually really rather good'. At this point, Mr Miles, often given to clumsiness, nudged his menu off the table, so that it fell, and fell, and fell, down on to the floor, so many yards beneath us.

A shiver ran down my spine as I remembered those tales of pennies dropped from the top of the Empire State Building splitting passers-by in two, but, luckily, the menu missed any passing diners and landed safely on the floor. 'And wh-wh-wh-what were your mushrooms like?' I asked my wife, still quaking from the shock. She said that they were explosive, with juices bursting everywhere the minute the outer layer of breadcrumbs was penetrated, but that this was, on the whole, probably a point in their favour.

Main courses were equally so-so, my own chicken Kiev decidedly unexplosive and rather dry; pub-standard but no more. Mr Miles's liver was overcooked 'but not too bad', and his bacon uncrisp. The only part of the meal which really got him going was the cucumber in his salad, which he described as 'vile'. As I think that cucumber, with its creepy texture and its taste of disinfectant, is vile at the best of times, I felt that he had only himself to blame. My wife, still sticking to her hardline vegetarianism, chose the *ratatouille*, which seemed perfectly ratatouill-ish, veering towards dullness.

Puddings were rather more wholehearted. Much smarter restaurants think that they can get away with offering only cold puddings, but the King's Road Jam at least takes a bit of trouble. Two and a half cheers, then, for the apple crumble, pleasantly stodgy, with quite a few raisins billeted on it to lend it glamour. My own *crème caramel* was a disappointment, but I had stupidly been imagining *crème brûlée* when I ordered it.

One of the many concepts the King's Road Jam seems to have kept going since the Seventies is the Seventies' rate of inflation. I had remembered the Jam as being cheap and cheerful, but a bill of £75.90 for three people with just one bottle of wine doesn't strike me as remotely cheap. The main dishes look cheap on the menu, but you should watch out for the extras – salads, vegetables, Perrier, and so on. But then time-travel has always been something of a luxury and, for me, there are few places groovier to be than up a tree-house in the Seventies. Regardless of the bill, regardless of the food, I came away singing 'Billy Don't Be a Hero', that marvellous 1974 chart-topper by the immortal Paper Lace, at the top of my voice.

'Micro the Dainties, Tina'

How To Get On In A Classless Society

Micro the dainties, Tina,
    The colleagues are soon dropping in,
For a bit of a chinwag and confab
    And the bunfight's about to begin.

Are the CD's all in the cabinet?
    We'll save the Lloyd Webber till pud
We've got Country-Style Cheesecake from Sainsburys
    (You know, their selection is ever so good).

Do you fancy a coffee for starters?
    That's the trimphone buzzing us now
Hi Gavin! Give us a bell soonest
    Okey-dokey? Ta-ra old mate! Ciao!

Tell you what, these eats are so super
    Once you start, you can't stop, don't you find?
My waistline's gone for a Burton
    I've lost weight? You're just being kind.

The bleep of my watch reminds me,
    We're just about ready for offs,
There's red, white or lager for allsorts
    And bubbly on tap for the toffs.

'Ding-Dong' the doorbell is chiming
    (Ravel's Bolero in D)
Sharon! Oh, but you *shouldn't*!
    Darren! Long time no see!

To the boys-room with coats and what-have-you
    And then straight thru to the house
Do mind your heads as you enter
    As the lady said, Duck or Grouse!

I see Craig's brought his cam-corder
  Do help yourself to cham-poo!
With 'Cats' on the music-centre
  We're having a bit of a do.

Where *did* you get that blazer
  What fab gold buttons it has got!
Quite casual enough for the wine bar
  And sufficiently posh for As-cot.

Nice to meet you again, Terry
  As the actress said, Put it there!
I must hand it to Nigel and Linda
  They make the most fabulous pair.

Your lapel badge tells me you're Andy
  A computer analyst from Tring
Please excuse us for asking,
  But what make of saloon did you bring?

Ford! Lovely vehicle! What reg?
  All the trimmings? Stereo? Phone?
Garfield? Jacket hangers? Wheel-cosy?
  Come and say a big hi to Tone.

Andy – Tone, Tone – Andy,
  Tell me, Tone, from whence dost thou hail?
Convenient for the motorway, I'd imagine,
  Have you met the lady wife, Gail?

Get what you were after for Yule?
  Aftershave? Moccasins? Jogging gear?
A China figurine, hand-crafted?
  The *Chronicle Book of the Year*?

Jasper Carrot's video's amazing
  He always has us in fits
The wife got the new Jackie Collins
  And Elaine Paige's 'All-Time Greatest Hits'.

Barry! What's your poison?
   Take a pew, if you'll pardon my French
A pint of best and a Snowball?
   Bide a while, and I'll locate the wench.

Do I spy Sue over yonder?
   Cooo-eee, Over here! Yoo-hoo!
No top-up for me please, I'm driving,
   Okey-doke, don't mind if I do.

Super quiche! M and S? Can't beat 'em!
   As I say, you can't help but laugh
Whoops! I'm repeating! Beg pardon!
   I've just spotted my other half.

Jill does put herself round a bit!
   A smooch with Bill, then Ron too!
The pizza's untasted, the coleslaw's all wasted
   And nobody's touched the fon-due!

The invite said half six to eight,
   And it's still wall to wall beyond nine
There are birds of the unfeathered variety
   And not a bad drop of wine.

The queue for the small room is lengthy
   But the blokes love to wee out door
The lager is flowing, the dances are slowing
   And the red wine is smooth Piat D'Or

Cheers! Bye now! Take care!
   Don't do anything I wouldn't do!
Ciao! Let's have lunch! God Bless!
   Be good! Adios! Toodle-oo!

Now let's curl up with a hot drink
   (Ovaltine's an excellent buy)
Then soak in a luxury foam bath
   And unwind with a weepie on Sky

Mmm, nice to be under the duvet,
   Switching off our Snoopy light,
To dream of Panatellas in Bournemouth
   Time for zizz! Ta-ra! Nighty-night!

'Money Talks'

Paul Getty and The Parrots

I am quite often sent biographies of characters in whom I have little interest to review. Books on Mae West, Robert Mark and George Harrison sit on my shelves. A couple of years ago at Christmas, I was sent two long biographies of J. Paul Getty, one of them subtitled 'The Richest Man in the World'. The odd thing about these books was that I had once met their subject: aged 16, I had spent a strenuous and awkward hour talking to Getty himself. That was back in 1974. He had died two years later, leaving me with the slightly unplaceable kudos of having been the last person, as far as I know, to interview him.

The two biographies made me think that perhaps I'd missed something. One of them claimed that, during the period in which my interview took place, Getty was of the belief that he was the reincarnation of the Emperor Hadrian. I had not scented an inkling of this. The other said that he had been a Nazi sympathiser. Both agreed that he was mean to an absurd degree; that he had destroyed his sons; that he had no sense of humour; that he cared more for money than for people; that he was a paranoid and a megalomaniac; that he was extraordinarily vain; that he juggled cruelly with avaricious women; that . . . and so on. I gave both books a bad review, not because I felt that my memories – or absence of memories – were more accurate than the strenuous research of the authors, but because of their snappy, nasty, journalistic style. Perhaps I am lying: book reviewing is as hard as any other area of writing for one to judge one's own motives. Perhaps part of me disliked the books for creating a demon out of one I remembered as a dull old gent.

A month after I had sent the review in, I found a copy of the interview, which I had written for my school magazine, the *Eton College Chronicle*. It was a dullish résumé of Getty's career, with his very few quotable quotes scattered here and there. But then I found the cassette tape of our meeting. I had not heard it for twelve years. I prepared to listen to these voices from the past: my sixteen-year-old self interviewing this old, old man who was now dead and buried.

This is how the interview had come about. On the Fourth of June – Eton's equivalent of sports day or prize-giving, though Eton is so superior that there are few sports and no prizes – I had been loitering about near the statue of

Henry IV waiting, I think, for a roll-call, when my eyes caught sight of two very large, burly men. Then I saw, some yards behind the two burly men, another two burly men. In between these two pairs of burly men, who I remember now as wearing sunglasses and looking this way and that, was a smart-looking woman in late middle age and, with her, a very old man in a smart suit, walking very, very slowly. I pointed out this peculiar sight to someone. They replied that he often came to Eton, he loved Eton: he was Paul Getty. Soon after this revelation, I had sent a letter to Getty at Sutton Place asking for an interview and his secretary had replied saying yes.

I always remembered getting in much better than what happened when I got in. My mother drove me up the A3 (we lived only half an hour away). At the gates, a security man with a walkie-talkie approached us. He then walkie-talkied through and eventually pressed the device that electronically opened the gates. I think there were signs saying something like 'Warning: Guard Dogs Patrolling: Do Not Leave Your Vehicle'. At the end of the drive lay the beautiful Sutton Place. No one was about. Leaving my mother in the car, I walked to the front door. I couldn't see a doorbell or a knocker, so I waited awkwardly. Eventually, I heard the sound of keys and bolts, a sound I have only otherwise heard in Dracula movies. A butler admitted me. My mother told me later that, bored with sitting in her car, she had ventured outside. Sure enough, Alsatians had come bounding towards her, and she had nipped back in. Police guards had told her, through the window, that it would be safest if she didn't get out again.

Meanwhile the butler had showed me to a secretary, and the secretary had shown me to a large and impressive room, where I sat, slightly nervous and toying with my tape-recorder, saying 'One, two, one, two' into the microphone. After a few minutes, the old man entered. I stood up and we shook hands. He walked slowly, and he spoke even slower, in a deep, drawling voice which sounds to me now most like Marlon Brando's voice in *The Godfather*. Unlike the Getty of the biographies, he smiled at definite moments throughout our interview, but the smiles might have been imperceptible to the camera, had one been in the room: his normal face was set in a dour mask, and a smile constituted the movement from dourness to indifference; nevertheless, it was a smile. We sat in armchairs, quite a few yards away from one another, the tape-recorder between us, both of us looking into each others' eyes. He is dead and I am a different person: the tape is what we were.

'Can I start by asking how you amassed your fortune? A difficult question.'

My voice is much higher than now, more chirpy. I don't sound embarrassed.

'Difficult question. I suppose little by little.'

There is silence, a long silence.

'How . . . er . . . quickly?'

'Well, I started working when I was in my late teens and that's 60 years ago, over 60 years.'

'And . . . you worked for your father's firm did you?'

'Sorry?'

'Did you work for your father's firm?'

That last question is delivered in a high-pitched, cosy, rather patronising way, as if I were addressing a very dim geriatric.

'I worked for my father, yes.'

The brevity of each answer obviously meant that my prepared questions ran out within a few minutes. As the tape goes on, the sound of paper being crumpled in between each answer and the next question becomes steadily more frantic. But I get through.

'Erm . . . Erm . . . are you now in the position that you have always wanted to be?'

'I didn't always want to be 80 years old.'

The sound of Getty laughing. A grunt with a twist. A nervous giggle from me: adolescents don't want to talk about death because they think of it so much.

'But haven't you got any further ambitions?'

'No. Not particularly.'

More paper being crumpled. The sound of my voice, almost to myself, saying, 'Right.'

Then, at last another question:

'Could you tell me a bit about your museum.'

'It's a reproduction of a Roman villa and, er, there's so much modern architecture that I thought I'd make an exception and try to re-create an ancient building.'

'It's exactly along the lines, is it?'

'It's exactly on the lines, yes.'

'And, er, do people pay to go and see it or what?'

'No, it's free. No entrance charge.'

'And do you have a house nearby?'

'My home is nearby.'

'In California?'

'In California.'

By this time, I must have sensed that my story (Getty rarely or never gave interviews) was not going to set the world on fire. In moments of desperation (I couldn't possibly leave after just ten minutes) one's true character comes out. We begin to discuss his art collection. He admits that he has one.

'Are you expanding your collection all the time?'

'Not recently. Prices have gone so astronomically high that I'd rather sit in the audience than on the stage playing a part.'

To which I – 16 years old, with a pound a week pocket money, saving up for the new Fairport Convention album – reply:

'Yes, I agree.'

I then fall back on Eton, as Etonians do.

'Did you visit Eton on the Fourth of June?'

'I was at Eton on the First. The First of June.'

'It's called the Fourth though.'

'Yes.'

'Did you enjoy that?'

'Yes. Very much.'

'Was that the first Fourth of June you'd gone to?'

'No, I'd seen it before.'

'I see.' (*Long silence*) 'Erm, do you like the idea of public schools and . . .'

'Yes I do, I do indeed. I think that there's an old saying, "The Battle of Waterloo was won on the playing fields of Eton".'

Silence.

'So you'd be very sad to see Eton disappear?'

'Yes.'

At this point, it might be worth wondering what we were both doing there. I was there so that I could say that I'd been there and seen him: within minutes I must have realised that he would say nothing of interest to me. He was, after all, just a rich old American sitting there talking to me. Why? Eton was probably more like Oxford had been when he was there, before the First World War, than Oxford was now, and his biographies say that his time at Oxford was the happiest of his life. But this long-haired, tieless boy cannot have reminded him much of Eton or Oxford. The boy was there asking him questions. Why?

'Erm. How would you describe your own character?'

'I'd best describe my own character as having a great talent for idleness.'

'That can't be true.' Again, the patronising comment. 'You can't be an idle man . . .'

And then comes his longest reply: 'Well, er, I have a tendency that way but also I have a conscience and, er, I don't work hard because I love hard work. I suppose that my character could be described, as, if you said you have 50 parrots and I said I don't particularly like parrots, but if I promised you that during your absence I would look after the 50 parrots I would consider that I have made a promise. If I was looking after the 50 parrots I would see that they were fed and watered and had what they needed even though I didn't like parrots.' Again there is a long pause, presumably while I digest what the richest man in the world has told me about parrots. I then change the subject. I was, at the time, a communist, and wondered whether the old man shared my sympathies:

'Erm. What do you say to people who say money is the root of all evil? How do you reply to that?'

'Well, er, some people have corrected it to saying that the lack of money is the root of all evil.'

'And that's your answer is it?'

(This reads aggressively, but sounds somewhat deferential.)

'Erm,' I continued, 'do you think that a world without a basis on money would be a happier world?'

'Well, there's always the best hotel in town and there's always the best room in the best hotel in town and there's always somebody in it. And there's always the worst hotel in town and there's always the worst room in the worst hotel in town and there's always somebody in that room too.'

'So communism can never work?'

For the second time, the odd sound of a Paul Getty laugh – the expansion of a Paul Getty chuckle inspired by his own previous statement – interrupts the crackle of the tape. I plough on.

'So you think that communism can never work?'

'Well, I think that's a fact that has to be faced. Nature doesn't seem to believe in equality.'

A short discussion then follows on the subject of British politics, the only type I knew anything about. He has never studied British politics, he says.

'So you're not firmly set beside one party or another?'

'No.'

Then I ask a question that may well be the only one he had never been asked before:

'Erm . . . So would you say you had quite a large social conscience?'

To which he replies:

'A what?'

Obviously thinking that he might not have come across the term before, I seek to explain it:

'Social . . . you have a . . . sort of . . . erm . . . feeling for your fellow human beings?'

To which he replies:

'Yes, I suppose so.'

We talk about the pressures of publicity and his pleasure in having given employment to so many people, and then there follows an interlude which I probably then found embarrassing, but which I now find quite touching, on both our sides:

'Er, do you have any regrets about your life, about the way it's been shaped?'

'Yes, I do. I regret that I haven't seen more of certain countries in South America. I've always wanted to travel in South America. And India. I regret that. I regret that I'm (*long pause*) not younger.'

'I'm sure you've got a long way to go. You'll be able to visit India will you?

Are you planning . . .'

'I could have done more in my time, I've wasted a lot of time.'

'But then, if you've wasted time, some people haven't started living.'

'Some others might have wasted even more time.' (*Laughs*)

'I wouldn't have thought that you could start getting depressed about things you haven't done, really. You've done a lot, haven't you?'

'Well, I don't know.'

Our talk then swerves towards his love of animals and the arts ('Do you like things like Shakespeare?' 'Yes, I do.'), the threat of kidnapping ('I don't take unusual precautions.') and personal publicity ('And so you keep out of public life?' 'Yes.'). We then talk of American and British education, and for some reason I ask him once again if he has visited Eton, and then whether he had seen the *Eton College Chronicle* on the Fourth of June.

'No, I'm sorry, I've never seen a copy of the *Eton College Chronicle*. I wish that you would promise that you'd send me a copy.'

'Certainly, but it won't be out for some time as it's the summer holiday . . .'

'Thank you.'

'Have you got a photograph of yourself I could . . .'

'A what?'

'A photograph of yourself that I could take?'

'Have I a what?

'A photograph.'

'Oh, a photograph. Yes, I think I have. Would you like a photograph?'

'Oh, that's very kind. Shall I come along?'

'Come along.'

A secretary found me a photograph. I shook hands with Mr Getty and walked across the drive to my mother in the car. I sent a copy of the *Chronicle*, as promised, to Sutton Place when the interview was published. I can't remember receiving any acknowledgement. I later discovered that I had been putting insufficient stamps on the *Chronicles* I sent out, and some had not reached their destinations. Mr Getty would have looked after my 50 parrots, but I could not deliver him his *Eton College Chronicle*. But I was young, and he is now dead, so perhaps it doesn't matter.

'Mr Cool'

Degsy's Memoirs

Until now, it has been easy to tell the difference between the auto-biography of a politician and the autobiography of a football star. Political autobiographies favour photographs of handshakes with international statesmen and are full of grave decisions not lightly taken, crises surmounted and recollections of grandeur. Their message tends to be: 'It would have been even worse without me, you know.'

A typical football autobiography, on the other hand, has pictures of silver cups held high, personalised number plates on flash cars and the wife in her bikini, whilst the text, full of exclamation marks and bad jokes, would all point to one thing: 'What a lad am I!'

Derek Hatton, one-time deputy leader of Liverpool City Council, has writ-ten a footballer's autobiography, or rather, like a footballer, he has had it written for him. His wife Shirl, pictured in her bikini, is allowed the odd page for her own memories of Degsy, as he calls himself on his numberplate, or 'Mr Cool', as she calls him. 'What a honeymoon! We laugh about it now . . .' 'With Derek, there's never a dull moment!' 'He was always there to change the nappies.'

To a large extent, Degsy goes along with this chummy view of himself, cracking jokes ('What's more, when I play football you'll usually find me on the right wing!'), relishing the family portrait ('I have a pleasant home, an attractive wife and four bright kids, two of whom enjoy riding horses') and describing friends as either 'legendary' or 'gentle and caring'. It is only when these friends turn out to be Tony Mulhearn ('very gentle and caring') and Peter Taaffe ('legendary . . . I am convinced he is the greatest political thinker I have ever met') that the laddish picture starts to go skew-whiff.

This is not to say that Degsy the Footballer is simply a front for Hatton the Militant. There are many moments in the book where Degsy's enjoyment of his own fame has a childlike enthusiasm to it, an enthusiasm which stuffier politicians might well share but would always do their best to disguise. For instance, his wife describes travelling with Degsy to London to appear on *The Wogan Show*. Degsy could think of only one thing. One of the best moments of his adolescence had been when he had appeared in a school production of *The Merchant of Venice*, and now he was convinced that the famous Wogan would want to ask him about it. To this end, he spent the whole train journey relearning his lines. Such innocence (why in the world would Wogan want to hear Hatton reciting Shakespeare?) is genuine and rather touching.

But arrogance and solipsism are rarely far away from innocence, and in Degsy they are cheek-by-jowl. 'When the history books are written for the 1980s, the names of Militant and Derek Hatton will be right there, alongside those of Kinnock and Thatcher,' he boasts, adding, somewhat misjudging the resolution, 'as a reminder that the working classes can and will win.' However much he rants against famous politicians, he can never disguise the thrill he feels at being in the same sentence as them. 'Whether it was against Thatcher, Kinnock, Patrick Jenkin or Kenneth Baker, people thought twice before taking me on,' he writes.

His description of the three years of Militant rule in Liverpool has all the hallmarks of a comic classic. Though both Hatton and Militant have been portrayed as fiendish and sinister, it seems more likely that they were simply a bundle of cranks and yobs, Liverpudlian Pooters, all convinced, as they bungled about, that in years to come their names would be mentioned in the same breath as Marx and Lenin.

Like Richmal Crompton's William selecting a make-believe cabinet from The Outlaws, Hatton's choice of government officers is hilariously inappropriate. 'The Chairmanship of Finance went to Tony Byrne. His grasp of economics was second to none,' he writes, 'and he wasn't blinded by facts and figures.' In a similar vein, he appoints 24-year-old Dominic Brady as Liverpool's chairman of education, enthusiastically detailing Brady's CV: 'A first year Town and Country planning student of the Liverpool Polytechnic who had left school at 16 after taking his O levels. For a time he had worked as a school caretaker.'

Though he makes it quite clear that Militant is indeed a party within the Labour party, and that he is a dedicated member of one while loathing the other, Hatton still believes his expulsion to have been unfair and 'a witch-hunt'. His hatred for Mr Kinnock ('disgusting') is matched only by his admiration for Mrs Thatcher ('still demonstrating that she is an effective leader'). In many ways, his respect for the powerful and his contempt for the powerless put him on a par with right-wing Tory backbenchers like Geoffrey Dickens. He writes approvingly of a school-master giving a child a 'clip about the ear' and derides 'the shouters, the screamers, the agitators', with their interests in black and gay rights, who form 'the stupid revolutionary groups on the fringes of the party'. Of his own experiences with the press, he says huffily: 'Society and democracy are seriously undermined by that kind of behaviour.'

Having brought his city to a standstill, having served redundancy notices on 31,000 council workers, having been thrown out of the Labour party and having had to resign from the council, Degsy immediately sets up as a 'public and industrial relations consultant'. This forms a brilliant comic ending to a consistently funny book.

'My Rounded Prose'

Clive James's Diary

People have been kind enough to call me sharp. To be blunt. I am sharp. It was probably Rilke who first taught me that if ever a man is to be sharp, he needs also to be blunt. This was a revelation to me, and partly because I already knew it. The sharp man must make pointed statements in rounded prose, remaining careful that the points emerge from his heart, and not from his head, or they will come out flat. Voltaire, too, taught me to square my feelings with my thoughts, particularly when talking among my circle.

If I am a master of the easy paradox, it is essentially because no paradox is easy to master. My prose style is the style of a pro(se). The clever effect is achieved by reversing the first half of a sentence so that the reversal achieves an effect of cleverness. This has gained me an international reputation for being smart, though I am not one to smart at the international reputation I have gained.

Ronald Reagan is a man who walks tall, and, walking tall, the free world looks up to him. Looking up to him, the free world walks tall, walks as tall as Ronald Reagan. Ronald Reagan may walk tall, but he also talks walls. The Berlin wall was also a Burly Wall when Ronald Reagan came to the Presidency of the United States of America, but by the time he left office it was a Hurly-Burly wall, not a tall wall at all but a short wall which had just had a short-fall. Now people could step over it, in a way that they could never step over Ronald Reagan.

Ronald Reagan met me a few weeks back, and he seemed pleased to shake my hand. My hand, in turn, seemed pleased to shake his. But there was nothing shaky about the way he addressed himself to my probing questions, and sure enough my probing questions were asked at his address. Even Shakespeare might have felt a little 'Shaky' on meeting Clive James, but not Ronald.

If I am known at all, and there is no reason other than my worldwide popularity to believe that I am, it is as a fearless and incisive champion for truth. Too thin on top to be compared to Einstein with complete accuracy, I am nevertheless humble enough to admit to having been born with a dazzling armoury of wit and an impressive command of the language. Small wonder, then, that the ex-President was ex-pressing himself a little dented by my presence in his ex-tremely im-Pressive den.

My questions were carefully judged to be hard-hitting without hitting hard, forceful without being full of force. In this manner, Reagan ended up getting more out of me than many a more aggressive interviewer. Of course, many of the most interesting answers were never screened. For instance, when Reagan said, 'Did you come far?', I replied with a brief but mercilessly funny resumé of my biography. I began with an anecdote concerning the condition of my donger after I had plonked it once too often in the sheep-dip. I then talked him through the lighter side of the notably incautious acne I experienced throughout a prolonged adolescence. I spoke movingly of the moment as a wide-eyed and gifted Cambridge undergraduate when I first realised that I was not only wide-eyed but gifted. I spoke as briefly as humility would allow of my television reviews from the early 1970s, with extracts from my classic 'Game for a Laugh? Game for a Bath, More Like!' review (since reprinted in many anthologies). And I wound up by telling the great man that I was now proud to dine out on a regular basis with the Duke and Duchess of York. 'So, yes, Mr President,' I concluded, 'I think you could indeed say I've come far!!' And you know, under that gently sleeping exterior, I think I detected a chuckle.

My first question to Ronald Reagan – 'You were undoubtedly the best-loved President in the history of your country' – lacked for nothing save, perhaps, a question mark. My second question – 'Would you mind awfully, Mr President, if I were to declare that you were a hero not only to countless millions of your fellow countrymen but also to me personally?' – was intended to soften him up for the third question – 'You are undoubtedly an excellent horseman. What is it about horse-riding that you find so appealing?' This one took him aback a bit. I could tell that he hadn't been expecting anything quite so piercing. But the old charmer forgave me afterwards with another warm handshake. 'Pleasure to meet you, Mr-er-er-' he said, in a revealing aside, too overcome with joy at our meeting to be able to splutter out my name.

I am sometimes fiercely criticised for being able to write as brilliantly about the great French poet Eugenio Montale or the revolutionary Italian composer Wittgenstein as about TV commercials for Maxwell House Instant Coffee. Solemnity, I am well aware, is not my best vein. Lacking all pomposity, it is pomposity that I find myself most lacking. Low subjects or high, I find myself saying 'Hi' to subjects others see as low. And to subjects that are high I trust I have learnt the humility to say 'Lo!'

If my reading of Dietrich Bonhoeffer – much of it in the original Russian – has taught me anything, it is that Instant Coffee granules and Eugenio Montale differ only in the things that make them unalike: it is in their similarities that one finds them much the same. You may not be able to spoon Montale into a cup and stir him up without making an old man very cross, but still you may find yourself saying 'ah!' and asking for more upon sipping his dark brown prose.

The youth who once hoped for royalties is now the man who dines with royalty. The student who once read *Nietzche* in sobriety is now the guy who has found his *niche* in society. Born to the upper crust, Princess Margaret now counts it a privilege to be borne to eat pastry crust with myself. The bloke from the outback who satire weaned is now the sophisticated *litterateur* whose attire gleams. These and other brilliant, caustic aphorisms have earned me my place at life's top table, but I know that human nature is various, and I have never been pleased enough about my own nature to feel contemptuous about anybody else's. I therefore take pride in offering a helping heel to those still struggling, and, as for those few still above, I do my best to help them cross their 'T's' and lick their 'R's'.

'My Way'

Richard Nixon and The Think Tank (Wallace Arnold 6)

When I began writing my major new tome, *Richard Nixon: Husband to Pat, Father to a Nation* (Weidenfeld £25), I was well aware that the media (dread word!) remained hell-bent on indulging in the vilification of this most honourable of citizens. This made me more than ever determined to paint an accurate pen-portrait of the Nixon I knew, a Nixon – patriot, family man, wine-lover, amateur piano accordionist, keen Morris-Dancer – many miles removed from the ruthless monster of popular imagination.

I had first met Richard Milhous Nixon in 1978, a full four years after he had resigned from office under something of a cloud. We had invited him for a private discussion with the Conservative Philosophy Group, a select gathering of like-minded academics, politicians and editors who met from time to time for a lively debate of like-minded opinions.

Throughout that historic meeting, we were impressed by the ex-President's dazzling mastery of foreign affairs. He spoke to us quietly and with great courtesy. 'It's nice to be here in –' (at this point he took only the most cursory of glances at his prepared notes) ' – England.' he continued, and we awarded this outstanding display of international expertise with rapt applause.

He then embarked on a *tour d'horizon* of foreign policy developments, leaving us all quite literally flabbergasted at the breadth of his knowledge. 'China,' he reminded us, 'is one helluva big country. Full of one helluva lot of people. And who are they? Mainly Chinese.'

At this point, my old friend and quaffing partner, the distinguished columnist Peregrine Worsthorne, chipped in. 'And Japan,' quoth Perry, 'that's very much the same, from the sound of things, would you agree?'

'To some extent, but not entirely,' replied Nixon, with the greatest possible courtesy. 'You see, Japan is, comparatively speaking, a small country, with rather fewer people. An interesting point, nevertheless, Mr Horne'.

'Quite, quite,' replied Perry, 'but the point I was making is that Japan is also populated largely by Chinese'.

'To some extent,' replied Nixon, 'But mainly by Japanese, to be absolutely frank with you'.

'My point entirely,' exclaimed Perry, obviously delighted that he and Mr Nixon should be seeing eye-to-eye. Needless to say, we were all stunned by Mr Nixon's bravura display of international know-how. In the question-and-answer session that followed, he was even able to tell us, without conferring, the name of the longest river in Africa, how glaciers are formed, the capitol of Canada and the rough whereabouts of New Zealand, brain-teasers compiled from learned textbooks by my young *confrère* Mr Jonathan Aitken.

Three years later, in June 1981, at Mr Nixon's behest, I was to arrange an intimate dinner-party at The Dorchester. Mr Nixon had requested beforehand that, aside from the most distinguished parliamentarians of the day, the cream of sympathetic intellectuals and influential columnists should be invited. From all over the nation, the great and the good turned up to pay homage, so that eventually we were forced to change our booking from four persons to six, after last minute acceptances from Lord Kagan and the self-styled Bishop of Medway, with Messrs Worsthorne and Aitken in charge of drinks, 'nibbles', coats and so forth.

Contrary to the sneers of the chattering classes, Mr Nixon proved himself a most civilised dining companion, and something, I might add, of a wine buff. 'This is white wine, am I right?' he said, taking a sip. 'Almost entirely correct, Mr Ex-President!' I confirmed, leading a small ripple of applause while topping-up his claret.

Over coffee and petits-fours, Mr Nixon stunned us with his insight into world politics. 'I always say,' he intoned, 'that every clock must tick before it tocks. Furthermore, no alarm will ever ring without a bell'.

'A penetrating insight into foreign affairs,' I nodded sagely.

'Who said anything about international affairs?' replied Mr Nixon. 'I was talking about my goddamned alarm clock. It's done gone bust on me.'

'A most apposite metaphor nonetheless!' I purred, and as Peregrine rounded off the evening with his celebrated rendition of 'My Way', we all sensed that the rehabilitation of Richard M. Nixon was steaming ahead with due aplomb.

'No Business Like Showbusiness'

Bill Board and The Smash Hits

The recent publication of the Collected Letters of the impresario William 'Bill' Board sheds fascinating light on the ups and downs of the theatrical calling.

Board first made his name as an expert in the art of topping and tailing lukewarm reviews for public presentation. In his hands, even the dowdiest review could be turned into a full-blooded rave with a discreet cut here and a few dots there.

Alas, the talent that was his making was also to prove his undoing. Witness Bill Board's reply to this letter from his bank manager at the end of last year, in response to his plan to launch another two West End musicals – *Fowler!* – *The Life and Amazing Times of Sir Norman Fowler* and *Gazza The Musical* starring Robert Hardy in the title role. In late December, his bank manager had written:

'Dear Mr Board, I am afraid I must refuse all requests for more money for your forthcoming projects. Yours faithfully, W. P. Binns.'

Ordinary people might have regarded the above letter as a firm refusal, but Board's reply reveals his optimism undented:

'Dear Mr Binns, Thank you for your encouraging letter in which you state *'ALL . . . MONEY . . . FORTHCOMING'*. I take pleasure in enclosing two seats for the first night. When would you like to hand over the money? With very best wishes, W. Board.'

By return of post, Mr Binns makes it clear that his earlier letter has been subject to misinterpretation:

'Dear Mr Board, At no time have I suggested that you would be receiving any money. I would not like you to think that I have. For the present, my bank is stopping all further loans to you. Yours faithfully, W. P. Binns.'

But Board hadn't been 30 years a theatrical impresario for nothing:

'Dear Binns, *'NO TIME . . . LIKE . . . THE PRESENT!'* Excellent news!! On the strength of this firm promise of finance for my next two productions, I have initiated a third, *Verses!* a musical for all the family based on the best-selling book, *The Satanic Verses*, for which I enclose more tickets. Best wishes, Board.'

Similar sleight of hand with words and punctuation was exercised by

Board in almost every area of his life. For instance, whenever he received a letter from the council headed 'Parking Fine', he would send it back altered to *'PARKING? FINE!'*, thanking them profusely for their kind permission.

Readers of Mr Board's love letters might well imagine that the impresario had struck up a perfect relationship with the girl of his dreams. The following letter, for instance, seems to suggest mutual bliss:

'Dear Miss Joy, I am bowled over. You say, '*I AM ALREADY ATTACHED TO . . . YOU*' and you then add, '*I MUST HAVE . . . YOU*' before ending with those longed-for words, '*I WILL WAIT FOR . . . YOU . . . FOREVER!*' Oh, Miss Joy, your words fill me with hope: let us swiftly to the altar!'

Only when the reader turns to the original of Miss Joy's letter, with words later underlined by Board for added emphasis, does a very different picture emerge:

'Dear Mr Board, Thank you for your letter. *I am already attached to* another. *You* must understand this. *I must have* a private life of my own, keeping my professional life as secretary to *you* quite separate. *I will wait for* your reply before seeing *you* again. My refusal is final and *forever*. Yours sincerely, Miss Geraldine Joy.'

Following Board's reply, this section of the correspondence ends with a curt letter from Miss Joy, again underlined by Board:

'*Please* do not write to *me* again; *anyway*, I will not reply, whether *you like* it or not'. But Board's relentless optimism was eventually to prove his undoing. Motoring fast along a country road, he happened to mis-read the warning sign 'LEVEL CROSSING AHEAD' as simply '. . . SING AHEAD'. At the inquest, the unfortunate engine driver was to report hearing echoes of 'There's No Business Like Showbusiness' shortly before what Board was to describe in his dying words as 'the greatest smash of all time'.

'Not At All Dull'

The Fowler Years

From time to time over the next 30 years or so, this column will be printing exclusive extracts from ex-Cabinet Ministers' memoirs of the Thatcher era. We will be printing three memoirs a week for the first 12 years, the figure rising to four a week thereafter, so as to prevent a log-jam; some of the less notable ministers, who led remarkably similar careers, are being asked to 'double up' on joint autobiographies. Today's extract is taken from Sir Norman Fowler's account of his years at the helm, *Not At All Dull: My Years in Office 1979-89*:

Part One: My Far From Dull Departure from Office

Number 10 was quite literally abuzz with rumours concerning my request for a one-to-one meeting with Margaret Thatcher. When I arrived at that familiar door, to be greeted by the same cheery constable who had greeted me daily for the past ten years, I felt my heart quicken.

'You'll be from the Yugoslav Farmers Delegation, sir,' said the constable, 'Vegetables, isn't it?'

'Fowler, officer, Norman Fowler. I have a one-to-one meeting with the Prime Minister,' I announced, adding, with no little pride, 'On a strictly one-to-one basis, you understand'.

The cheery constable consulted his schedules. 'Ah, yes,' he said, obviously impressed, 'You are pencilled in from 10.45 all the way through until 10.46, allowing for a minute either way. The Prime Minister will see you now'.

I explained my position to the Prime Minister: I had served with her for 15 years, including more than 10 in her Cabinet. I had enjoyed it. But I felt that the time had come for a change.

She was visibly shaken. 'It's a blow, Kenneth,' she said.

'Norman, Margaret – the name's Norman.'

At first, she looked stubborn, as if she were not prepared to back down. But, contrary to popular belief, Margaret has great respect for those who stick up for what they believe to be right. After much eye-to-eye contact on a one-to-one basis, she looked at her timetable. '10.45: Norman Fowler. You're quite right. I *do* apologise. Kenneth's the next one. So sorry. You were saying?'

I explained that politics prevented one from spending much time in the company of one's children.

'And it has plenty of other advantages too,' she replied, 'So why leave?'

I departed Number 10 that morning with a sense of relief. At last, I would be able to spend more time with my wife Eileen and family. Later, I was to meet her for lunch at an Italian restaurant. I told her of my decision. 'At least it'll allow me more time for one-to-one meetings with our sons,' I explained, enthusiastically.

'Daughters.' she replied.

I faced the day of the public announcement of my resignation with a certain measure of foreboding. Sure enough, the newspapers had a field-day. 'FOWLER RESIGNS' screamed the headline a quarter of the way to the top of page 16 in some of the early editions of *The Daily Express*. For the rest of the day, our house was besieged by the press. Amidst all the upheavals my wife Gillian had forgotten to pay our newspaper bill, and the local newsagent had come round to pick up the cash in person.

Might I add one final point on the vexed question of the leadership election? My views on this have always been crystal clear. I believed, as I still believe, that Margaret Thatcher would have won a second ballot, and that Michael Heseltine had all the makings of a great Prime Minister, and so I voted for John Major as a measure of the respect in which I held Douglas Hurd. I am glad to have been given this opportunity for clearing this matter up once and for all. I now look forward to a future in industry, ably assisted, as always, by my wife Veronica.

Part Two: The Early, Even Less Dull, Years

The time I spent as an undergraduate at Cambridge was by no means uninteresting, not to say seldom dull. I had long entertained ambitions to take part on a one-to-one basis in the world of Cambridge politics. Those who have read political memoirs of the time will have grown used to seeing me in group portraits, my head always clearly circled. From the start, I had worn a hula-hoop around my head for all group portraits. In this way, I would be ready-circled when the photograph was developed, so that all could marvel at such a mark of destiny on one so young.

By repeated use of the hula-hoop, I soon rose to committee level on the Cambridge University Conservative Association. Ours was an outstanding generation, with a shared vision of Britain's future in the world. 'By the time I leave politics,' John Nott announced one day, 'I want this country to be very similar to when I went in.' And the motion was passed without further ado.

One morning, strolling along the Cam with the young John Gummer, hands in shorts, I confided for the first time exactly the type of politician I wanted to be. 'My ambition,' I said, 'is to be remembered for being, well, not dull exactly. No: if anything, something slightly less flashy than dull . . .'

'Unmemorable?' he said.

'That's it.' I said, adjusting my spectacles with a modest flourish, 'Unmemorable.' And I determined there and then to become the single most unmemorable politician of my generation. But I was already well aware that with such stiff competition this would be no easy task.

I was never a flashy politician, never one to go for the crowd-pulling gesticulation, the unneeded 'quip', the interesting 'remark' or the original 'opinion'. Even now, come Christmas, I can walk into my own home, packed with family and friends, and still pass unrecognised through the merry throng. This, I need hardly add, remains a source of quiet pride.

In the Cambridge of the 1950s there were others every bit as unmemorable as me. A group of about 10 of us – myself, Leon Brittan and John Gummer among them – would stay up late at night, sometimes not going to bed until some good few minutes after 11 p.m., discussing Conservative issues over mugs of warm Ovaltine and a selection of assorted biscuits. We had so much in common – we all eschewed the colourful neckties that seemed to abound, and we favoured sober socks – that we found it hard to tell one another apart. I need hardly add that we got up to our fair share of student 'larks'. As well as the inevitable yo-yos and conkers, our favourite game would consist of one of us leaving the room and the rest all racking our brains to work out who it was.

One of the hardest parts of a politician's life lies in getting selected. Conservative selection committees are always on the look-out for a first-rate candidate with nothing too unusual about him. They are well able to ferret out at interview stage those who say or do anything too memorable. It was a proud day indeed when I was selected for a safe seat somewhere up North, in the Yorkshire area as I recall, which I was to hold for the next thirty years. Three of my contemporaries – Gummer, Brittan, Nott – were on the shortlist with me, and I knew that it would be close-run. I had picked my wife from the Central Office approved list of Candidate's spouses, so I was safe on that score, but some of the questions could be very searching.

Leon, for instance, had fallen at the last fence. When asked for his favourite colour, he had replied 'Lilac'; it was a full three years before he would find another seat. When they asked me the same question, I knew that my whole future was at stake. 'It would be invidious to single out any one colour in particular before consulting my constituents and the country at large over this very important issue,' I replied. 'But let's first and foremost be realistic in this matter.' The committee rose as a man and shook me by the hand. I was on my way.

'On The Button'

Cecil Parkinson's Comeback

He had lost the top button of his shirt earlier in the morning, and was a little put out. 'Perhaps we'll be able to encourage someone to do a bit of sewing when we get there,' he said as we both got into the back of his small chauffeur-driven car. The cuffs on his well-cut blue-and-white striped shirt each had a third, spare button which, I thought, might come in handy later.

His family had been part of the strong Northern working-class Conservative tradition, he explained, as we smoothed our way away from the Tarmac building in Mayfair, but he had been a socialist at his grammar school. 'Socialism appealed to one's radical instincts but also to one's idealism,' he said. 'And it's easy now to forget what an idealistic concept nationalisation once was.'

Cecil Parkinson has a way of screwing up his eyes when talking, as if he is looking constantly at the sun. His hands, with their bitten nails, are rarely still. They smooth down his already neat hair; they run themselves up and down his tie; when cupped, they lend emphasis to a statement of political conviction; and, every now and then, they play anxiously with the buttonless collar.

'What was your early ambition?'

'Oh, I've been around this course many times before.'

'I'm sorry . . . I just wondered.'

'You know already, don't you?'

'No, I don't think I do.'

'I didn't realise that this would be a soul-searching interview. I didn't realise that those were the terms.'

'Well, I was just asking because I was interested.'

He pulled at his tie. 'It's been written before, but I was thinking of going into the Church. But that's old hat, it really is.'

We moved on to his Cambridge days. Reading English, he never missed a lecture by Leavis. 'He was so rigorous, you know, and his influence carried way beyond one's attitude to literature. He taught one to look for the difference between the imaginative and the contrived in one's daily life; between artificiality and conviction. And one can apply that attitude in the House of

Commons too.'

'How?'

'Benn, for instance. He believes in what he says. It's not a charade. He may be deadly but he's earnest.'

'What about Kinnock?'

'I think most people would accept that he's the genuine article.'

'And Hattersley?'

'He's obviously a very able person with a wide range of interests. I think he's an exceptional writer, by the way . . .'

'But does he represent artificiality or conviction?'

'I think we'd better draw stumps on this one.'

He picked up his car telephone and punched out a number. 'Just getting some figures,' he said to me as it was ringing. It was the day after the council elections . '. . . Is that you, Paul? Have you got the figures? . . . Oh, I'm sorry, Could you tell me your number so I don't make the same mistake again? . . . Thank you.'

He turned to me as he was redialling. 'It was my father-in-law's number,' he explained, the right-hand side of his mouth smiling briefly before returning to place. He smoothed his tie. Paul answered. The figures were tremendously encouraging.

His head shakes very slightly while he talks. The surrounding demeanour of the rest of his face makes the scrunched-up, bewildered eyes sadder than they might appear on someone less manicured. Like many politicians, when he talks of others he talks of their personalities rather than their politics, but, on the subject of himself, he pooh-poohs what he calls 'soul-searching' questions, as if somehow one was being clumsy or naive in asking them.

'What would you say were your faults, and what are your qualities?'

He looked straight ahead along the M3. There was such a long silence that I thought he might well not have heard me. Then he turned.

'That's for others to say.'

'But what would you say?'

Another long pause.

'I suppose some people would say that I was bland and that I lacked conviction, but others who know me better would say I have very strong political conviction.'

He could be harder on others, from all parties, than he was on himself, but never for quotation.

Throughout the day, he would say 'off the record' or 'I'd ask you not to put this in, though' with the almost flirtatious air people adopt when confiding the secrets of a circle they see as charmed, and as theirs. What would follow would be no more than a little off-the-record anecdote about Willie or Norman especially designed for affecting intimacy with journalists, for creating an air of complicity while actually establishing ground rules for superiority.

The Rt Hon. Cecil Parkinson was due to speak at a grammar school in Portsmouth. We had set off late and when we got to Portsmouth we lost our way. There were many people in the streets whom we could have asked the way without leaving the car, but, once the chauffeur had brought the car to a halt, Parkinson leapt out in his shirtsleeves and strode along the pavement to an elderly couple. I can't remember ever having seen anyone bothering to do this before. The chauffeur and I stared through the car window as Parkinson and the elderly couple talked animatedly and hands were shaken. 'He's made their day!' said the chauffeur, but the freshly contented look on his face made me feel that, in another way, they were making his. Before we found the school, Parkinson had leapt out of the car a second time, to be recognised by three businessmen.

In the headmaster's room before the lecture, Parkinson chatted with a select band of boys and staff over sandwiches. He obviously felt easy talking light-heartedly with groups of six or seven, drawing them into his stories of power, asking them for information about the school and about themselves.

He had something to say to everyone, and he was evidently going down well. A few minutes before we were due to climb the stairs to the lecture hall, there were words in the headmaster's ear, and, seconds later, a boy and three masters were ushered with a certain amount of bustle into the headmaster's study. The miscreant had let off a number of stink-bombs in the hall.

Meanwhile, a master told me that, on the whole, pupils these days were different from those he taught a decade ago. They were more interested in careers, in money and in getting on.

I asked the ambitious 17-year-old chairman of the Politics Society whether we could expect heckling. He looked a little sheepish and said that they'd all been told not to say anything they shouldn't.

Parkinson spoke about the fundamental differences between socialism and conservatism. As he speaks of all the achievements of the present Government, his chin thrusting to and fro, his hands gesticulating towards the ceiling, a sense of ease emerges that is rarely evident in ordinary conversation with him.

There is a refuge in public life and public issues, a refuge where everything is simple and certain, untinged with contradiction and desperation. 'That's all very well, you might say . . .'; 'The truth of the matter is . . .'; 'People want to stand on their own two feet . . .' Here, everything is momentarily straightforward. '"I don't want to play the fuddle-fiddle in the muddle-middle"', he recalls Roy Jenkins saying, years ago, '. . . and he got it right; absolutely ON THE BUTTON!' Everyone joined in the laughter.

At the end of his speech, there were questions. A girl asked, 'What motivates politicians: a lust for personal power, a desire to serve the people, or something else?' Parkinson seemed ruffled by this. 'I can't honestly claim that I had political ambition . . .' his reply began. 'Some people have a burning ambition to be Prime Minister. I can't honestly claim I had . . . then one day the Prime Minister asked me down to Chequers and asked me if I would be Chairman of the Conservative Party. I don't know who was more surprised – me or her!'

There were more questions, on defence and economics, and then: 'When the Conservative Party claims to be the party of moral values, how is it that some of its members fail to live up to these values in their personal life?' There was a feeling of embarrassment. Cecil Parkinson replied, 'We all have ideals which we can't always live up to as human beings, and I should guess that, by the way you're blushing, you're the same.' There was relief, and much applause.

As we were leaving the hall, the headmaster said, 'Not a very clever question, but a clever answer,' and, to Mr Parkinson, 'I thought you handled that one very well.' 'You won't mention that, will you?' said Parkinson to me. I said that he must get a lot of questions and heckles of that nature. He said, no, hardly ever. Sometimes at universities, maybe.

We went to tea with the Conservative agent for Portsmouth South, a seat at the moment held by the SDP with a 1,300 majority. In the drive there was a green Jaguar with a car telephone. In the sitting-room there was an abundance of scones and cream cakes, an upright piano and a local newspaper with the headline 'SOUTH TURNS DEEP SHADE OF BLUE'. 'Tremendous isn't it?' said the agent. 'Tremendous,' agreed Parkinson. Parkinson mentioned to one of the women in the room that he was afraid he'd lost his top button in the morning. She offered to mend it later. 'Oh, could you?' he said, smiling pleasantly.

Having lost to Paddy Ashdown in Yeovil, the Conservative candidate had been selected for Portsmouth on condition that he lived there. 'He lives in a good middle-style house in a middle-style road in a middle-style part of the constituency,' explained the agent. 'You've got to be careful in that respect.' While we had tea, Parkinson told stories of his dealings with Mrs Thatcher. Every time her name was mentioned, the women would hide their smiles with another sip of tea.

We moved to the study, where a journalist and a photographer from a local paper, *Street Life*, had an appointment for a brief interview. After talk of his time at the school – 'I was interested to hear from the headmaster that many of the pupils there were on the assisted places scheme' – and election prospects – 'very encouraging' – the journalist said, 'I must ask you this, Mr Parkinson: it was announced today that Gary Hart has given up being a candidate for the presidency.'

'Oh, really.'

'What are your feelings about that, Mr Parkinson?'

'I have no thoughts about Gary Hart.'

'Because his situation is very similar to the one you experienced yourself a few years ago.'

'I really have given no thought to Gary Hart.'

'So you've not nothing to say about him?'

'Nothing.'

'Because you also had a political career and a supportive wife and so on . . .'

'I have nothing to say, I'm sorry.'

'Well, if you don't want to talk about Gary Hart, perhaps we should move on to Trident . . .'

But after the first couple of sentences on Trident, the photographer, who had been silent, said, 'You still talk like a Top Tory.'

'Do I?' said Parkinson. 'I can't tell. Do I?'

'Well, you're still one of Maggie's favourites, aren't you?'

'The Prime Minister is a friend of mine, yes.'

'Do you think you'll get back to the Cabinet then?'

'Whether she includes me or not is entirely a matter for her.'

'You must have suffered a lot of heart-ache and trauma, Mr Parkinson. How have you kept going?'

'I've done a great deal of public speaking. I think I can help the Party in numerous ways. I'm involved with a number of charitable organisations . . .'

'Would you describe yourself as a happy man, Mr Parkinson?'

'Yes,' he said. 'Yes. Very.' Though even the happiest of men would have found difficulty in smiling after those questions, Mr Parkinson smiled. 'You should be on television,' he said to his photographer-inquisitor as they shook hands. The photographer seemed gratified by the compliment.

After a photo-session over a bottle of coins on a Union Jack collected for a baby-care unit by local Conservatives, we went on to our final engagement, speaking to Conservatives at a Trusthouse Forte hotel. The full list of Mr Parkinson's posts was listed by the agent, including secretary and chairman of the Anglo-Swiss parliamentary group since 1972. Elderly women beamed with admiration. Again the achievements of the Conservatives were listed with unaffected enthusiasm.

Roy Jenkins was pictured playing the fuddle-fiddle in the muddle-middle, but now a reference to the coming election and Portsmouth: 'I believe we can win it back and we will win it back and we have just the candidate to win it back!' He pointed to the small, neat man in the Prince of Wales check who lived in the middle-style part of the constituency. The applause was vigorous. After polite calls for the return of the death penalty and for life to mean just that, the meeting was brought to a close.

In the car in the dark on the way back, Cecil Parkinson seemed to be pleased with the way in which the day had gone. He was matey and relaxed. His hands no longer fidgeted with such vigour. The lost button seemed forgotten. In the dark, the sad eyes in the executive face were less noticeable. 'I've had a song on my mind all day,' he said, just before his chauffeur dropped me off. 'Very powerful song from *Paint Your Wagon*. D'y'know it? "I'm On My Way".'

The thought occurred to me later that, relaxed and matey as he was, he had mentioned 'I'm On My Way' because he thought it might be an optimistic note on which I could end my article, a catchy summary of the day's events. After all, everything looked tremendously encouraging, and prospects were excellent.

Postscript: *Following the June 1987 General Election, Cecil Parkinson was appointed Secretary of State for Energy. He is now Lord Parkinson.*

'Pop-Tarts'

Yelly Telly

If things went exactly as planned at breakfast this morning, then all well and good. But if a little bit of coffee spilt from your coffee-pot, or you accidentally knocked your elbow on the table, or the plastic monster in the Cornflakes afforded you an unnecessary shock as it fell unexpectedly into your cereal bowl, then you must write to *Watchdog* without further delay.

At times, Watchdog appears less a consumer affairs programme than a peak-time therapy session in which malcontents and paranoids the world over can air their grumbles while the presenters go 'There, there,' and call for immediate government action.

Did your hairbrush catch in your hair this morning? Well, a clear warning should be printed on each brush. When you attempted to walk on the ceiling last night, did you find that you fell over and hurt your head? Well, research shows that this is a growing problem affecting up to 75% of all households, and surely it's high time that clear safety guidelines were printed on every ceiling in residential properties.

Monday's programme was a classic of the genre. The co-presenter, Lynn Faulds Wood was surrounded by a semi-circle of gloomy consumers, some sporting plasters and bandages on their hands. Their complaint? Even the keenest satirist could never have predicted it: they had all been injured by Pop-Tarts.

For those who haven't watched the ads on breakfast telly for more than a year, Pop-Tarts are pancakey things, filled with sweet, highly-coloured stuff, which you press into a toaster whenever you feel like something really disgusting for breakfast. Minutes later they pop up, and are ready to eat, or rather, if the *Watchdog* whiners are to be believed, ready to burn your fingers. After their Pop-Tart injuries, one of the grumblers couldn't go to school for days, another couldn't drive, and so on and so forth. Out to a science lab, where a man in a white coat is toasting a Pop-Tart under laboratory conditions before measuring its heat with specialist implements. Yes indeed, the Pop-Tarts are *far too hot*. Absolute disgrace! Concerned faces! Send for more bandages! Calls for compensation! Should be a clearer warning on the Pop-Tart packages!

Now that they have reached this Pop-Tart pinnacle, where can *Watchdog* go? I am hoping that next week there will be a semi-circle of people with hot-water bottles held to their cheeks after suffering the grievous shock of finding that ice-cream is very cold when placed in the mouth, or more people with their legs all painfully trapped in single trouser-legs after their trouser manufacturers neglected to print clear instructions that both trouser legs should be employed when putting them on. And why are there no instructions on the Pop-Tart packets making it quite clear that Pop-Tarts are for eating? How many people, I wonder, have bought them as hats or even boots, only to find that they grow disgracefully soggy when it starts to rain?

Food scares also cropped up in two food programmes this week. On *Food and Drink* it was revealed that salmonella is 30% up since Edwina Currie's warnings five years ago; and on *Food File* the scare concerned the potential death-trap of undercooked beefburgers. The problem with all these food scares is that they are now such a part of food programming – rather like the chart run-down on *Top of the Pops*, or the Things to Make on *Blue Peter* – that it is hard to know which to be truly scared by. There is a danger that when a real report comes along saying you will drop down dead if you drink a cup of tea, we will all go tut-tut before nipping into the kitchen to comfort ourselves with a nice cup of tea.

But both programmes contained more obviously enjoyable items. particularly *Food File*'s investigation into shoddy cookbooks, conducted by an admirably forthright woman called Clarissa Dickson-Wright. The cookery writer Claudia Roden revealed the extent to which her recipes have been plagiarised by others, so much so that nuggets of autobiography such as, 'My mother always used to add coffee-beans to the dish' have been repeated, word for word, by other writers. Alastair Little, the chef, also made history by becoming the first person in history ever to utter a word of criticism against Elizabeth David. 'A lot of the recipes in Elizabeth David,' he said, 'don't actually work.' Hurrah!

I find that, against all expectations, I am developing rather a soft spot for Jilly Goolden on *Food and Drink*. Her post-sipping exclamations are now reaching the outer stratosphere of probability, and are becoming collector's items. 'Absolutely sumptuously gorgeously malty,' she bubbled this week after sipping one malt whisky. 'It's like smouldering Tarmac, it's very, very haunting,' she enthused of another. Given that most people I take out for meals say only 'very nice', I have begun to value Jilly's increasingly brave and bizarre range of epithets. How I long for the day when I can hear what she says as she places her fingers on a freshly toasted Pop-Tart.

As part of last night's *A Night of Love* the enormous Barry White introduced Sounds of Love. Dressed from top to toe in green silk, looking like nothing so much as a domestic version of Glastonbury Tor, Barry spoke of how 'we make love in bedrooms and living rooms and bathrooms . . . throughout the ages, artists have always wanted to perform love songs.'

Meanwhile, a ticker-tape across the bottom of the screen revealed that *Time* magazine once suggested that Barry White's love songs were responsible for the baby boom of the 1970s.

It all left me feeling slightly queasy. Frankly, I preferred Mr Humphries' artistic claims prior to a cultural evening arranged for a Mongolian delegation in *Grace and Favour*. When Captain Peacock asked him whether he had any experience in the arts, Mr Humphries replied sweetly, 'Well, I once turned over for Sir Malcolm Sargent.'

'The Power Tea'

Hitler's Favourite Meal (Table Talk 7)

Like so many of the grander Trusthouse Forte hotels, the Waldorf camouflages its ownership quite excellently. Those THF initials, so evident in lesser establishments, are nowhere to be seen. Matchbooks, plates, saucers and spoons remain untarnished with the logo, and are instead allotted the dainty disguise of a fancy 'W'. This is just one of a number of un-Forte-ish aspects to the Waldorf, principally to do with generosity and joie de vivre, which have managed to convince even the most worldly hotel troupers that it is owned by some other group, or even, oh happy day, by a one-off proprietor.

The Waldorf's Palm Court is one of the most bizarre and triumphant anomalies in the Trusthouse Forte empire. A vast and beautiful space, it remains vast and it remains beautiful. Its upper reaches have not been converted into luxury dinette suites superbly equipped to satisfy the demands of the busiest international executive, its ceiling has not been lowered so as to offer an intimate, echo-free setting for inter-personal commerce; THF refurbishment has quite simply passed it by. Why, there are even such anachronistic delights as *thé dansant* on Fridays, Saturdays and Sundays, and, on all the other days, a pianist to accompany a full afternoon tea.

How has the Waldorf managed to retain so much of its identity, separate from the THF factory? I suspect that the reasons may lie in sentiment. In 1958, the Waldorf became the very first hotel ever bought by Charles Forte. 'Forte's was then concerned solely with catering and entertainment,' Forte writes with characteristic lack of zip in his autobiography *Forte*. 'I was intrigued by the hotel business. I wanted to broaden the character of our activities and indeed I believed we could apply the methods which worked so well for us in our current business to the running of hotels. I also felt that the addition of a hotel would make us a more balanced concern . . .' Over 30 years later, THF owns upwards of 800 hotels, and has even managed to get a discreet but unyielding foot in the door of the Savoy group, but the Waldorf remains peculiarly special, a jewel in their cardboard crown.

Like the interview with Barbara Cartland and the night spent under the arches at Charing Cross, covering the *thé dansant* has, in recent years, become a standard part of the journalist's repertoire. Nevertheless, I simply couldn't face it. I am all for people swooping around the dance-floor during those dull hours between lunch and dinner, but I haven't the stomach for it myself. *Thé sans dansant*, on the other hand, is a far more attractive prospect, so I nipped around to the Waldorf at 3.45 on a Thursday, when the five-piece band was lying low.

Somewhat to my surprise, tea in the Palm Court was already well underway, with foreign businessmen and ladies up from the country (which country?) chomping and pouring to their hearts' delight. Perhaps it was just me, but I thought I detected a slightly seedy edge to our fellow teapersons, a tinge of the Frank Warrens, but then I have always suspected men with hair that is too short and too neat who carry briefcases with gold locks. My companions told me that I was barking up the wrong tree, and that everyone was perfectly normal, but, quite frankly, I wouldn't be surprised to discover that at least half of them were up to no good, afternoon tea being the perfect cover for all manner of roguery.

In many ways, afternoon tea is the most bogus of meals, even more than the cooked breakfast. For this reason, I imagine that it is very popular in somewhere like Jersey, but in Britain afternoon tea is eaten only by people in hotels who wish to think of themselves as typically British. When was the last time you were offered a fresh scone, cream and jam in someone's house? And a cucumber sandwich? End of argument: afternoon tea exists only in the make-believe land of the hotel, and is as much a flowering of the caterer's imagination as the towelling robe, the DO NOT DISTURB sign, the mint on the pillow case and the single sachet of shampoo.

As I was helping myself to a bridge roll spread with tuna paste, and thinking to myself that tea was probably not such a bad idea after all, one of my companions informed me that it was Hitler's favourite meal. 'He ate nothing but,' he added. Perhaps the decline in afternoon tea in post-war Britain might be attributed to this association. Even breakfast now carries more kudos: I have never heard of a Power Tea for instance, but then nor have I ever heard of a Power Elevenses.

After the tuna paste bridge rolls (v. nice) came a selection of crustless sandwiches made with Mother's Pride but none the worse for that. I grabbed all the cream cheese and prawn paste sandwiches I could, having no liking for the glassy taste and creepy texture of cucumber, and I awarded them all top marks. The Waldorf offers a wide choice of drinking teas. My companions both plumped for Earl Grey, but I went wild and ordered orange pekoe. To be quite honest, I must be one of the few restaurant critics in the land who cannot tell the difference between China and Indian tea. I only drink about two cups of tea a year, and when the next six months comes round I find myself unable to recall the taste of the previous cup. This meant that the excitement and subtleties of orange pekoe were quite lost on me, though I managed to finish a whole cup.

Next up – service, by the way, was remarkably efficient – was a plateful of what were described as toasted English muffins. One of my companions declared that they were not muffins at all, but teacakes. I tend to avoid this type of debate. Like the vexed problem of whether photography is art, the question of whether a muffin is a teacake is doomed to go round in circles, leaving everyone feeling miserable in the end. Muffcakes or teacins, we thought that they could have been a little warmer, though we appreciated the extremely real cream that came with them.

Already feeling a trifle full – I had finished a three-course lunch only an hour before – I found myself slumping back in my chair and listening to the music emanating from the piano in the corner. 'Send in the Clowns' and a medley from *Les Miserables* followed *On Broadway*, all performed with those extra little tinkles between each note so beloved of lounge pianists.

Throughout the bridge rolls, the sandwiches and the muffcakes, I had been hearing the 'Oooh, I really shouldn'ts' and the 'I'm being awfully naughtys' that have now become obligatory amongst people faced with a trayful of creamy cakes, but we all jumped in at the deep end without so much as a backward glance. Two of us had cute little fruit salads on pastry – 10 out of 10 – while the third member of our group went for a small éclair. 'I could have done with more chocolate,' she declared, 'but otherwise good.' After we had finished, the betailed waiter came back and offered us seconds, but by this time we were all feeling very full and rather queasy. In many ways, tea at the Waldorf is less dainty than it sounds, and it would go a long way towards satisfying the ravenously hungry.

There are few rooms in London where it would be possible to hold a festival of boomerangs or a fork lift truck rally, but the Palm Court is one of them. With its great open space comes a sense of privacy alien to more ostentatiously intimate (ie small) hotel lounges. We took advantage of this privacy to pocket the remaining pots of Baxters Jams. 'No need to feel guilty,' I kept whispering, 'we have paid for them, after all.' Hotel theft is a vexed moral question – obviously it would have been ethically wrong to leave the Palm Court draped in a linen tablecloth, one of the smaller armchairs stuffed discreetly down my trousers – but I think that few tears will be shed over a small jampot, even by the frugal Lord Forte.

'Pull Its Wings Off'

Tam Dalyell and Bernard Ingham
(Political Sketch 7)

Mr Bernard Ingham is an odd fellow who sits slumped at the side of the Press Gallery during Prime Minister's Questions, immoderately busy. He is large and craggy and rather loopy-looking, like one of the background soldiers who used to be employed on *Dad's Army*. He takes notes with such diligence that it is as if he were sitting an O-level. Afterwards, the press circle around him listening to his every word, like schoolboys touting for Mars bars from a demobbed prep school Latin master.

There is something so comical about his appearance, and so unremarkable about his location, that it is hard to get very worked up about him one way or another. Somehow, the proximity of such a colourful cove – his hair is a peculiar red, like a carrot with anaemia – to the Prime Minister is rather reassuring, just as the presence of a parrot on Mr Long John Silver's shoulder was rather reassuring: with him in tow, passers-by tend to think, nothing too devilish could occur. Or so it would seem.

But others think differently. For Mr Tam Dalyell, Mr Ingham is forever up to no good. Most calamities in public life, and quite a few in private life, find themselves attributed to Mr Ingham by Mr Dalyell. Judging by Mr Dalyell's questions in the House of Commons, Mr Ingham is here, there and everywhere. He it was who weighed down Mr Eddie Edwards's skis, he it was who whispered faulty messages just prior to the Charge of the Light Brigade, he it was who was spotted blowing hard and mighty at a secret location on the night of the October 1987 hurricane.

Mr Ingham first entered Mr Dalyell's life at around the time of the Westland saga, and ever since then he has been unable to stop thinking of him. In many ways, they are strikingly similar. Ungainly figures both, in another life they might hike around picturesque mountain scenery together, clad in shorts, rucksacks, Aertex shirts and sensible shoes, swapping train-spotting experiences and offering each other cups of Bovril brewed in the open air.

But fate has set them at odds. Everything that Mr Ingham does, and much that he fails to do, finds it way into Mr Dalyell's black book. At the weekend Mr Ingham seemed to have a harsh word or two to say about the press, whom he deemed to be inadequate to their task of toeing government lines. After a seething Sunday, Mr Dalyell screeched into the Palace of Westminster the very next day, his complaints at the ready. Luckily, Monday found 10 minutes allotted to questions to the Minister for the Civil Service, so Mr Dalyell could sing his grievances in an appropriate setting.

Mr Dalyell always speaks as if he were a Victorian minister foretelling the very gravest of dooms for the assembled congregation, and when he enunciates the name of Mr Ingham it is as if he were pronouncing the most iniquitous sin of all. 'Mis-ter . . . Ber-nard . . . Ing-ham,' he booms, and a shudder bolts around the quaking multitude. To the mild-mannered Minister for the Civil Service, Mr Richard Luce, he suggested that Mis-ter Ber-nard Ing-ham ought not to be classified as a Civil Servant. He wished to know, he said, 'whether those who talk in the terms he did about the hysteria of the press ought not to be paid out of Conservative Party funds.'

The mild-mannered minister suddenly learnt aggression. It was as if St Francis of Assisi had just screamed, 'Pull its wings off!' Mr Luce accused Mr Dalyell of always seeking to 'dredge up old issues', and he sought to offer a reason why. 'He does it because he recognises the Prime Minister has been such an outstanding success and is of very great integrity and because of that he is trying to undermine the whole position.'

Judging by Mr Dalyell's expression – bafflement, exasperation, indignation and outrage all jostling on to his face at the same time – it seemed as if he disagreed with at least some of the main gist of Mr Luce's diagnosis. Unbowed, he began to rub his chin with his right hand, ready to fight another day, sure in his belief that as long as the madman Ingham walked the world, not a living soul could sleep in safety.

10 May 1988

'Quite Frankly, Dick'

Sir John Harvey-Jones's Diary

The alarm goes at 7.16. I had set it for 7.15., so it is abundantly clear to me that there is something seriously wrong somewhere. The alarm clock is in desperate need of a radical re-appraisal by someone who cares passionately about its health. So I pull off its back and take a bloody good look, levering out all sorts of unnecessary springs and screws to strip it down to its bare essentials. It turns out the whole thing's a load of bloody cobblers. The problem is that we as a nation care too much about all the tiddley little springs and screws without bothering to look at the larger clock beyond, so there's absolutely no doubt in my mind that the best plan is to eject all the tiddley bits, bung the rest back into the clock and reset the alarm for 7.28.

My worst fears are confirmed. Despite my intervention, the clock has now deteriorated so badly that it never manages to get to 7.28. In fact, it no longer ticks at all. If I have learnt one thing from my years as one of Britain's leading industrial entrepreneurs, it is that a clock that does not tick will give off no alarm. Frankly, it's a lesson the rest of British industry badly needs to take on board, and it's a lesson I take pains to repeat in my first book *Making It Happen* and in my subsequent bestsellers, *Pulling It Out* and *Wiping It Down*.

Down in the kitchen, I focus my attention on making a halfway bloody decent cup of coffee and a slice of toast. As always, I favour the commonsense approach. I spoon two tablespoons of coffee granules into the toaster and place a slice of bread into the mug. I boil some water in the kettle, and then pour it on to the granules in the toaster. But then, once again, the whole thing goes up in smoke. Frankly, it saddens me very much indeed that so many of our homegrown toasters explode at the first drop of boiling water. It's simply not good enough, and it's a problem British industry really must get to grips with fairly and squarely in the years ahead.

Luckily, The Chairman of the firm that made the toaster is a very close personal friend of mine, and a fellow for whom I have an immense amount of admiration. I straightaway go round to his office to offer him the benefit of my experience.

'Quite frankly, Dick,' I say to him. 'In this day and age you simply cannot ask the consumer to accept exploding toasters. These days, the toaster market is highly competitive, and if we're going to beat our foreign rivals, we've got to generate nothing less than a complete sea-change. Forgive me for saying this, but at the moment your management methods are thoroughly out of date and, if I may say so, utterly ludicrous!' I then give off one of my endearing cackles, smile heartily, light my pipe and sit back, notebook in hand, to see what poor old Dick – for whom, incidentally, I have a very great deal of respect – has to say.

In fact, he says nothing, but sits bolt upright in his chair, his index finger on a buzzer beneath his desk. He is obviously pondering the far-reaching implications of my vision for the future. 'I know,' I continue, 'that there are an awful lot of poor buggers like you in industry simply crying out for my help, so I came over as soon as I could'. Before he can utter a single word of thanks, his office door bursts open, and a uniformed security guard marches in.

'You must be a uniformed security guard!' I laugh, setting him at his ease. 'Now tell me, what's the view like from where you're standing?'

'Okay, fattie, you've had your fun, now OUT!' he replies, helpfully lifting me out of my chair with both arms. He is obviously highly skilled at his job.

'What we're really talking about here, if I may say so, Dick, is what I call the Feelgood Factor,' I remark over his shoulders to my old friend and fellow Captain of Industry.

'OUT!' says the uniformed security guard, and I must say I can't help but chuckle.

'We've got a bit of a chicken-and-egg situation on our hands,' I shout to Dick as I am escorted with robust efficiency into the street. 'And we must remember which are the big ducks and which are the little ducks, or else we're in danger of letting the lion out of the fishtank like a headless chicken.'

These are hard times for the toaster industry, but I am left with the distinct impression that Dick and his senior command team will be implementing my advice, and that a toaster producing good, fresh coffee at a reasonable price is now one step further to the drawing-board.

Time, I think, for a bite of lunch, so I queue up at a shop around the corner which has a sign outside saying 'FISH AND CHIPS'. When I get to the front of the queue, I say to the charming woman behind the counter, 'You must be the woman behind the counter!' This puts her at her ease. 'What d'you want, love?' she asks me. 'Medium-rare steak, a good dollop of mash and a side-salad, please!' I say. But to my absolute horror and bewilderment, she tells me that she doesn't serve steak.

'Well, I must say I'm simply AMAZED!' I laugh incredulously. 'This really is an eye-opener! By golly! I'm sorry, but I'm literally gob-smacked, I really am! So you're really telling me that in this day and age I can't buy a perfectly simple medium-rare steak, a good dollop of mash and a side-salad in a fish-and-chip shop?'

'Just fish and chips, love,' she replies.

'And, tell me, little woman behind the counter, where do those fish come from?' I inquire, bluntly, taking out my notebook.

'Out of the sea,' she replies.

'The sea! Can you believe it?!!' I reply, utterly flabbergasted. 'You mean to tell me someone has to take them out of the sea, and then someone else has to transport them all the way here, and then someone else has to cook them?!' I hoot with laughter. 'I'm literally gob-smacked!'

I take out my pipe, write her a Three-Point Agenda for Action, and hand it to her over the counter. 'I'm arrogant enough to think I know British industry pretty well, and, quite frankly, I think you'll go completely bust in the next 18 months!' I laugh pleasantly. She seems grateful for my advice, bidding me goodbye with a cheery wave of her ketchup bottle.

On my return after a busy day, I remove my jacket. I find that it has the words 'PISS OFF FATSO' inscribed in tomato ketchup all over the back. This, I feel sure, is the charming lady's immensely jocular way of thanking me for the great deal of time and effort I have devoted to sorting out her problems. Well, I like to do my bit, and frankly it's the sheer gratitude of ordinary, decent people like her that keeps me going. You know, sometimes I don't know how they'd get by without me.

'She Didn't Just Walk Into The Room'

Bubbles and The Private View

The obituaries of Lady Rothermere have made interesting reading. The obituary in the *Daily Mail* was a classic of its kind. Phrases I particularly treasure include, 'She didn't just walk into a room. She made an entrance.' 'She made most other people seem slightly shadowy,' 'Young and old were drawn to her like a magnet.' 'She was a great connoisseur of champagne, and woe betide any host who tried to serve her the wrong marque.'

Two mentions were made of the fact that, as an actress, she had once played Sally 'the girlfriend of Douglas Bader' in the film *Reach for the Sky*, but the obituarist's sense of propriety prevented him from adding that Sally is in fact the feckless girlfriend who, after Bader's disastrous crash, says something along the lines of 'No legs? I'm off'.

There are moments when we in the British press can show extraordinary sensitivity; these moments usually coincide with the death of a proprietor, or a proprietor's wife. Many of the scrupulously generous obituaries of 'Bubbles' Rothermere have paid tribute to her wit, all latching on to the same example. When asked for her verdict on the new nightclub 'Regine's', situated just off High Street, Kensington, she said, 'This place will never succeed because it's far too far out of London'.

But was it wit? For me, wit is based on some kind of imaginative or ironic leap. From my small experience of her, I would say that Lady Rothermere's remark was wholly sincere, even innocent, and owed nothing to wit. I once witnessed her at a party in a house on the border of South Kensington and Fulham, and she behaved with the type of panic others might feel upon finding themselves bundled into a sack to emerge blindfold in a dungeon in downtown Panama. It is a tale perhaps worth retelling as a pleasing parable of the problems created by an excess of wealth.

The party was being held to celebrate the opening of an exhibition of paintings. As I entered, Lady Rothermere was in the centre of the room, champagne glass in hand, dressed in one of her extraordinary bulbous creations, a sort of upmarket 'Baby Doll' negligee in bright red, with additional bows, flounces and what-have-you. There is always a tendency at such openings for guests to chat among themselves, forgetting to study the paintings on display, but for Bubbles this seemed not so much a tendency as a point of principle. Nevertheless, she was obviously enjoying herself – no bad thing at any party – when suddenly she was summoned to the telephone.

Within seconds, pandemonium had broken out. 'What are you SAYING?' 'What's the point of having you if you can't understand A WORD OF ENGLISH?' 'Oh, what's the POINT?!' Such exclamations wafted their way from the telephone area on to the floor of the exhibition, though everyone sensibly carried on as if such fraught conversations were quite routine at all the best openings.

'Here – YOU,' Lady Rothermere beckoned a young man – as far as I know, a total stranger – to the telephone, 'For God's sake, tell her where we are!'

The young man took the phone, and tried to spell out the address. Lady Rothermere snatched back the telephone. 'Have you got that then? What? WHAT?' She looked around the room in exasperation. 'Someone else! Quick, quick!' Again, she hauled someone to the telephone, and again the poor person tried to struggle with her problem.

The problem, it emerged, was this. Lady Rothermere had been driven to the flat by a chauffeur, and thus had no idea of where she was. On the telephone was her maid (Portuguese, if I remember rightly) who in turn had Lord Rothermere waiting on the other line. Lord Rothermere, due at the party, was speaking from his own chauffeur-driven car, with no idea of where he was meant to be. Thus the husband who wanted to know where he was going was asking the wife who didn't know where she was, and all via the maid who couldn't speak English. Meanwhile, guests were being dragged to the telephone one by one, only to be replaced by someone else at the first sign of any muddle. 'With the instinct of the born hostess,' wrote her obituarist last week, 'she always knew when to move people on or create a diversion'. Hear! Hear!

'She Took It Out Inch By Inch'

Julie Burchill with Sir Harold Acton (Wallace Arnold 7)

I feel quite sure that most people who know anything (three? four? I jest!) will know that as the dappled dew of May makes way for the juniper-clad glow of early June, the cream of British literary society heads west for *Firenze*, there to sojourn with Sir Harold Acton at that divine *palazzo* 'La Pietra'. It is a time for friendship; it is a time for reflection; but perhaps above all else, it is a time for *books*.

Let me aspire to the briefest pen-portrait of such a house party, so that those who, candidly, stand no chance of receiving an invitation this year, next year, sometime, ever, will be able to relish the crumbs dropped from the table of those of us upon whom fortune has seen fit to smile. Popping one's head around those lacquered doors on to the verandah at *petit dejeuner*, one might glimpse Dr Rowse fingering an old Graham Greene; beside the terrace fountain, Kenneth Rose will be reciting passages from his splendidly entertaining *The Wit of the Titled* to an enraptured gathering of local tradesmen and rustics; and – lo! – up there on the balcony, his head all but shrouded in the morning mist, whom should one espy but my Lord St John of Fawsley busily perusing an exciting young British novelist!

By the evening, we 'early birds' have been joined by the 'married couples', and our reading grows apace: John Julius is tackling the quietly amusing memoirs of an 18th-century cleric; Johnny Mortimer trades literary badinage with the estimable Sir Roy Strong; Antonia Pinter is genning up on the prose-poems of Daniel Ortega, and way down in the scullery, Harold P, never what one might call a 'mixer', is challenging the trusty staff to an arm-wrestling competition, but only after they have finished the washing-up. And over this redoubtable treasure-trove of cultural leaders presides the inimitable figure of Sir Harold himself, clad, more often than not, in jim-jams of the finest silk, highly polished 'platform' boots and his charismatic pom-pom, reciting for those of us at a loose end a selection from his excellent collection of verse, *Of Ponies and Peonies* (1941).

Following a sumptuous repast, our solitary pleasures become communal. Each guest is expected to come up with a 'little something' from his knapsack of literary gems for the delectation of the company therein assembled. A smidgin of Brontë is followed by a soupçon of Drabble; a favourite Johnson anecdote is exchanged for a wicked witticism from Firbank; Johnny Mortimer scintillates with a new story about the incorrigible Rumpole (*what a character!*). This, one finds oneself declaring annually, is Civilisation, and we, it gladdens me to acknowledge, are the Civilised!

It is with no little sadness, then, that I feel impelled to recount the sorry events that overtook yours truly during my stay with Sir Harold *cette année*. This act I perform not from spite nor from resentment, but so that others might learn. Those who are excluded from such a glittering circle – I speak now principally of the Editor of this journal – are too often hell-bent on destroying the standing of those at its centre. I am now possessed by severe doubts as to whether Sir Harold will welcome me back next year, and through no fault of my own. Thanks, Bron. Thanks a lot.

Allow me to take a deep breath and explain. I had arrived with a large travelling suitcase choc-a-bloc with tomes both plentiful and various, all scrupulously selected to reflect my famously Catholic – yet occasionally idiosyncratic! – taste. Following dinner on the night of my stay, while poor Kenneth Rose was pausing briefly for breath as he entertained the assembled company with a reading from his own *The Wisdom of the Marchioness of Abercrombie*, Sir Harold took advantage of the *hiatus*, and, turning to me, fedora ever so slightly askew, said, 'Might we now be blessed with a little something from the Wondrous Wallace?'

Amidst many an encouraging chuckle, I piped up that Sir H had caught me 'on the hop'. Little realising that I would be 'called', as it were, I had left my tome-filled bag at the foot of my bed. Swiftly excusing myself with undoubted ease and charm, I leapt the marble stairs two-at-a-time. Reaching the main landing, I could hear the distinctive tones of Kenneth Rose attempting to 'bag' my spot, as it were, with what he described as 'a few paragraphs' from his recent *Darling Duchesses*. If I failed to act fast, I had no doubt that my opportunity to enthral the gathering with my own renderings from literature would be lost for ever. I thus scooted with all haste into my bedroom, and, without so much as turning on the light, plunged my hand into the aforesaid bag, pulling out the very first volume upon which I stumbled.

Hurtling myself downstairs with unprecedented gusto, I arrived back in the drawing room in the nick of time. Kenneth had just embarked upon his oration. 'The philanthropy of the British aristocracy has long been renowned the world over,' he began.

Alas for dear Kenneth, my re-entry encouraged Sir Harold to interject. 'Aha! The Return of the Artful Arnold!' he exclaimed. Turning to Kenneth, he added, 'If you would be so good, Kenneth, as to read that to yourself some other time, I think we are all awash with excitement to discover with what literary *bonbon* Wallace has chosen to entertain us!'

The eyes of the civilised world were upon me as I gazed for the first time at the book upon which my hand had alighted with such haste. It was a novel I had never read, by a woman of whom I had never heard, the unknown *ouvre* having been foisted upon me by the irresponsible editor of the prestigious *Literary Review* as being 'very much your sort of thing, Wally'. It would never do, of course, to admit to my host and fellow guests that I had no knowledge whatsoever of the work in my hand, so I decided, there and then, to, as it were, 'bluff it out'.

'Thank you for that kind introduction, Harold,' I said, for we have been on Christian name terms for yonks. 'I have with me a book by – by – by –' (at this point I cast a stealthy eye to the dustjacket) 'by one Julie Burchill, a sensitive young novelist, who is, I feel, erm, erm, doing no more and no less than erm, erm, re-inventing our very language and culture, erm, erm, in a way that is both, erm, life-enhancing and erm, erm, yes – paradoxical.'

'Mmmm. Paradoxical.' An appreciative whisper rushed around the finely-carpeted room. With my famous 'second sense', I could perceive instinctively that the interest of my audience had been awakened.

Now, it is not done at these *soirées chez Acton* to blunder into a book at Chapter One, as this might raise the suspicion amongst one's fellows that one possessed insufficient taste to select a particularly haunting passage from the work in question. Thus, I carefully pulled the said tome open a few pages in.

'I trust that you will all find this passage both moving, and, above all, erm, erm, plangent,' I said.

'Mmmm. Plangent,' echoed the distinguished gathering. I had them in the palm of my hand. After a suitably dramatic pause, I plunged in at the first paragraph on the page.

'*Ever since Susan Street could remember,*' I began, allowing the warm expectation of a well-honed trip down memory lane to seep through my enraptured audience. '*Ever since Susan Street could remember,*' I repeated, and, from the glow in Roy's eyes, I could tell that there was much warmth in his heart for the trinkets of childhood memories: picnics o'er moss-cloaked glens, piggy-backs for Mr Teddy, steam pud with lashings of custard, and so forth.

'*Ever since Susan Street could remember,*' I continued, '*men were launching themselves like ground-to-air missiles at your groin with their tongues hanging out the second after they'd first shaken hands with you.*'

There followed a stunned silence, punctuated only by a high-pitched cough from somewhere deep in the throat of Sir Roy Strong. John Julius began to untie and tie his shoes in quick succession. Antonia looked frankly aghast. I had to think fast.

'So sorry,' I blurted. 'Wrong passage. Silly Wallace! Ha!' I flipped the leaves ever onwards until my eyes were caught by what seemed to be a far more charming passage, and all around breathed a sigh of quiet relief.

'*The two girls were into their stride now, reaching a plateau beyond mere professional pride,*' I intoned. I had already drawn a rich smile from Norman Stevas.

'Adore girls' school stories,' he enthused. 'Always have, always will. More, maestro, more!'

'Two dears on a hearty mountain hike,' chuckled Roy. 'Just my cup of tea!'

'Now, where was I?' I said, suitably gratified. 'Ah, yes: . . . *reaching a plateau beyond mere professional pride, working as one body with two heads, licking and plunging in and around her, the noise of the three liquid orifices filled the huge room more deafeningly than the most sophisticated sound system.*'

Silence descended. To my left, Kenneth Rose withdrew a hand-woven mauve hankie and began to wipe the sweat from his brow.

'Frankly, I'm lorst,' proclaimed Leslie Rowse, somewhat pettishly. 'Will someone tell me what they're all up to? Pot-holing is it? Cleaning a drain, perchance? Hardly the stuff of anthologies, one would have thought.'

Sensing that I was losing their confidence, I skipped yet more pages, but, by now, there was, as Mr Bond might have put it in one of his more elegant moments(!), no turning back.

'Another of my favourite passages from this . . . experimental, yes *experimental* work, is to be found a little further on,' I announced, flipping like billy-oh through the pages in search of something seemly. 'Aha! Here we are!' I said, and began to read.

'*She took it out inch by inch – not believing that there could be yet more and more of it. It must be a trick, like those long strings of coloured kerchiefs conjurors kid children with; she felt the same wonder now as she handled it. It was like a cosh wrapped in plush pink velvet: ten inches easily.*'

'Delightful! Delightful!' exclaimed Sir Harold encouragingly. 'Rarely have I encountered such a felicitous description of the nefarious delights of the Christmas Cracker! Onwards, ever onwards, dear Wallace!'

I continued, "*Do you like to eat pussy?*" *she asked.*'

'Pardon me,' said Roy, 'but did you say "pussy"? I'm very sorry, but I have a natural fondness for animals, unfashionable though that may be. May I ask why any character brought up in the central tradition of European literature would enjoy eating a cat? A bit off, I would have thought.'

Happily Sir Harold sprang to my defence. 'Misprint, my dear Roy,.' he chipped in. 'Must mean "purée" – "Do you like to eat purée?" Some people don't, y'know. Never liked pineapple m'self: most uncouth of fruits. Proceed!'

I continued with my reading. '*Have you ever – er,*' I hesitated for my eye had caught a glimpse of my impending doom. '*Have you ever -*'

'Have you ever WHAT? One two, one two, my dear, can't wait all day,' barked Leslie, his usual tetchy self.

I played for time. 'I really do feel I mustn't hog too much time with my recitation, and Kenneth reads so very beautifully,' I argued.

'HAVE YOU EVER WHAT?!!!' roared Leslie once more, and the others seemed to share his curiosity.

'Naughty, Wallace, naughty! No time for tenterhooks! Conclude the passage, s'il vous plait.' It was Sir Harold, demonstrating his easy acquaintance with the French tongue. Alas, I had no option.

'*Have you ever fucked a donkey?*' I said.

Needless to say, I rushed shame-faced to my room, and it was early nights all round. In the morning, I was informed by a senior butler that my breakfast had been set at the end of the garden, some 200 yards from the others. Sir Harold was very good about it, allowing me to leave by the earliest possible train, but he gave me no hint of any subsequent invitation. No doubt this was the effect on civilisation Miss Burchill intended when she set pen to paper. If that be the case, civilisation will not lightly forgive her.

'So Sorry Surrey'

Jane Austen and Ronald Biggs

The other day, I received a letter from an Italian restaurateur in Surrey, inviting me to come along and give his restaurant a good review. As a way of showing that we were on the same wavelength, he threw in a few snooty remarks about his regular customers, whom he called 'the Surrey crowd'. Around the same time Jonathan Meades, reviewing a restaurant in Ripley, wrote of Surrey as a county pullulating with white-collar fraudsters and showbiz golfers, all daintily spooning avocado and prawns to the sound of Jack Jones.

No other county in Britain is treated to such derision. The merest mention of Surrey draws a knowing titter from the most sophisticated lips. Humorists struggling for punchlines need only insert the word 'Esher' to be guaranteed cackles galore, perhaps saving 'Chobham' or 'Chertsey' for an encore. Wales is the land of song, Yorkshire is a-bustle with real people, Somerset has its cider and Kent is the garden of England, but Surrey is just the place where stockbrokers live in mock-Tudor houses.

Perhaps now would be the best time to declare my own position in the matter. The son of a stockbroker, I was brought up in a mock-Tudor house in Surrey. What roots are these for a writer? Could any credentials be less pleasing to the ear of a researcher on *The South Bank Show*? Whilst it is deemed seemly for the sons of Cumbria and Yorkshire and Lancashire and Scotland to parade their backgrounds before them, the son of Surrey must remain sheepish. Judging by documentaries, every other county in the land is awash with a rich and wonderful heritage of plain-talking grannies and big-hearted landlords and hills and valleys soaked deep in history. But Surrey just has its avocados and prawns.

Few are the autobiographies with titles like *Surrey in my Bones*, *Born on Surrey Soil* or *A Surrey Lad*, fewer still the popular songs called 'On Leith Hill B'Tat' or 'A Surrey Poacher' or 'Dorking on My Mind'. At any given moment, there will be at least half a dozen travel writers negotiating the heart of Bradford, or zipping up Mount Snowdon on a donkey, but Surrey is doomed to remain the great unexplored territory. Of the 50,000 new books published this year you can be quite sure that not one will be titled *Woking: A Sentimental Journey* or *Into the Heart of Godalming*. Late night television chat shows are congested with avuncular politicians and earthy comedians growing dewy-eyed as they rattle on about the qualities to be found in Liverpool or Hackney, yet no one has ever spoken up for the native wisdom and ready wit to be found in Haslemere. Similarly the food products of Surrey tend to have their origin hushed up. Cream is never described as 'Real Surrey Cream', nor are cakes ever baked 'to an old Surrey recipe'. Surrey is the great neglected county, a county rich in history and culture that is treated, more often than not, like a nouveau-riche dullard. It is as if Mr Meades' own home county of Dorset were to be remembered solely for the fact that Poole is the birthplace of Tony Blackburn. Had you been passing through the village of Witley in 1878, you might well have caught the sound of the distinctive yelps of George Eliot as she was taught to play tennis in her grounds by John Cross, and had you paused while ambling past The Greats in Esher in 1859, you could have overheard Mr Swinburne reading the newly published *The Rubaiyat of Omar Khayyam* to his host, Mr Meredith.

Lewis Carroll lived, preached and died in Guildford, the place which Malory believed to be the Astolat of Arthurian legends. Tennyson wrote 'The Holy Grail' in Haslemere, where he died, and the great Thomas Love Peacock lived in Gogmoor Hall in Chertsey. Matthew Arnold spent the last 15 years of his life in Cobham, E. M. Forster had a house for more than 40 years in Abinger Hammer, Disraeli wrote *Coningsby* in Dorking, John Evelyn lived in Wotton and even Stephen Crane, the author of *The Red Badge of Courage*, lived at Oxted for a time. Just along the road from my family's mock-Tudor house, Agatha Christie had deserted her Morris at Newlands Corner before staging her mysterious disappearance. Keats, Donne and Gerard Manley Hopkins also have strong associations with the county. Beside Surrey, the Lake District, which enjoyed some small vogue in the late 18th and early 19th centuries, looks small fry indeed.

Closer investigation of books celebrating the gritty heritage of the real, folksy counties tends to reveal that they are more often than not written from a mock-Tudor house in Surrey, for Surrey is so convenient, and few writers can resist a top-notch avocado and prawns. Surrey is a particular favourite of those who have earned sufficient money singing the joys of working-class life to be able to move house. The first action of John Lennon on coming into money was to purchase Kenwood, an expensive mock-Tudor mansion on the exclusive St George's Hill estate at Weybridge. In these congenial surroundings, he was to compose 'Strawberry Fields Forever' and 'Working Class Hero'.

The joke shared by the rest of the country about Surrey is that it is dull and conformist. Such jokes do not explain how it has been the home county of quite so many extremely loopy people. Few English writers have been so conventional in appearance yet surreal in their work as the Reverend Dodgson, and few painters can have been so acclaimed by society yet so extravagantly vulgar as G. F. Watts, whose home-made mausoleum at Compton still shines as bright red as ever. The landowners of Surrey, too, have a history of worldly savoir-faire combined with bizarre broodings. At Pains Hill in the 18th century, Mr Charles Hamilton advertised for a hermit to occupy one of the many follies on his estate, specifying that the successful applicant would be required never to talk to anyone, never to shave, and never to cut his hair or nails. (Alas, his appointee was discovered chatting over a pint of beer only three weeks into his seven-year contract and was dismissed, never to be replaced.)

The Surrey air can have a weird effect on inhabitants, an effect not immediately noticeable to outsiders. As a teenager, I once had tea at Sutton Place with Paul Getty, whom I judged to be something of a dull old cove. Only some time after he died did I discover from a biography that, at the time of our meeting, Mr Getty had been under the firm impression that he was a reincarnation of the Emperor Hadrian.

In many ways, Box Hill stands as a fitting monument to the true character of Surrey. Its grass is neat and close-cropped, but its shape is quite outlandish. It was the setting for the picnic scene in *Emma* and, 150 years later, for some loot-dumping by the Great Train Robbers. Where else in England could boast such disparate group activities? Under the avocado, something stirs.

'So Very Negative'

John Cleese and Dr Robin Skynner's Diary

John: Let me ask you something that has puzzled me a lot over the years. What do we mean when we say that someone is 'a bit of a bore'?

Robin: I suppose, John, that on the deepest level we mean that he or she is going on and on about something quite 'boring', something of interest only to themselves. And, of course, repeating himself.

John: 'Repeating himself'?

Robin: Repeating himself.

John: I see. So someone who 'repeats himself' stands in danger of becoming 'a bit of a bore'.

Robin: Certainly. If he repeats himself, then –

John: – He could become 'a bit of a bore'?

Robin: Quite. If he repeats himself.

★★★

John: One thing I've always wanted to know, Robin, is why quite intelligent people – comedians and so forth – often like to talk in public about themselves all the time: their problems, their innermost thoughts, their feelings about themselves, and so on?

Robin: Good point, John. In layman's terms, this is what we call 'talking about yourself in public', often to the exclusion of all others. Broadly speaking, the world can be divided up into two groups of people: people who always talk about themselves, and people who never talk about themselves. Research shows that though quite a few people always talk about themselves, and about the same number never talk about themselves, most of us are in a third group, somewhere in the middle, of people who occasionally talk about themselves, but certainly not all the time.

John: So what you're really saying, if I've understood you correctly, is that the vast majority of people occasionally talk about themselves, but certainly not all the time?

Robin: Correct.

John: Yes, I know what you mean. I used to talk about myself all the time – my 'problems', my 'innermost thoughts', my 'feelings about myself' and so on – but, thanks to psychotherapy, I now find that I talk about myself in public only very occasionally –

Robin: And another thing worth mentioning is –

John: I'm sorry, if I could just finish, Robin – I was just saying that, speaking personally, I now find that psychotherapy has helped me 'come to terms' with my past need to 'talk about myself', and that I can now be much more objective, showing an interest in other people. What do you think about me and the way I've overcome this solipsism, for instance?

Robin: I –

John: Because, speaking personally for a second, I feel that I have somehow 'got out of myself', and can now concentrate on spiritual, psychological and philosophical matters outside my own little world. 'Me', if you like, is now less important than 'You'.

Robin: I –

John: – But, forgive me, I'd like to hear what you have to say for a second! How would you describe me, for instance, to someone who had never met me?

★★★

John: What do we mean when we say we feel 'happy'?

Robin: It's probably best described as feeling the opposite of 'sad'. Most people are 'happy' some of the time and 'sad' some of the time, but most of the time they feel something 'in-between'.

John: Neither very happy nor very sad?

Robin: Quite so.

John: And what comes after the letter 'D' in the 'ABC'?

robin: For most people, 'E'.

John: And then 'F'?

Robin: Usually.

John: And is 'E' a happy letter? Or a sad one?

Robin: Probably somewhere in between.

John: I suppose that in many ways it's infantile and regressive to talk about letters as 'happy' or 'sad'.

Robin: Certainly.

John: After all, they're only letters. They have their off-days like everybody else.

★★★

John: Why is it only married couples who divorce one another? Is there something about marriage which encourages divorce, do you think?

Robin: In the vast majority of cases, divorce comes about after married couples 'fall out' with one another. But of course, if they had remained single, they would not then be in a position to get a divorce.

John: Or if they had never met one another in the first place?

Robin: Certainly.

John: So it follows that the two people – let's call them Person 'A' and Person 'B' – should never actually meet if they want to avoid the awful prospect of divorce?

Robin: They are certainly increasing their chances for a potential divorce in the years ahead if they first get to meet one another.

John: And what's the best way for 'A' to avoid meeting 'B'?

Robin: Well, if they live in difficult parts of the world, and in different socio-economic groups, then that's half the battle won.

John: But surely they might still meet? On holiday, for instance.

Robin: Certainly, that's a risk.

John: So what's the best place to go on holiday in order to avoid meeting your future wife, and the whole thing ending in a distressing divorce, awful for the children and potentially ruinous to the inner psyche?

Robin: We're venturing into very difficult territory, here, John. It's advisable to consult a qualified travel agent on this one, I think.

John: Quite.

★★★

John: Why are so many people these days so very 'negative'? For instance, a lot of humour these days seems extremely satirical and cynical and 'non-positive'. Shouldn't we be encouraging our young comedians to be more caring, healthy and 'upfront'? It upsets me, for instance, that so few young comedians are writing books telling people to enjoy better, richer, more fulfilled lifestyles. Instead, they're just telling jokes, often just for a laugh. To put it in a nutshell, what kind of a world are we living in, Robin?

Robin: Surveys suggest that we're living in a world full of people of all nationalities inhabiting a variety of types of domicile in a great many different countries, John.

John: You mean there are literally millions of different people in the world, apart from me, of course?

Robin: At a rough approximation, yes, though I'm sticking my neck out a bit here.

John: So the expression, 'it takes all sorts', first used by Gurdjieff – or was it Fromm? – has a ring of truth to it?

Robin: In a nutshell, yes.

John: And what in layman's terms is a 'nutshell'?

Robin: Broadly speaking, it's a shell containing a nut.

John: And what advice would you offer middle-aged comedians with too many destructive or 'negative' feelings, who can't be bothered to do funny things any more?

Robin: Well, if they are household names I'd suggest they consult a psychotherapist, who will put them in touch with a good publisher. You'll find a good many problems can be profitably solved by sharing them with the paying public.

John: Even the more boring ones, Robin?

Robin: *Especially* the more boring ones, John.

'Square Dealer'

Francis Kyle, Princess Margaret and The Encyclopaedia Britannica

He is, I was told, a man who eats a lot of bread and butter when eating out in restaurants. I was told, too, that he is the kind of person who would never get his hair wet in a rainstorm: he has a large and varied collection of umbrellas, mackintoshes and assorted rainwear. People also kept reminding me that he had started life as an *Encyclopaedia Britannica* salesman, that his nickname was Brad, that he has never been seen to dance, that he probably takes an immense amount of sugar in his coffee, and had I heard the story about when Princess Margaret came to the gallery? Everyone has something to say about Francis Kyle; not very much, maybe, but something all the same.

To call him charismatic would be wrong, I thought to myself after formally interviewing him for two-and-a-half hours; and then I smiled at my own thought as he went on about the dangers of too much diversification. He must have noticed my smile, because he returned it in his lopsided way, perhaps worried that I would be offended if I suspected that he had realised that I had smiled when he had not been making a joke. To call him charismatic would be wrong. As the waiter asked us if we would be wanting more coffee, I thought that this conclusion was good as far as it went, but perhaps it didn't go far enough. 'FENS' I wrote in my little notebook. I had had the idea that Francis Kyle was like the Fens, an area of land so flat and featureless that it gave birth to innumerable stories and legends, so reliant were those who crossed it on the more miraculous features of their own imaginations. Perhaps I was hallucinating by this stage, for on my return, I reflected that Francis Kyle was nothing like the Fens at all. As I was going to sleep I had this idea that maybe a gallery-owner grows to be like his pictures, as a dog-owner grows to be like his dog. In years to come, will Francis Kyle become like an exhibit in his own gallery? At private views, instead of standing awkwardly by his desk while others frenziedly consume the drink that he himself does not touch, will he be seen draped in a colourful French table-cloth, a potted plant or two placed perfectly on his head, a glass of red-wine, a stray daffodil and a jug of water lingering gracefully on his outstretched frame? Will a pretty, somewhat sexless girl in a Pierrot costume eat a small plate of mussels off him? Will he, at very least, come to incorporate those relaxed qualities of old-fashioned charm, gentle colour and end-of-meal composure that have become the hallmark of the paintings in his gallery?

There are one or two details about Francis Kyle upon which rumour and legend cannot alight. He definitely owns the Francis Kyle Gallery in Maddox Street, where he holds 10 shows a year. He definitely does very well for himself. For some time, he definitely stepped out with one of London's most popular women, Ann Barr, and, through her, he definitely came to know many people – smart people, bohemian people, media people – whom he would definitely never have known without her. But they are no longer together, and, for many, as one of them put it to me, 'our Francis Kyle years are over'.

The details of his appearance must also be beyond dispute, though the neat parting of his well-trimmed hair, the expressionless face offset by a sloping mouth some have compared to Prince Charles's, and the glasses so solidly affixed to that prominent nose, might lead casual observers to conclude that at least one part of the whole was a mask. He is soft-spoken, or at least deep-spoken. He dresses conservatively, though with care. He is not known as one of the 'great character' school of art dealers. At private views he does not radiate bonhomie and savoir-faire: rather, he stands close to a wall, his head peering downwards rather than about. On potential buyers he practises charm, but most would agree that it will be some time before this reaches performance standard. This is what is known of Francis Kyle; the rest is rumour.

Glynn Boyd Harte had reassured me that it was he who had thought of the nickname 'Brad' for Francis Kyle. Brad, you will remember, was the name of the Mr Normal character in the *Rocky Horror Show*, a no-nonsense guy who is transformed into something wild and unearthly by the peculiar inventions of others. A smile tends to play across his artists' lips when they talk of Francis Kyle, and you can see why: he is a humorous figure, in the tradition of Sybil Fawlty: that is to say, he himself would not get the joke, because it's a joke about being normal, about taking yourself very seriously, about the disparity between your own self-image and the image the world has of you growing ever greater as your capacity to notice that disparity grows ever smaller; it's also a joke about trying too hard in England.

I had not set eyes on Francis Kyle for three or four years – in that respect, my Francis Kyle years, too, were over – and I had never spoken to him in a room containing less than 30 people, so it was quite odd to think of spending an evening alone with him, just so that I could write about him. 'It's a prospect I view with some consternation,' he had said to me over the phone, his peculiar choice of words – prospect! view! consternation! – making me think that, yes, there was a joke here, there was something out-of-kilter and faintly abnormal about him, there was something to put into my 3,000-word bucket. One of the things I thought funny, in my malevolent way, was that the more guarded he became – prospect! view! consternation! – the more comical he sounded.

I see most of the pictures are sold!' I said, I thought reassuringly, as I arrived late for my appointment at the Francis Kyle Gallery. Glynn Boyd Harte had had an opening night before; 44 pictures (*Sunday Lunch, Charlecote; Young Man and Pomegranate; Sweet Peas and Swags; Caffe Pedrocchi, Padua*), average price £2,500, estimated dealer's commission 50 per cent, only two or three without red dots.

Kyle, who had finished shaking my hand and was doing up his mackintosh, paused, obviously thinking that this could be a tricky one.

'Yes,' he replied.

He took me out of the gallery, along the street, round the corner, through a doorway and up some stairs. Halfway up, we passed what looked like a seedy red-velvet drinking club.

'What else happens in this building?' I asked.

'I don't know,' he replied. 'Nothing to do with me, though.'

In his business flat at the top of the building there were low-lying sofas and tables, primitive African sculptures, a notepad and paper, a Buddha, daffodils, posters of past exhibitions and a slight smell of what might have been after-shave. Before he poured me a drink, Kyle passed me an article he had written recently in an art magazine on the rôle of the dealer. Its thrust was that good artists benefited from good dealers. But those odd words again – fully-fledged! spectrum! fulfilling! – and long sentences using those phrases that attempt to combine strong emotional appeal with business-like jargon. On the relationship between artists and dealers: 'It is a challenge which carries deep responsibility and commitment; in a sense it is almost a marriage – with the artist's output as its progeny.' The conclusion: 'Its creative sustenance comes, however, from another source: it lies in the friendship he shares with the artists to whom he is committed, which is based in its turn, on deep mutual trust and respect.'

An hour before, Kyle's longest-standing artist Adrian George had told me that he had never been invited either to Kyle's house in London or his house in the country. Wasn't this rather odd, I ventured, after nine years of partnership with him? Yes, I suppose it is a bit odd, said George, but perhaps he considers his private views to be his private parties. 'I don't think he has much of a private life.'

Adrian George was being very solidly pro-Kyle. He had met him, he said, nine years ago, when Kyle was working at the Thumb Gallery. Kyle had struck him as very bright, energetic, aggressive and highly motivated, with a strong ambition to succeed. George thought that one of Kyle's motivating forces was to prove himself to his father, who looked like Douglas Fairbanks and had made a lot out of something indeterminate. He didn't think Kyle went in for leisure activities: his enjoyments were 'work, publicity, success'. Yes, he had one or two faults: 'He lacks delicacy with new artists, but I don't think he's intentionally cruel.' After another drink, George told me that he had a theory about people who went to Harrow as Kyle had done. They always swing between being bullies and being suck-ups, depending on who they are talking to: they can't strike a happy medium. He also thought that Kyle was rather shy and nervous, and that this nervousness sometimes came out as sycophancy. 'He's supine in the face of people he admires,' he said. 'Because he doesn't have vices himself, he doesn't think of the vices of others.' George explained. Then he paused, took a sip, and said, 'Have you heard the story of Francis and Princess Margaret?' I had, from many people, but I said I hadn't.

I put down the article from the arts magazine, thinking that in its stress on companionship could be detected the self-encouragement of the solitary. Before me, Kyle spread posters for this show and that show on the carpet, talking enthusiastically about the vision of each painter, about the excitement aroused by such-and-such an exhibition. Every now and then I would slip in a direct question.

Direct question: Which of your exhibitions has been your favourite?

Answer: 'Like artists, I tend to feel that the most recent picture is the one I like most.'

Direct question: When do you let an artist have a new show?

Answer: 'An artist is ready for a new show when some kind of evolution has occurred since his last show.'

Direct question: How do you price the paintings?

Answer: 'I work harmoniously with the artist.'

Direct question: Will your artists still be around in a hundred years' time?

Answer: 'That's a bit of a luxury to ask oneself. The question is really: "Is what they're doing unique?" If it is – and I believe it to be so – then, yes, they will survive.'

Direct question: Is there a definite style of painting that you have come to be associated with?

Answer: 'What do you mean?'

I didn't know quite how to put it. Those who like them call them charming, those who don't call them bland. Those who like them call them skilled, well finished, beautifully composed, lovely to look at. Those who don't, such as one art dealer I spoke to, call them illustrations, or 'a soft confection for the demi-intelligentsia'.

'Your pictures tend to be very polished, very well finished.'

He looked doubtful. 'If something's raw, there's got to be good reason,' he said, adding, 'I love craft. That's one of the ingredients I will admit to liking.'

'And by and large you don't show abstract work, do you? So at least we can say that a Francis Kyle painter is figurative?'

'I think that the best abstract work is large,' he replied. 'And, on the whole, I don't like very large work.'

He had booked us a table with a companionable half-moon seat in the restaurant at the Westbury Hotel. His artists had been intrigued to know to which of his three grades of eating-place he would take me: this was obviously the best, but a rather peculiar best, I would have thought.

I wanted to know about his father, a key figure in all the legends about Kyle. Someone had told me that at Harrow Kyle's name had been F. F. Kiel, spelt like that, and that his father was an antiques dealer with a shop near South Kensington tube station. Someone else had told me that his father had made a pile of brass up north and had financed Francis's gallery. Someone else had told me that his father was a Maxwell-type figure with a publishing business, and someone else again that his father was from Transylvania and was in clothing.

'Tell me about your father.'

He told me that they no longer talked to one another; clash of personalities, he supposed. I felt guilty for having asked the question and surprised at the alacrity of the reply. It was something he meant, and something he felt: there was no patter to it at all.

'What does your father do?'

'He's a company director.'

'What company?'

'A kind of conglomerate really – it evolved into all sorts of things.'

'What sorts of things?'

'Well, it started in advertising and electrical, and then it evolved.'

We talked of his mother, who was Welsh, and his father, who was Czech, and how they met on an Alp in Bavaria. His family had lived in Pinner and Dorset. His prep school, he said, was 'pretty hellish'. One or two people I had spoken to had said that Francis Kyle was the kind of person who was bullied at school. I asked him more about his prep school, but he wouldn't tell me much, and then about Harrow, which he ummed and erred about. Out of nowhere, he suddenly said, 'At Harrow, I won the General Knowledge prize. I must tell you that.' He took a sip of his Perrier. I took a sip of my wine. In the silence was a sense of sorrow.

One of the most popular rumours enjoyed by Kyle's enemies is that he was an *Encyclopaedia Britannica* salesman. You can see why this rumour appeals to those who dislike him: it suggests a lowly origin, but not so low as to make his flight from it glamorous; it has him as a salesman – and a door-to-door salesman at that; and it suggests the origins of a career based on the selling of that soft confection to the demi-intelligentsia.

Oddly enough, when I checked with Kyle, I found it to be correct. In fact, in many ways, it had not gone far enough. Art dealer Andrew Dickerson had told me with a laugh, 'Yes, I'm the man responsible for launching Francis Kyle into the world of art.' This is how the story went. On Good Friday 10 years ago, Dickerson opened his door to an *Encyclopaedia Britannica* salesman, having expressed an interest in purchasing a set. The salesman became very interested in some Peter Blake prints Dickerson had hanging on his wall, asked where he could get some, and, when Dickerson revealed that he was Blake's dealer, asked if he could borrow one or two on a sale or return basis. The salesman's name was, of course, Francis Kyle.

'You see,' says Dickerson, 'he had tremendous gall, even in those days.'

And then Dickerson asked me if I knew the story about Princess Margaret and Francis Kyle.

Would Kyle admit to all this? Our conversation about his career had seen him leave Oxford and enter publishing. He had reached Heinemann. What did he do there? 'I was involved with rights – paperback rights, book-club rights . . . I found it very constricting.' And how did he make the move into the world of art? 'I began borrowing a painting here and there, finding out who wanted what, selling one here and there, that sort of thing.' Not true, but certainly not false: like so much of what people tell each other every day.

While he told me of his time at the Thumb Gallery ('I talked to people, learnt from them, listened hard, listened to the critics . . .') and of the early days ('doing something entrepreneurial was definitely what I was moving towards in some small way . . .'), of his young ambitions ('I did think at that stage that total control was what I needed . . .') and of setting up on his own ('My local bank were very sympathetic. I had built up a very good working relationship with them . . .'), I began to wonder what I was doing listening ('So I thought, there's a certain kind of tradition that I like and a certain kind of tradition that I can judge and that's the tradition that I'm going to put across . . .') to this man I hardly knew ('It's difficult these days to imagine what cool there was, suspicion even, towards figurative-based work . . .') pattering on ('I have an extraordinary memory for people's faces . . .') and on ('Internationalism for me means a levelling out . . .') and on ('With the art of the past – and I love the art of the past – it's already there, you can't discover it . . .'). Who was he and what was he? A comical figure full of mackintoshes, decanted wine and gawkiness? Or a sad figure, fighting some solitary battle with his powerful father? Was he still the boy bullied, the boy who had got his own back by winning the General Knowledge prize? Or was he just another art dealer, pushy and sycophantic by turns, telling yet another person yet more drivel? Was he very interesting or very boring? My mind began to blur.

Perhaps gossip lives in London for the same reason that parables live in the New Testament: it makes things clear and simple, it allows people to believe that things happen in stories, with a beginning, a middle and an end, when we all really know that everything's far too confusing to make out even the blurred outline of a story. Have you heard the story of Francis Kyle and Princess Margaret?

Here it is then.

Princess Margaret had come to the gallery for one of the openings and Kyle had offered her a choice or red or white. 'Haven't you got a proper drink?' she had replied. A proper drink for Princess Margaret! Out Francis Kyle had bounded into the cold, finding all the off-licences in Mayfair closed, before returning, exhausted, with a half-bottle of whisky.

As Princess Margaret stories go, it's pretty fourth division, but it's a perfect Francis Kyle story, suggesting a comic beginning, a bit of stinginess, a level of desperation, a touching unworldliness, a desire to get things right, a panting, lonely struggle, and, in the end, some small triumph.

'Subtract 12 and Bob's Your Uncle'

British Rail Fayre (Table Talk 8)

Soup of the day, half a grapefruit, choice of fruit juice (orange or tomato). Starters used to be so simple, with no language worries and nothing fancy. Of course, even such a clear-cut choice of dishes soon presented its own problems: the grapefruit would be inexpertly cut, so that the unprepared diner employing just a little spoon would find himself in a life-and-death struggle with the thick string attaching the fruit to its outer peel. While this tournament between man and fruit was going on, another place-setting would see a diner engulfed in steam as he waited for his boiling-hot soup to cool down. Meanwhile, the person who had chosen the fruit juice would have finished his meagre glass in one furtive gulp, and would be busying himself with trying to look occupied.

Now that eating out in Britain has become so sophisticated, with kiwi fruit and mangetout wherever one turns, the dining car on British Rail has become the last refuge for those with a yearning for times past. The buffet car on the 125 Intercity trains is now chock-a-block with the tastes of today, including burgers in buns with those horrid green things lurking on them, chocolate chip cookies, and a range of expensive sandwiches 'designed' by Sir Clement Freud. Only in the dining car are things roughly as they once were.

Taking the London to Edinburgh service a week or two ago, I groaned when I heard the conductor begin to blather over the intercom. Nowadays, British Rail conductors all seem to take the Radio One disc-jockey Mr Dave Lee Travis as their role-model, speaking gibberish at every opportunity, replete with quips and cackles and bossy advice. On the other hand, it could well be that Mr Dave Lee Travis spends his weekdays moonlighting from Radio One on behalf of British Rail, who, recognising his talents for motor-mouthing banalities, have secured him a position as a professional irritant on board their main-line services. Either way, I suspected that I was in for a grim and crackly time.

But then, through the muffled caterwaulings, I heard the final call for all those wishing to partake of luncheon in the restaurant carriage. As I have never failed to enjoy a lunch on board a train, however tacky the food might have been, I rushed helter-skelter down the central aisles, pushing one and all out of my way, intent on grabbing a place.

My wife and I managed to capture the last two seats, and we found ourselves opposite a middle-aged husband and wife who had already been served their first course. 'What sort of soup is it?' the woman was saying to her husband. 'Not sure,' replied her husband, taking another sip. 'Tomato?' suggested the woman. 'Yes, mainly,' replied her husband.

I tend to find soup on a train almost as troublesome as soup on a pogo-stick, with great waves of the stuff sloshing all over me, so I decided against. My wife took the traditional second choice, and went for the half a grapefruit, which arrived with a thin slice of orange twisted daintily on top of it. Bamboozled to see anything more cosmopolitan than a Brussels sprout on British Rail, I leapt at the choice of mushrooms *á la Grecque*. It was a bit of a mess, cold and splodgy and uninviting, but it didn't really matter, such is the romantic joy that still attaches to being served food by waiters at a table covered with a white cloth while the world whizzes by.

Sitting opposite one another in a railway dining car is one the few public locations in British life in which etiquette permits, and even encourages, total strangers to strike up conversation. This can, of course, lead to tears, as a high proportion of bores travel in the dining cars of British Rail in the hope of trapping a stranger into listening to their eternal prognostications on the way of the world. I once found myself on the train to Bristol opposite a real corker of a bore. 'Does this train arrive at 15.17?' he asked. I told him that I wasn't too hot on the 24 hour clock, which was a relatively new concept at the time. For the next hour and a half, he proceeded to teach me all its various ramifications ('subtract 12 and Bob's your uncle'), ending with an examination session ('What's 23.11?' 'What's 12.01? Aha! Trick question! 12.01 *is* 12.01!!!') in which he managed to inveigle other passengers, including a group of Japanese students, into being his fellow-inquisitors. By the time the train was passing through Bath, people on all sides were shouting '17.23!' '19.47!' '21.09!' at me, like a scene from a particularly distressing Hitchcock movie.

Happily, the couple on our present train were far more presentable, keeping themselves to themselves until way into the pudding before politely engaging us in a conversation about the relative merits and disadvantages of First Class. They were under the impression that only First Class ticket-holders were allowed to eat in the restaurant car, and even though I told them authoritatively that this was not the case, they still seemed to think that we had somehow diddled British Rail. On a 125 train there seems to me no point whatsoever in travelling First. All you get for a vast amount more money is a paper doily behind your head and a complimentary copy of *Intercity* magazine.

Back to lunch. Our friendly Geordie waiter, who, incidentally, addressed my wife as 'Lady' and the woman opposite merely as 'Madam', lurched up bearing a silver plate upon which was a gluttonous portion of loin of lamb. There is a curious, perhaps partly sadistic, satisfaction in watching a waiter on a train trying to keep his balance while dishing out a meal. First, he spooned out the lamb, then the parsnips, then some pleasantly old-fashioned, over-cooked and flabby beans, and then a vast mountain of excellent, very greasy fried potatoes, with not a drop touching the tablecloth. A waitress appeared with haddock in sauce for my wife, with vegetables, vegetables and yet more vegetables.

The quality was a lot higher than expected: the lamb was chewy but very tasty, the fish solid and lively, with a sensible sauce. The wine list, which used to consist of red or white, now has some variety, with good red rioja and Californian chardonnay.

The highlight of the meal was a sweet of *tarte tatin*, which was almost supernaturally delicious. My wife went for a slice of Camembert, which was a disaster, so chalky that if there had been a blackboard on the train one would have been able to conduct a maths lesson in every carriage all the way to Edinburgh Waverley.

When they came to serve our coffee, our waiter and waitress had changed back into civvies, perhaps as a discreet way of telling us to get a move on. With the abandonment of uniform a slight surliness entered into the picture, with complaints that I had just used the toilet reserved for staff only.

It used to be the case that you could loiter in the dining car until way past lunch, but no more. We were shooed out with relative politeness. As we passed the buffet car, a bundle of Scottish drinkers were cracking open more cans of McEwan's Export and singing 'Bye-Bye Miss American Pie' over and over again, an ambitious choice for a communal sing-song, and quite an improvement on ''Ere We Go'. At this rate of progress, it'll only be another couple of years before they're going in for a selection of Gregorian plainchant, with Sir Clement Freud's poached salmon sandwiches served as a little something in the interval.

'Such A Shame'

The Queen Mother's Diary

My favourite chocolates are Orange Creme, Strawberry Creme, Nougat and – you must think me *awfully* wicked – a Brandy Truffle. In bed, I stick with Maltesers, in the bathroom it's always a Marathon bar, but never more than three. I find Sherbet Fountains go deliciously well with my 5.30 Whisky(s!) and Soda with *Neighbours*.

Have you watched *Neighbours*? You *must*, I've always had a special place in my heart for the poor people in the East End of London and that's where it's set. They all have the most delicious Cockney accents, reminding me of the time I visited the brave little East End during the war. It seems much sunnier now, I must say, so perhaps I will visit it again soon. They absolutely adore the Royal Family there, you know, bless them, because we lend colour to their lives.

What an awful brouhaha there has been in my *Daily Express* about the way an odd little man called Woodrow Wyatt has published snippets of conversation with me. Alas, I remember thinking he was rather small and rather fat, very, very pompous and – forgive me – a little nondescript. And he would *insist* upon puffing his cigar into my face as he held forth about this and that. If he is going to tell tales, then I'm afraid I've instructed my people to strike him off my list of possibles.

At the same dinner, I met another writer – A. N. Something-or-other, who seemed much more the ticket, certainly not the 'blabbing' sort, but discreet and respectful. I wonder if he'd care to write my biography?

I have always loved writers. And waiters. Writers and waiters, waiters and writers. Too adorable. Of the two, I think I prefer waiters, because at least they bring one things. We occasionally hire a waiter called Worsthorne who manages to write in his spare time and will *insist* on regaling us all with what he has written that week when he should be clearing away, the poor thing. Once, he even sat down to table with us!! Marvellous old character, though. I rather think he comes from the East End. It's full of them, you know. He may well be a 'Pearly King'. So exciting.

In my time, I've had the very great pleasure of entertaining some of the most superbly brilliant men and ladies this nation has ever produced. Sir Noel Coward, Sir Cecil Beaton, Sir Hardy Amies, the lot. I recall one dinner party with particular pleasure. Sir Roy Strong, the gifted painter, sat to my left, with Lord St John of Fawnsley, the impersonator, to my right. For some reason, artists have always been so very fond of me, and others present had been hand-picked from the cream of the arts, including Mr Eric Sykes, the comedian, my granddaughter, lovely Sarah York, who has written children's books, poor girl, and Sir Kingsley Amis, the actor. They simply couldn't stop singing my praises, perfectly sweet of them, and as Worsthorne brought around the Toffee Crisps and the top-ups I decided to award a dear little prize to whoever could praise me most beautifully in a maximum time of 60 seconds.

Oh, the fun we had! I kept time and scored whilst my dear guests "pitted their wits" against one another to come up with the most adorable compliments. The winner? Lord St John of Fawnsley, who called me many charming things, comparing me to a jewel, a flower, a perfectly formed young tennis champion, a rhododendron in full bloom, a mint edition *Almanac de Gotha* and a *crème caramel*, all in one breath. Bless him. Amis, poor little man, could think of nothing better than to say I wasn't half as bad as Major Ferguson. I'm awfully sorry, I don't think we'll be inviting him again, not if he doesn't know how to behave, such a shame.

Items in my handbag: tissues; chocolates (Rollos, Wrigley's Spearmint 'Gum'); one miniature Gordon's (for emergencies!); one spare string of pearls; one copy of the *Sporting Life*; a toothbrush; spare pair jeans for leisurewear; the day's 'horoscope' from *The Daily Express*; one tin, Heinz 'Alphabetti Spaghetti'; one 'good luck charm' (darling dolly of dear Mrs Simpson, plus the sweetest little pins!); yesterday's slips from my bookmaker; two packets chocolate eclairs; twelve thousand five hundred in cash (just in case).

I'm a great collector of words. It's one of my interests. One is so often so lucky to be in the company of very, very brainy people (Nicholas Soames, my grandson Edward, and many more) and they are teaching one new words all the time. 'Kew' for instance. Did you know that there are some parts of the world where if everyone wants something at the same time – a Bittermint, say – they have to 'form a Kew', which means standing in a line for a little while. Such fun. And 'Soupymarket', that's another, based on *the* most extraordinary idea. Obviously one knows about 'shops', where ordinary people – largely from our dear East End, I would imagine – offer coins in exchange for a Milky Bar – but a 'Soupymarket' is much, much bigger than a 'shop', with tins piled high, mainly of broth, hence the name. People – how I wish they wouldn't mutter about one so – sometimes criticise our wonderful Royal Family for living a 'sheltered life', but this is most unhelpful and quite untrue. I opened a 'Soupymarket' and walked around it six years ago, somewhere in the East End, I would imagine, my driver doesn't tell me these things! Their most charming aspect, I learnt from my experience, is that they let each individual 'shopper' walk along the aisles in the company of a manager with no one else allowed in until they have finished. *Such* a civilised idea.

One more very clever new word, if you'll forgive me, so kind. 'Dear Swosher'. I feel quite sure you haven't heard of that one! It seems that if the kind women who clean your dinner plates for you are on holiday or feeling a little poorly – you know what they are! – then it is possible to employ a 'Dear Swosher', which is sort of a mechanical appliance for cleaning dirty dinner plates. The modern world! Such fun, don't you think!

'The Sun Has Got His Hat On'

Don McCullin (Wallace Arnold 8)

As the marketing director of that fine and 'gritty'(!) paperback magazine *Granta*, I am delighted that the first book by our esteemed Editor, Mr Bill Buford, has drawn so many sterling reviews in all parts of our national press from some of his most loyal contributors.

It was nye on 12 years ago that I handpicked Bill for the post of Editor. For some time, I informed him, I had sensed an untapped market for a glossy paperback magazine which the general reader would feel happy to leave lying on his or her bookshelf.

The Contents page was, our market research told us, by far the most important, being the only page read by over 53% of purchasers. After thorough investigation, we discovered that our thoroughly 1980s target readership was after a fashionable young name in bold type beside a suitably stark, 'gritty'(!) title. To this end, I drafted a dummy Contents page for our first issue, 'Dirty Fingernails'. I have it with me now:

Martin Amis In the Launderette
Don McCullin Old Woman Eating Sand on Wolverhampton Beach
Raymond Carver Why the John Won't Flush
Richard Ford No Ketchup, No Relish Tray, No Burger, Nothing
Redmond O'Hanlon On Bruce Chatwin
Bruce Chatwin On James Fenton
James Fenton On Redmond O'Hanlon
David Hare Taking Brecht to Nicaragua
Hanif Kureishi Milton Keynes
Don McCullin Cross-Eyed Man With Empty Shopping Bag

Alas, Bill's first reaction was somewhat iffy. Was it not a little too . . . bleak? he asked.

'My dear boy,' I replied, taking a deep puff on my trusty pipe, 'The bleaker the better! Our marketing men assure me that the poor old bookbuyer is simply *crying out* for a spot of bleakness. First, he buys his black polo-neck from Next, then his matt black cafetière from Conran and then – Bob's your proverbial uncle – he nips out to buy his pile of *Grantas* for his matt black bookshelf. Hey presto: business booms!'

Within a few weeks, all the pieces had been commissioned and knocked off, and within a couple of months 'Issue 1: Dirty Fingernails' was on the bookstands, selling like hot-cakes. This was followed by 'Issue 2: More Dirty Fingernails', and then by 'Issue 3: More Dirty Fingernails Again'. We had, it was now safe to say, tapped a rich vein: the young Briton, having left his public school and university (or polytechnic!) was only too keen to be seen with an easy-to-handle glossy status-symbol, replete with vivid pen-portraits of nervous breakdowns in Notting Hill laundromats and elegant descriptions of working-class murders in out-of-the-way places.

At around this time, with sales blossoming, Bill began to get twitchy. Perhaps, he suggested, the readers were getting bored with the delightfully-named 'Dirty Realism'. Perhaps they would prefer all the same writers, but writing about something a little well . . . different?

Frankly, I slapped him down pretty sharpish: 'Such as what, may one ask?'

From out of his matt black briefcase, Bill brought forth a dummy contents page for 'Issue 4: Introducing Clean Realism'. I stared at his list in growing dismay:

Martin Amis The Magic of Julie Andrews
Don McCullin The Sun Has Got His Hat On
Raymond Carver It's a Funny Old World It Really Is
Richard Ford Welcome to the Fabulous World of Fondue

Frankly, I could read no further. Our customers, I retorted, would not tolerate such a revolution. They expected consistency from a market leader, and, in the case of *Granta*, this meant a rich diet of unfortunate occurrences in faraway countries written in straightforward prose. Bill ummed and erred for a time, but eventually he saw reason. 'Okay,' he sighed (he is – needless to say! – an American), 'I'll send Hanif to Guatemala again,' and with that he picked up the phone.

Ten years on, the 'Dirty Realism' format still thrives, and though I am, as you might imagine, more of an *Illustrated London News* man myself, the readers, some of them now grown-up and with children of their own, still can't get enough. Bill, too, has finally seen sense. He had wanted his first book to be called *Among the Toffs*, a witty guidebook to the English social season. I persuaded him to retitle it *Among the Thugs*, and I am delighted to say that his close circle of reviewers has made sure it is now available from all good second-hand book shops everywhere.

'Terrible Business, That'

The Koestlers and the Village Shop

The death of the great affects us all in different ways. The truth of this was brought home to me while I was reflecting on one of those lists of people who died during the past decade.

A few months before Arthur and Cynthia Koestler committed suicide in March 1983, I was pottering about in a small shop in a local Suffolk village. I have always felt slightly embarrassed about buying Kellogg's Variety Packs, thinking that onlookers might sneer at me for being unsophisticated for pre-ferring such childish cereals over the more grown-up cornflakes or the more earthy muesli.

With a Variety Pack in my hand, I slunk to the counter, half hoping that the other customer in the shop whose presence I had noted out of the corner of one eye would not start tittering, H. M. Bateman-style, at my purchase. Just as I had been given my change by the cheery shopkeeper and was about to hot-foot it out of the shop, the other customer came up and said, 'Hello Craig', his eyes all the time glancing down at my Variety Pack. Who should it be but Julian Barnes, arguably the most sophisticated novelist in the world, whom I had once known when we both worked along the same corridor. In front of the cheery shopkeeper, we chatted about what had brought us to the place. I lived nearby, I said, and had run out of breakfast cereal (how I wished at that moment that I had gone for the Alpen!).

Barnes said that he was staying nearby, writing a novel (the great *Flaubert's Parrot*, I now realise). He said he was staying with the Koestlers and asked me if I knew them. I knew of them, I replied, but I was not really on their level, at that time earning the bulk of my living by reviewing pop records for *Over 21* magazine. We agreed to meet for a drink the next day and left the shop to-gether, bidding the cheery shopkeeper goodbye.

It was quite some time later that I found myself in the same village shop. Once again, I was buying a Kellogg's Variety Pack (though they look big, even encyclopaedic, one pack lasts one person a maximum of only 10 days), and I was chatting animatedly with the cheery shopkeeper about the weather. I had all but forgotten about my previous meeting with Barnes. But suddenly the cheery shopkeeper said: 'Hey, weren't you friends with that bloke who was staying with the Koestlers?' I said that yes, I was, but I wasn't sure what to say next, for the Koestlers' joint suicide in Kensington a few weeks before had seemed particularly grim. 'Terrible business, that, ooh, terrible,' he said. I nodded my head in a mournful gesture. 'Terrible, terrible,' continued the cheery shopkeeper. 'You see, they always rang through from London with their order for the weekend, and I'd spent the whole afternoon packing up a big box of groceries for them. Then that night I heard the news on the television. Terrible business, terrible.

'The next morning I had to unpack the whole lot and put every single item one by one back on to the shelves.' The cheery shopkeeper shook his head in despair at the memory of it. 'Terrible business,' he added. I agreed with him, paid for my Variety Pack, wished him a cheery goodbye, and departed. As I said at the beginning, the deaths of the great affect us all in different ways.

'A Thingy Sort of Bloke'

An Old Codger Remembers (2): Kingsley Amis

One of Kingsley Amis' most commonly praised talents is to catch hold of words floating in the air in pubs and at parties and to hold them up to ridicule through constant repetition. No-one who read *Jake's Thing*, for instance, could ever again use the word 'Cheers' without first placing around it as many ironical quotation marks as he could muster.

Over the years, 'thing' itself has become an Amis word, along with 'sort of thing' and 'or something' and 'that kind of thing'. Having first been employed primarily in direct speech in his novels, largely by his confused male heroes, these shorthand symbols of robust good blokishness have gradually seeped into Amis' own voice. In his *Memoirs*, there is a thing on almost every page. In the very first paragraph of his preface, he writes that, 'Writing directly about my own (life) would anyway not appeal to me, even if I had a good memory for that kind of thing'. The fourth paragraph begins, 'The kind of thing I have written here . . . ' and a little later in the same paragraph we are told, 'I have invented dialogue, but nothing that is material or is not the sort of thing that would have been said at the relevant moment'. It comes as a pleasant surprise when the address and date at the end of this two-page preface is crisply given as 'Primrose Hill, May 1990', rather than 'Anyway, Primrose Hill sort of Hill thing, Mayish 19-bloody-90. Or something'.

The preface makes it clear that the book will not be a connected narrative, but a series of sketches, mostly about people 'I have known more or less well'. Amis will, he writes, be keeping himself 'away from centre stage'. The things and the more-or-lesses also make it clear that this stage-right narrator, this Amis bloke, will be rabbiting on in chummy anecdote, assuming the whiskery tones of a bluff and seemingly trusty retired major, of the type that so often crops up, somewhat sketchily drawn, in the works of Agatha Christie.

Amis' chosen tone, decked in the chumminess, tetchiness and naughtiness of the lounge-bar, appears relaxed and all-embracing, but is in fact extremely limiting. It is perfectly designed for prickly and very funny descriptions of self-aggrandising strangers. Among these strangers, each lampooned and dismissed in two or three pages, are Lord Snowdon, Arnold Wesker, Roald Dahl and Tom Driberg. Amis met them once or twice, found them abnormally irritating and/or absurd, and now wipes them out with blissfully nasty anecdotes, related with his singular skill for the mimicking of affectation. In these sketches, the author's irritation with his victims seems to raise his perception of conversational idiocies and physical peculiarities to almost astral heights, from where he looks down and cackles. Enoch Powell's eyes 'were gleaming, but not in the corners'. Roald Dahl, advising Amis to turn to children's books ('That's where the money is today, believe me') shakes his head and says, 'I hate to think of a chap of your distinction having to worry about money at your time of life'. Tom Driberg chases Martin Amis five times around a bed before clapping him on the shoulder, saying 'Fair enough, youngster' and departing. Lord David Cecil 'probably had a desk-compartment with a coded label meaning FORMS FOR FUCKING FOOLS WHO ARE FED UP WITH ME JUST POCKETING MY FEE AND WANT A SERIOUS SUPERVISOR'. Mark Thatcher is guilty of 'over-attentive conduct' with his cigarette lighter. These sketches of fleeting encounters with the famous are well-matched to the saloon-bar tones, for their mercilessness is not encumbered with friendship, and the targets fit well into the savagery of the anecdotal form. Any anthologist of twentieth-century gossip would find perfect examples of the genre in these sections of the *Memoirs*.

But when he ventures beyond the confines of gossip, Amis still remains lumbered with his blokish bad humour, his thingy sort of style. Occasionally, he hoists the white flag. Iris Murdoch has been, he says, 'a pal for decades' and there he stops. She is a woman, she is intelligent, and he likes her: these three qualifications mean, it would appear, that he is unable to find a way of including her. When he does write of old friends he admires – George Gale, Philip Larkin, Peter Quennell and one or two others – he either ruins it all by inserting a wantonly offensive piece of information into his appreciation, or else his prose puts on its Sunday Best, becomes stiff and formal, and cranks out the old hymns he elsewhere spends such care in lampooning. 'There is nothing to beat his welcoming smile and handshake' he writes of Quennell, 'his reliable cheerfulness undimmed by some nasty surgery a couple of years ago and its continuing effects'. This could be lifted from a speech by a rather distant personnel manager before awarding a watch to a cleaning-lady on the occasion of her imminent retirement. But at least here the personnel manager struggles through this appreciation without swerving into abuse.

In other appreciations, notably of Larkin, it is as if Amis is swimming slowly but surely under water, carefully slogging through the praise stroke by stroke, when all of a sudden he feels he can't go any further without rising to the surface and taking a quick slug of the air of misanthropy. Though he maintains that Larkin was his best friend and his favourite, or at least second favourite, poet, the only extracts he quotes from his verses are included to show that he wasn't quite all he cracked himself up to be. One extract is from a dirty verse, and is succeeded by the comment, 'That too I am fairly sure

Philip would not have wanted to see published in his lifetime, perhaps ever, but I think it comes in well here, before we get down to the serious stuff . . . ' Another is from *Aubade*, after which Amis scorns the extremity of Larkin's fear of death with this almost military wigging: '. . . depression among the middle-aged and elderly is common in the early morning and activity disperses it . . . so if you feel as bad as you say then fucking get up, or if it's too early or something then put the light on and read Dick Francis'. Having ticked off Larkin for meanness, and emotional parsimony, and fear of failure, Amis once again puts into print something that he knows his best friend would have hated, a silly story of drunken incontinence. 'He went on to extract from me some sort of promise not to go round repeating it, which I interpreted as a ban on any sort of publication,' explains Amis, 'But now I consider myself released from that undertaking . . . ' That 'some form of' in the phrase 'some sort of promise' is most telling: presumably it means that just so long as you throw a clubby sheet of pub lingo over any promise it is immediately transformed into 'some sort of promise' and can then be broken for a bit of a chuckle.

Amis' most venomous bitchiness is, however, reserved not for best friends, or family (though he describes his granny as 'a large dreadful hairy-faced creature') or even worst enemies, but for old friends who, for one reason or another, never achieved the success that once seemed their due. John Wain, John Braine, James Michie, Philip Toynbee and Bruce Montgomery are all kicked mercilessly, dead or alive, their main crime having been worldly failure. There are suggestions that the author even considers death itself as some sign of failure, for he takes a particularly repulsive pleasure in standing beside graves mouthing the language of mourning whilst all the time tapping a merry beat with his feet. 'Into limbo too went Philip, even before his death,' he writes of Philip Toynbee. Of Carson McCullers he simperingly declares, 'But one must not allow any sort of grin to enter here, in view of the sufferings and failures of Miss McCullers' short life; she died aged 50 in 1967, having evidently published only one book after the work I mention, which had come out when she was 34'. After a jaundiced appreciation of John Braine, in which he declares his embarrassment at having one of that author's 'unreadable' books dedicated to him, he recalls 'My last and saddest memory of John' which, inevitably, portrays him as a drunken bore at Bertorellis. Given the widespread view that Amis' first novel was also his best (even the most enthusiastic reviewers tend to gush with what must seem to the author depressing regularity 'His best since *Lucky Jim*') it seems that the special care he takes to beat up those contemporaries whose bright futures now lie behind them could be a means of bolstering up his own success, of rubbing that knighthood and those sales in their mouths, lest they question how far he, too, has progressed. Similarly, his extraordinary memory for times long past when A did not buy his round or he had to buy lunch for B eventually calls his own generosity into question. Which is the meaner, the man who forgets his wallet, or the man who 30 years later remembers the man who forgot his wallet?

Particularly when writing of his period as a don, Amis tries to have it both ways. It is hard to square the grouchy old philistine with the great educator for whom Cambridge supervisions 'offered the only context I have found in which serious, detailed and exhaustive discussion of literature is socially practicable', yet both rub shoulders in these pages. Almost every book mentioned is 'unreadable', or, as in the case of *Seven Pillars of Wisdom*, 'a piece of pretentious bullshit'. Donne is 'intolerably convoluted' and James' *The Aspern Papers* is 'the only work of his that I have ever read to its conclusion'. Yet Amis often boasts of his great interest in literature, 'a rarity then as now'.

One of the most bizarre side-effects of the formulation or simplification, of the Amis persona into a conduit for autobiography lies in his tailoring of the past so as to fit more comfortably his paunchy attitudes of the present. Respect, love, interest or understanding that he once held for others is now deemed never to have existed. Thus, in 1957, in an essay reprinted in *What Became of Jane Austen?* (1970) he was able to write this about his one meeting with Dylan Thomas, who, having grown too drunk, was cold-shouldered by Amis and his gang: 'I am ashamed now to think how openly we must have seemed to be dropping Thomas, how plain was our duty not to drop him at all. Our general disappointment goes to explain our behaviour, but does not excuse it . . . At the time I thought if he wanted to detach himself and talk to the students he would have found some means of doing so: I have since realised that he was far too good natured ever to contemplate giving anybody the cold shoulder . . . One of us, at any rate, should have found a way of assuring him that he was being regarded that evening, not with a coltish mixture of awe and suspicion, but sympathetically. Then, I think, we should have seen that his attitude was the product of nothing more self-aware or self-regarding than shyness'. Re-writing this same account 30 years on, Amis excises this passage, substituting, 'I will cut the account short at that point. There was a return to the pub but still no pub performances. Perhaps he thought we were not worth it. . . . Thomas was an outstandingly unpleasant man, one who cheated and stole from his friends and peed on their carpets'.

The style has slackened, the sympathy and the regret have been expunged, Thomas is written off, truth has gone tabloid, and all for the sake of a fancy dress posture. It is often said of actors that offstage they turn into their rôles, and of dog-owners that they grow like their dogs. Likewise, Amis has created his autobiographical persona along the lines of one of his most comically pitiless characters. I rather think it might be the elderly gent in *Ending Up* who pours urine over his old friend as he sleeps so as to foster the suggestion of incontinence, hoping that by so doing he will soon have the house to himself.

'Totally Out Of Date'

John Major and The Little Chef (Table Talk 9)

Just a few weeks ago, in the deep midwinter, Mr John Major made the headlines by stopping off to eat sausage, egg, bacon, toast and coffee at a Happy Eater near Doncaster. Mrs Thatcher once visited Harry Ramsden's fish-and-chip shop in Yorkshire, but as far as I can remember it was during the last election campaign, and her every cautious bite of chip was monitored by television cameras. Mr Major seemed to stop at his Happy Eater out of personal choice rather than political expediency, and this was what made the world gasp.

My own gasps were a little lack-lustre, I must admit. One of the few things that anyone knows about Mr Major is his penchant for junk food, and it would have been far more surprising – indeed, it might have led to his downfall – if he had been caught secretly scoffing pâté de fois gras with a glass of Muscat de Beaumes-de-Venise at the Hotel Posh. The Wall's sausage is to John Major what the pipe used to be to Harold Wilson; if he now abandons it for something more elitist, he will not be lightly forgiven.

This week I have followed the prime ministerial trail by stopping off at my local chain roadside café, the Little Chef on the A604, a few miles out of Haverhill in Suffolk. It would be silly to pretend that Little Chefs and Happy Eaters have no point to them. They are cheap, they are largely efficient, they welcome children and they are unsnobbish. How many of our more illustrious restaurants can lay claim to more than one of these qualities? They also exude a strange sense of security, perhaps because they all look the same and they all serve exactly the same food. I think that if ever I was put in charge of a country in the midst of a war and a recession, I too might find myself reaching out for one, just as a child reaches for a blanket. The tastes, too, aren't dissimilar.

The décor in the Little Chef is spartan, with stabs at cheeriness. The chairs and tables are stapled to the floor, perhaps to prevent any large-scale rioting. Three Chinesey flower paintings are pinned half-heartedly to the brick walls, and here and there some plastic greenery blossoms in the neon light. The carpet is inlaid with hundreds of Little Chefs running hither and thither. There is another Little Chef underneath a sign on a door saying TOILETS: NAPPY CHANGING FACILITIES. This Little Chef appears to be running off with a baby, and may well feature on a future *That's Life* special investigation.

There are plenty of comforting little extras, such as high chairs, the day's newspapers and fully illustrated menus. Our fellow customers, too, seemed rather more spick-and-span than one would find in the average London restaurant: with shirts, ties, jackets, conventional hairstyles and sensible shoes, many of them looked as if they could have stepped from a *Film on Four*, set in an English seaside town in the late 1950s.

The food is, I suppose, best described as disgusting, but then too few food critics realise that there are times when disgusting food is just what one craves. Most of the dishes have been captured in full colour by a Little Photographer, and when they arrive they look and taste precisely the same as their photos, neat and vivid to look at, rather like glossy cardboard to eat.

The starters come from a number of countries, some of them still undiscovered. We ordered a salmon terrine, a Mexican dipper, a mushroom dipper and a prawn cocktail. Five minutes later, the Little Chef sent a message that salmon terrine and Mexican dipper were off, presumably because Little Fisherman and Little Mexican were caught in the snowdrifts, so we doubled up on the other two dishes. The mushroom dipper ('crispy coated whole mushrooms served with a tasty dill dip') wasn't too bad for just £1.95, though as our companion said, 'This could be a mushroom, but on the other hand it could equally well be an eyeball.'

I had been looking forward to my main course, the chef's grill (beefburger, bacon, sausages, egg, tomato, chips), but in all the major departments it was pretty grim. The burger was horrid, thin and bitty like a Pekingese's tongue, the sausages tasteless and cased in plastic. Of the other two dishes, the gammon and pineapple was judged quite a success, though it tasted peculiarly of beef, and the scampi platter scored five out of 10, with complaints that the scampi were too glutinous. 'Nothing here could possibly fall off your fork,' commented my wife.

Puddings proved the high spot – presumably they are one area of a meal where you *expect* to feel sick. Outright winner was the jubilee pancake (red cherries and ice cream filling), with the 'mapleen' syrup pancake not far behind. These puddings were all around £1.30, the price of a glass of water in smarter places. Another interesting difference between the Little Chef and its big city cousins – for instance Chez Nico (Large Chef) and Harveys (Loopy Chef) – is that at 1.55 p.m. the Little Chef, full half-an-hour before, had virtually emptied, whereas in the others the lunch hour is often really a lunch three-and-a-half hours.

One of the reasons that people are so quickly in and out of Little Chefs must be the absence of alcohol. I ordered the only alcoholic thing on the menu, which was a low alcohol lager called Germania. This was 0.5% alcohol, which meant that I would have had to drink roughly 10 pints to loosen up, and another 64 pints if I wanted to become involved in a fist fight with a fishfinger. My wife later said that it was the first meal she had ever eaten with me where I didn't grow happier as it went on, and this may have had something to do with it.

As I was paying the bill at the till, I browsed through a book of customer's comments. These seemed divided half and half between complaints and praise. 'Music totally out of date', remarked one irate diner. It was only then that I realised that there was music at all. Quietly, very quietly, a discreet Neil Sedaka selection was being played by a combo which may well have been Sounds Orchestral. Very John Major, very Little Chef.

'Uncle Mac'

Ian Paisley and Peter Robinson

One of the many oddities about Mr Paisley is the amount of smiling he gets up to. He smiles so much, and so energetically, that in a better world he might have been usefully employed in advertisements for leading brands of toothpaste, or perhaps as a Northern Irish Bisto Kid. Another oddity concerns the speed with which his smile can turn into a scowl, and then back to a smile once more, without any of the conventional facial contortions or hesitations in-between.

His visits to the Chamber of the House of Commons are rare, but he puts them to good use. He sits on the Tory benches beside the eerie figure of Mr Peter Robinson. While Mr Robinson sits upright, thin and expressionless, Mr Paisley spends much of his time lolloping on his corner seat, his legs outstretched, a chuckle playing on his lips, perusing his order paper. Sometimes he looks for all the world like Uncle Mac rejoicing in fond memories of the last Teddy Bears' Picnic. But kiddies on all sides of the House would be well advised not to offer this particular Uncle Mac a cookie. His large and sudden bites can often incorporate a hand or two. Then, munching on the hand, he will issue one of his red-faced and scornful chuckles, and the whole House will shudder to its very bones.

Questions to the Secretary of State for Northern Ireland are a particular favourite of Mr Paisley. Over the years, he has shown a lively personal interest in the affairs of Northern Ireland, and he likes to seek a cheery word of advice from that nice Mr King whenever he can. Before he asks a question, he wipes the chuckle off his face, swallows any hands he might be chewing, leans forward in his seat and does his best to look fearsome. His best happens to be very good indeed. He then looms to his feet, his vast bulk casting a shadow over the Chamber, and that nice Mr King begins to look a little worried.

Yesterday Mr Paisley wished to know whether Mr King agreed with the Prime Minister, who believed Mr Haughey had been out of order in his recent speech, or the Foreign Secretary, who believed he had spoken as a patriot. Mr Paisley's questions are notable, among other things, for their volume. They are delivered at a pitch more normally reserved for the issuing of warnings at sea, or the take-off of a lunar rocket.

That nice Mr King replied that he agreed with them both, and that he saw no contradiction between the two points of view.

'Of course you wouldn't!' boomed Mr Paisley from his corner, his face reddening, his scowl growing ever more carnivorous. But within a few seconds he was back to his old smiling self, exchanging giggles with Mr Robinson – a process similar, one might have thought, to exchanging giggles with one of the less outgoing inhabitants of the Chamber of Horrors.

When Mr Kevin McNamara, Shadow Minister for Northern Ireland, bumbled to his feet, Mr Paisley looked as cheery as if Mr Pastry had appeared, which, in a way, he had. Mr McNamara is a white-haired figure of increasing comic potential, always opening barn doors so that horses may bolt, forever cooking up objections way after each issue has passed. Having failed to bat an eyelid at the original announcement of the Gibraltar killings, he has recently taken to batting both eyelids with such vehemence that many wish to call for a doctor. Make way! Make way! A doctor is at hand! Alas, it is only Doctor Paisley, laughing his guts out at Mr McNamara's every protestation.

A minute or two later, the Doubled-Up Doctor chose to megaphone his way through the ins and outs of a recent murder, 'a well organised inside job'. Again, the red-faced scowl, and again, seconds later, the vulpine cackling. Beside him, Mr Robinson took to his feet. During Northern Ireland Questions, there always seems to be one of them up and one down. The two of them resemble nothing so much as a grotesque Swiss weather predictor, forever presaging gloom ahead.

29 April 1988

'Very Dear Friends'

Jennifer's Retirement Diary

After a night in bed, I entered the kitchen of the flat to pour myself some quite excellent All Bran from one of Mr Kellogg's very sensible packets, beautifully designed, and then poured Mr Unigate's delicious milk on top of it, making a thoroughly pleasant breakfast, perhaps one of the most enjoyable I have ever attended.

I then began to plot my day. Looking up at my mantelpiece, I noticed that my invitations to parties thrown by my delightful and excellently-bred friends all stopped by coincidence on the very day of my retirement from the splendid *Harpers and Queen* magazine. Nevertheless, I knew that my presence would be required at five or six major society events, so, after a delicious cup of coffee courtesy of Mr G. Blend, I ventured on to the streets of our very own dear city of London.

My first call of the day was on a beautifully organised and most impressive Employment Exchange where glorious postcards let one know exactly the employment that is on offer in the Mayfair locality. Joining an impressive queue, I discovered that there were one or two fellow guests I failed to recognise, so I got out my notebook and inquired as to their names. These most helpful people included Quit Shuvvin and his son Piss Awf, Ooyoo Starin-Att, looking resplendent in a brown and dark brown 'boiler suit' with exotic phlegm inlay, Upyors Mite accompanied by his attractive wife Gorblimey Mite, the Fuck-this-Foralark family, looking better than ever, and the Hon. and Mrs Buggerov, who graciously offered me an antique "coca-cola" can to nibble while we waited. I was also delighted to make the acquaintance of O. God Almighty, sporting an attractive string vest and a pair of casual trousers just beneath the buttocks.

I then set off to a luncheon party thrown by some very dear friends at the Connaught Hotel. Oddly enough, Her Majesty's Postal Service had failed to deliver my invitation but I knew that if I put my head around the door I would be welcomed with open arms as I have been these past forty years. I was greeted, as always, by the head doorman, Charles, who most considerately placed himself in front of me and asked if he could possibly help. I informed him that I was expected at a party thrown by some very dear friends, and he checked a list he held on a most useful clipboard. He then called a larger doorman and most kindly asked him to escort me out of the door. Within a matter of seconds, I had been whisked off with utmost efficiency back out through the revolving doors, accompanied by charming wishes for my good riddance. I remained on the street outside the hotel – a most original idea for a party location, I must say, and very greatly appreciated – for the duration of the party, which, it emerged, was in Fancy Dress, such an amusing idea, with many people coming as road-sweepers, dustbin-men and the like. From my grandstand position just near the gutter, I spotted The Duke and Duchess of Abercrombie, The Hon. Miss Lucinda Northampton, Lord and Lady Theydon Bois and The Countess Ruislip, resplendent in a very pretty dress of azalea silk georgette, but they seemed to be going into another party indoors, so they obviously failed to notice me waving and shouting 'coo-eee'. All in all a delightful evening, and so clever to 'do away with' drinks and cocktail-eats, which so often lead to unnecessary expense for the host and hostess.

I then went to see my old friends the Sainsburys, picking up a most attractive metal 'basket' as I entered. I saw a lot of very old and dear friends in this charming building – so cleverly designed! – among them The Prince and Princess of Wales, Miss Annouska Hempel, The Count and Countess Spencer, Lady Tryon looking radiant in pink, Mr and Mrs Rolf Harris, Sir Hugh Casson, Lord Hailsham, Lady Olga Maitland, Lord and Lady Whitelaw, Mr Roger Moore, Lord and Lady Bollard and The Duke and Duchess of Westminster, looking younger than ever. A kindly assistant then asked whether I was planning to buy the copy of *Hello* magazine I had been observing all my very old dear friends in, but I decided against, and, with her encouragement, moved on towards the delightful 'Household Products' counter, with its excellent range of quality goods all most kindly packed in a tin wrapping: such a clever idea of the delightful Sainsburys and so handy for all their many devoted friends.

Returning to change at my flat, I found that my old friends the Bailiffs, Ron, Don, Len and also Ben had called in my absence, such a shame, but they had kindly left a small memento of their visit on the outer door, a padlock crafted in silver metal, with an enchanting chain. I then walked to the arches at Charing Cross, where I had watched our own dear Prince and Princess of Wales parade to St Paul's for their triumphant marriage in 1981 on the most memorable day in our nation's history. At seven o'clock promptly, the caterers generously served piping hot soup and a bread roll to all guests, who then returned to the relaxing and historic surrounds of the arches, where they each found a most welcoming cardboard box to keep out the slight chill of the evening. On the side of my own most effective box was printed 'HEINZ', a memory of very dear friends of that name who have entertained me so lavishly in Washington on each of my visits there.

The next morning, I was offered a delicious breakfast of Cider and Methylated Spirits mixed with one of Mr Carlsberg's most invigorating Special Brews by an old and very rank friend, but I regretfully declined. I went behind my cardboard box to change, and from there walked to Clarence House, London home of my very dear old friend, the tremendously youthful and much-loved by all the nations of the world possibly the most gracious woman who has ever lived the ever-radiant Queen Elizabeth the Queen Mother, and rang the front doorbell of this most delightful mansion. As a most original welcoming treat, I was then surrounded by four policemen in very smart uniforms, all pointing highly beautifully polished pistols in my direction. When I pointed out that Queen Elizabeth the Queen Mother was one of my very oldest and dearest friends, they told me that I was quite right ('A right one here') and they then summoned a motorcar to take me on a most comfortable and smooth drive to a large building. I appear in front of my very old and dear friend Lord Justice Shoveha'penny whose attractive wife Diana is so good with flowers, tomorrow afternoon, and from there to the Scrubs at Wormwood for an indefinite period. Bliss!

'Wakey! Wakey!'

Christmas Telly

Not long ago, television was regarded as the medium of the eternal present, a mad dog without memory barking away in the corner, always reacting to events as they happened, yet unable to recall them when they had passed.

But over the past few years, television has been developing something akin to a memory. Inspired, no doubt, by parsimony, it is raiding its own archives. There are now reruns galore of shows that are 10, 20, even 30 years old. There are even quizzes based on television nostalgia, such as *Telly Addicts* and *A Question of Sport*. And the most hip-hop supa-modern Street-Porter-style programmes are formed around repeats of *The Man From U.N.C.L.E.*

One of the strangest things about television looking back on itself is its ability to invest everything with a warm, cosy glow. The phenomenon first came to my notice when the BBC showed, reshowed, and then re-reshowed its spellbinding series *The Rock and Roll Years*.

Television news footage of the strikes, wars, riots, natural disasters and so on from a given year was accompanied by contemporary pop music. It was the news as rock video, and even the dingiest sight – great piles of rat-infested rubbish in Leicester Square during the Winter of Discontent, perhaps to a tune by 10CC – was afforded an air of nostalgia, even gaiety. The rubbish in Leicester Square has since become a much-loved part of the repertoire of most documentary makers, as it can be used to illustrate so many things – the unions, the Labour party, the rise of Margaret Thatcher, the end of the 1980s or what-you-will.

It has now become so popular that perhaps one day they will award it a show of its own. Just last week, the final episode of Michael Cockerell's four-part documentary series *Class Rule* featured another guest appearance by the rubbish, this time as an illustration, I think, of how Mrs Thatcher managed to win the working-class vote.

The thrust of Cockerell's message – that Britain has been and remains beset by class – was hampered throughout by the oleaginous charm of all the old television footage. Whether it was Hartley Shawcross explaining that he might be a swell sort of toff but he still voted Labour, or Macmillan on the grouse moors (another television favourite), or Wilson with his pipe and shorts in the Scilly Isles, the little screen made it all seem too cute for words. Only when back in the present, with Tebbit, Heath and Barbara Castle all barking to camera, did the issue seem at all raw.

My only other objection to this enjoyable Rock and Roll Class Years compendium was that it failed to acknowledge the complexity of class in Britain, never questioning the trite stratification into upper, middle and working class, perhaps being under the misapprehension that to do so would undermine its potency.

Thus Cockerell brushed over the lowly origins of Edward Heath so as to make Mrs Thatcher seem more timely. He also allowed Sir Peregrine Worsthorne to describe himself as 'upper class'. Anyone who feels he must go on television to describe himself as upper class is quite obviously nothing of the sort. In fact, Sir Peregrine is a stalwart member of the media class, like Ian Carmichael, Penelope Keith or Ray Allan's Lord Charles.

In *Behind the Headlines* a sparky review of the year showed footage of Saddam Hussein accompanied by a soundtrack of Gloria Gaynor singing 'I Will Survive'. How long ago the Gulf war seemed, and once again through the retrospective eyes of television, how quaint! As proof of television's power to mollify, it wouldn't surprise me if, in a year or two, I was to turn on *Pebble Mill at One* to find Saddam Hussein entering to a round of applause to plug his latest book, *Toujours Baghdad* ('Now, Saddam, you've been through a tough time, but I guess there must have been some pretty amusing incidents along the way'), before handing out some gardening tips.

Yesterday evening, BBC2 was entirely given over to television memories. My own favourite was the 1973 Christmas *Top of the Pops* which I had been prevented from seeing in its entirety on its original showing.

I was 16 at the time, and my family's 1973 Christmas lunch, like so many across the nation, was stricken by the knowledge that Christmas *Top of the Pops* was available in the next-door room. Should one wolf lunch down in an attempt to catch the last 10 minutes, or should one stage a scene and refuse to eat until it was over? I imagine that in 1973 I attempted my usual untidy compromise, darting out between bites to catch a snatch of Sweet singing 'Blockbuster', before being bawled back in again.

Last night, for the first time in 18 years, I was able to see what I had missed. 'The Sweet have had a fan-tastic year,' said Tony Blackburn. The Sweet then performed 'Blockbuster' wearing a selection of gold jumpsuits, sparkle, red satin loon pants, and foot-high platform heels. 'Fan-tastic,' said Tony.

Dawn then sang 'Tie a Yellow Ribbon'. Tony said: 'Gilbert O'Sullivan's had a fan-tastic year.' Pan's People danced to 'Get Down', dressed in platform heels and what looked like maternity smocks, with much animated arm circling and facial expression on the phrase 'Happy as can be!' Next, Gary Glitter sang 'Leader of The Gang', looking rather like an oven-ready

Terry Scott in aluminium foil.

While Tony was saying, 'What a fan-tastic year it's been for Peters and Lee,' I began to realise that despite it all I was enjoying every second, and I thanked God that my youth hadn't coincided with a period of good taste.

As Wizzard sang 'I Wish It Could Be Christmas Everyday', my wife came in and said, 'Does it have to be this loud?' the very same question my father used to ask all those years ago. My happiness was complete. 'That was Wizzard,' said Tony, 'Weren't they fan-tastic?'

A couple of hours later, *Christmas Night with the Stars* from 1964 seemed impossibly ancient. There were times when I expected it to be followed by a Christmas Message from King Alfred the Great. Billy Cotton kicked it all off with a shout of 'Wakey! Wakey!' and a rendition of 'Food, Glorious Food', waddling around with a carving knife and fork while girls in shortie gingham aprons danced around a kitchen table. 'Well, no need to tell you that that was Billy Cotton,' said Jack Warner, compèring. 'Billy's one of our oldest friends – no offence, Bill!'

Kathy Kirby sang 'Silent Night', the Black and White Minstrels a high-spirited medley including 'South of the Border', and Ralph Reader's Boy Scout Gangshow a song in praise of walking, which went: 'A motor car is phony/I'd rather have shanks's pony'. Ah, such innocence, such naivety, such utter ghastliness! And why did so many Boy Scouts in those days look like the Kray brothers?

The comedy on the show proved far more durable. Among the situation comedies, Hugh and I and The Likely Lads were still funny – much funnier and closer to life than their equivalents today. Marriage Lines and Meet the Wife, while not particularly rib-tickling, had a certain sweetness. Benny Hill's parody of a concerned documentary on disaffected youth ('We couldn't go and live with her parents because like, they're living with theirs') hit home again and again.

In the never-ending festival of telly memories, Benny Hill was also the subject of celebration in this week's *Omnibus*. He was, they said, the first comedian to be made by television. Made, and then dismayed: a few years ago. Thames stopped making his shows on the ground that they were considered sexist. I was never a great fan, but many of the gags they reshowed on *Omnibus* were hilarious, and one of them – a macabre striptease by a clown, going down to the skeleton, ending only with a dancing hand – seemed touched by genius.

Of all the things to worry about in the world, the sexism or otherwise of Benny Hill should rate pretty low. Perhaps Carlton TV, the inheritors of Thames' franchise, might invite him back. Personally, I am thinking of starting a far more urgent campaign, calling for a ban of all repeats of Billy Cotton shouting 'Wakey! Wakey!', on the grounds of rampant sleepism.

'Walking the Dog'

An Old Codger Remembers (3): John Junor

These may well be the last of the school of Fleet street memoirs that are loomed over by the all-powerful figure of Lord Beaverbrook. After a childhood in working-class Glasgow, three years at Glasgow University, a good war and a stint as Editor of the Fleet Air Arm magazine *Flight Deck*, John Junor was welcomed to the court of Beaverbrook, whom he remembers, as so many have done before him, with the fearful adoration of the acolyte.

'I will put on your head a golden crown.' Beaverbrook reportedly said to Junor. That this golden crown turned out to be the editorship of *The Sunday Express* might seem to some yet more evidence of Beaverbrook's grim humour, but not to Junor, who wore his crown proudly for no less than 32 years.

Like so many crowned by Beaverbrook, Junor grew to ape not only his master's voice but also many of his little ways. His 'JJ' column in *The Sunday Express* – now in the *Mail on Sunday* – is as blunt as a truncheon and as full of prefabricated indignation as Beaverbrook could possibly have dreamed. Its sentences are as short as nails, its words largely monosyllabic, and it can be relied upon to quake and to quack with all the wrath of a toytown God. It has been said of Junor as an editor that he would chastise his reporters for wearing beards (sinister) or drinking rosé (effeminate); in Fleet Street, where those who were not hacks were necessarily legends, such trumpeted foibles soon enabled Junor to join the massed ranks of the latter.

Those who surrender their prose and their attitudes to the demands of popular journalism are doomed to find that, when the wind changes, they are stuck with them for life. Despite its whimsical title, *Listening for a Midnight Tram* is constrained by an unrelenting journalistic snappiness. The short, sharp stabs of paragraphs that might keep the Sunday newspaper reader awake for a thousand-odd words grow exhausting and absurd when transferred to a book. It seems, also, that Junor can keep his mind on the same subject for only a handful of sentences. His childhood and adolescence are completed by page seven, he is the Editor of *Flight Deck* by page 17, and from there on the book is one anecdote after another, generally concerning the tittle-tattle that has emerged between mouthfuls from those men of destiny he has managed to wheedle to his lunch table. There is virtually nothing about

Junor's private life, though we are told, in one curious aside, that Lady Junor 'has never been interested in money. Unhappily, and it is all my fault, for some years she has not been much interested in me either.'

Junor's bullish lack of introspection allows his underlying egotism to prance about without restraint. Like many journalists, he lacks any ability to observe others, perhaps because he is too busy gauging the impression he is making on them. A particularly comical example of this occurs when, as the guest of Lord Beaverbrook, he sits next to the Duchess of Windsor at dinner: 'I found her absolutely fascinating and enchanting. She made a man feel as if he, at that moment, were the only man in her life. She allowed me to do the talking, even prompted me to, and she seemed fascinated by whatever I had to say.'

The Duchess of Windsor's fascination with Junor is all he remembers about her. Of Beaverbrook himself, he remembers rather more, though there is a disparity between Junor's commentary, which treats him as divine, and his anecdotes, which make him seem rather closer to Dr Fischer of Geneva. This disparity has an icy comedy of its very own, a comedy all the richer for passing unnoticed by the author. In 1954, Junor was suffering the first pains of a duodenal ulcer, an agony exacerbated by drinking champagne. 'Although he himself drank only whisky,' writes Junor, 'Beaverbrook insisted that his dinner guests drank champagne. I have never much cared for champagne. In 1954 it was torture for me even to touch it. But I dared not tell Beaverbrook.' Later, listening to Beaverbrook's last speech – 'The man who is not true to himself is not a journalist. He must show courage, independence and initiative' – Junor in all innocence records that "tears of pride came to my eyes". This, from the man whose courage, independence and initiative did not stretch to refusing a glass of Beaverbrook's champagne.

Dr Fischer emerges even more strongly in the description of Beaverbrook's 1954 birthday celebrations, at which each guest had an envelope containing £100 placed at his dinner setting. What was the secret price paid for such a gift by each of the merrymakers? 'If you walk over a man once you can walk over him any time you want to,' Beaverbrook once told Junor, appropriately enough while taking him for a walk.

After Beaverbrook's demise, the book loses all shape, turning into a gossipy record of the author's various luncheon companions, coupled with magisterial and often batty character assessments. Macmillan is 'as phoney as a two-dollar bill', Nigel Lawson is 'more like a little boy lost than an intellectual snob', and Somerset Maugham is ' the best writer of this century'. Some of the gossip is first-rate, the rest quite extraordinarily dull; it is odd that, after such a long time wearing the golden crown, the author cannot tell the difference. Thus, half a page is devoted to the revelation that the forgotten figure of Lord Matthews used to buy his shirts from Marks and Spencer; on the other hand, it is as well to know that Enoch Powell sang the Te Deum in full during his morning bath after Heath's routing in the February 1974 election, that Tom Driberg had an affair with Johnny Ray, and that F. E. Smith successfully sought Beaverbrook's help when caught by the police with a prostitute in Battersea Park. I have never seen the full extent of Harold Wilson's loss of memory catalogued in print before (nor the triumphant mirth it seems to have inspired in Edward Heath), and Rab Butler's claim to Junor that while the government didn't mind Prince Philip seeing State Papers, the Queen wished otherwise, is an almost perfect piece of gossip, mixing royalty, conspiracy, politics, marriage, and the suggestion of treachery.

Why were quite so many Cabinet Ministers prepared to have quite so many lunches with an editor of a dull and declining newspaper who wrote a column of such barking ferocity? These memoirs do at least demonstrate how those in power crave the attention of journalists, and the complementary relish with which journalists like to hobnob with the powerful. The clammy intimacy of the two professions is caught in a remark Harold Wilson made to Junor in 1969: 'The other week I read a story (in *The Sunday Express*) that I was going to sack all junior ministers over 52. Wondered where it came from, and then suddenly remembered I'd leaked it myself.'

'Wallace in the Sky with Diamonds'

The Garrick Trip (Wallace Arnold 9)

I note a sinking feeling in the old tum that it is 50 years to the day since a bespectacled boffin clad in white overalls invented 'LSD', as it has come to be known. Might I make a confession? Back in the Sixties, whilst still a young man making my way in literary London, I found myself partaking in this least reliable of substances.

For hour upon hour, sprawled upon a leather armchair, not knowing whether I was coming or going, I witnessed the strange, unearthly apparitions of thespians, politicians and authors barking at me from every corner of the room, some on the floor, some on the ceiling, but all talking in high-pitched screeches of their successes and achievements, their weird, strangely distorted faces framed by psychedelic ties bursting with every hue under the sun. Nothing new there, of course, for this was The Garrick Club on a regular Thursday evening. But what, I found myself wondering, would the same thing look like under the influence of drugs?

Something within me yearned at that moment to escape from the narrow confines of The Garrick Club into another world, a world beyond anecdote and opinion. My old friend and dousing partner Aldy Huxley claimed to have discovered – and I quoth – 'eternity in a flower, infinity in four chair legs and the Absolute in the folds of a pair of flannel trousers'. I found myself longing to share his vision, for up until then the only thing I had ever managed to discover in the folds of a pair of flannel trousers was a piece of half-sucked Barley Sugar, discarded in error.

I then remembered that, during a pre-prandial stroll, I had been approached by a hairy creature – male or female, I know not! – who had urged me to 'tune in, turn on and drop out' before handing me a most mysterious dot. Might this be my route to Huxley's Absolute? Against my better judgement, I decided to swallow it, right there in The Garrick Club.

Here is a small selection of the notes I scribbled haphazardly over the next five and a half hours:

6.15p.m.: I – Wallace Arnold! – feel myself transported into a realm beyond my wildest imaginings! I look at my trusty pipe and it has turned into two trusty pipes, both puffing most smoothly! I think I have discovered the Absolute!

7.25p.m.: I – Wellbred Armhole! – find myself floating, floating, floating! I have now landed in the vegetable selection on the central table of The Garrick Dining Room! To my surprise, my body has transformed itself into a Brussels Sprout! . . . Oh, no! I have just been speared with a fork by my old friend and quaffing partner Kingsley Amis, who is in the midst of a pricelessly waspish anecdote about a very dear old friend! . . . Agh! He is swallowing me! . . . Oh no! I find myself sitting in his stomach, unable to hear the punchline of his waspish anecdote! This must be what they mean by a 'Bad Trip' . . .

9.30p.m.: Who am I? Wishful Ankle, Intergalactic Chameleon! I look down at my feet, but they are no longer my feet, they are stretchy pieces of elastic, and my hands – my hands! – they are thin and silky and all pink with mint stripes! I realise I have become a Garrick Club bow-tie, stretched around the next of my old quaffing partner Robin Day! And he always claimed that he wore REAL bow-ties, not ready-mades! THE HORROR! While regaling the assembled company with an anecdote about his legendary encounter with Ted Short, Robin has let a spot of gravy dribble down his neck on to me! I am STAINED! STAINED! STAINED!

10.55p.m.: At last, I am 'coming down'. I struggle to adjust myself to the normal world. Thank goodness no-one suspects I have been 'high'. I am now behaving quite normally. The Duke of Edinburgh – estimable fellow – enters the room and looks around. I want to reassure him that all is well with his favourite broadcaster so I approach him, man to man. 'My name,' I say, 'My name is Waxy Angel. I am a beautiful orange tulip, sent from Heaven to make you happy. Smell me!' The Duke turns around on his heels and leaves the room without a word. I feel sure he didn't suspect a thing . . .

Dread words, indeed. Never again, never again. From now on, I stick to the port, the brandy and the large gins. At least you know where you are with them, or my name's not, or my name's not MEMO TO SELF: INSERT NAME IN MORNING.

'We Want Jelly'

Nancy Lam's Enak Enak (Table Talk 10)

My cousin Caroline – no mean foodie, being the guiding hand behind the famous Porkinson's Sausages – told me, long ago, that I might well enjoy a marvellous little place in Battersea called Nancy Lam's Enak Enak. Alas, I instinctively shy away from marvellous little places in Battersea, and somehow the title 'Nancy Lam's Enak Enak' made me shy away still more. When my cousin Caroline added that Nancy Lam was a terrific character, I thought to myself that I would make every effort to give it a miss.

Time passes, and, many months later, I found myself trying to think of somewhere to eat in Battersea. Looking down a list of restaurants, I saw 'Nancy Lam's Enak Enak', and I remembered that old cousinly recommendation. Very well, I thought: Enak Enak it is and off we set.

My companions for the occasion arrived before me. They are, I would say, Chelsea people, more used to San Lorenzo and Meridiana than to Indonesian restaurants in Battersea, so I was expecting long faces and bitter taunts. Far from it, 'As far as I'm concerned,' declared one of them when I arrived, 'this is the best place I've ever been to.' This was uttered before a mouthful of food had come. The casual, jolly atmosphere of this scruffy little restaurant and the cheeriness – kiss, kiss, kiss, ho, ho, ho – of Nancy Lam were, he thought, just what the doctor ordered.

From the outside, Nancy Lam's Enak Enak is pretty unprepossessing. Situated on a dank part of Lavender Hill, it resembles nothing much more than an average greasy spoon café. Inside, there is a thin grey carpet of the type found on the floor in pawnbrokers' offices and there is a fridge situated somewhere around the middle of the eating area with a plaster cat on top of it. The walls are whitewashed, the bright green chairs available in job lots from any kitchen warehouse. Shelves are scattered with a variety of keepsakes, with postcards and greetings cards stuck at random to the wall, alongside little pictures of exotic birds and flowers. A blackboard hangs above the opening to the kitchen, on it chalked, FISH MENU £5.50 COD SQUID AND SALMON. 'Enak, Enak', one of our party had discovered, means 'Yummy, Yummy'. This, I realised, was no place for a blind date with The Countess Spencer.

A message on the table menu sets the tone, that mixture of business and chumminess which, I have often noticed in the past, is often to be found in a good kitchen. 'Nancy cooks with love using the very best and freshest ingredients. As no monosodium glutamate or preservatives are used some dishes take time to perfect, so please be patient, relax and enjoy.' Another message, on the front of the menu, announces, 'Birthday or business celebrations our delight.' My brother-in-law, with many years experience of the advertising business and its assorted celebrations, scoffed 'I bet!' The very idea that even the most liberal restaurateur could actually be delighted by the prospect of a business celebration, with all the whoops and gropes and wolf-whistles it would entail, seemed to him perfectly ludicrous.

While Nancy Lam herself could be seen over the counter toiling in the kitchen, a less forceful, equally smiley waitress came and asked if we were ready to order, calling me "Massa". We ordered a bundle of things to start with, helping ourselves from each others' plates. The satays – six generous sticks – earned high praise, particularly the crunchy peanut sauce. "As far as I'm concerned the whole thing is absolutely fab," said the other Chelsea friend, thrusting a satay into his mouth, without, so far as I could see, removing the stick.

I have never really seen the point of spare ribs. They seem to me a rather exhausting way of getting your hands all clammy and ending up with a luminous red Russell Davies-style goatee beard around your mouth. If Nancy Lam's barbecued spare ribs didn't quite win me over, they were at least chunky and meaty and extremely tasty. I would imagine that their hearty, outdoorsy quality might appeal to The Duke of Edinburgh, though his delight might be offset with corresponding distaste for the slovenly behaviour and general attitude of some of his fellow customers, not to mention the staff.

My brother-in-law, whose reputation within the international advertising community has, alas, been fatally damaged by my vivid description of his short-tempered behaviour in a Balham Indian restaurant a couple of months ago, was making every effort towards geniality. He pronounced Nancy Lam's Herbal Soup 'excellent – one of the oddest I've ever tasted. It's clear chicken soup with odd bits and pieces in it – a sort of Indonesian consommé, and very good indeed. Mmmm.'

By now we were all purring merrily away. My Chelsea friend declared the batter of her deep fried prawns to be 'paper thin and the prawns delicious', a silly mistake, as then we all wanted one.

As we were about to plunge into our main courses, Nancy Lam began making the rounds of her little restaurant, laughing and joking with those she had not met before, and hugging those she had. Alas, I'm very English about Great Characters, especially when they own restaurants. Tremors leap up and down my backbone when I see them begin to circulate, and I blush and whimper when they finally arrive at my table, closing my eyes, muttering 'lovely, lovely' and hoping that they'll push off. My brother-in-law, though, is very good with them. There is nothing he likes more than repartee. This meant that when Nancy Lam arrived at our table, he was happy to take the main brunt of her jollity. A beaming, plumpish figure, she was wearing a brightly-coloured apron illustrated with a page from the Bash Street Kids. In one of the scenes, Smiffy and the others are chorusing 'We Want Jelly'. During an awkward silence, during which we were smiling at Nancy and Nancy was smiling back at us, my brother-in-law read off Nancy's apron, 'We Want Jelly'. This, it turned out, was like a red rag to a bull. 'Yeeaaah!' exclaimed Nancy, placing a hand over each of her bosoms and wobbling them around, 'These jellies never set!!!' I doubt whether this is part of the suggested small talk one is taught at the Prue Leith Restaurant School, but I may be wrong.

Our main courses were way up to standard. Like the starters, many of them had cheerful, almost Hooray Henry, names. Treasure Hunt Chicken is a chicken breast cooked with lemon grass and fairly hot spices, its taste nipping back and forth between spicy and savoury. Nasi Goreng takes the biscuit for off-putting names ('mmmm . . . I could murder a Nasi Goreng') but turned out to be a great mound of fried rice with an ample sufficiency of prawns, and all very delicious.

I was just jotting a few of these names down when who should loom up once more but Nancy Lam. 'You writin' love letters?' she said, laughing. Then she had second thoughts. 'You writin' about us?' she said. I ummed and erred. Generally I have found that if a restaurateur suspects that you are a reviewer he will start to fawn all over you, offering you drambuies on the house, dinner dates for two, free money, and so on. Not so Nancy. 'Well, you can F**K OFF,' she said, and I instantly warmed to her. Only my brother-in-law, diverting her attention with fresh recitals of the 'We Want Jelly' joke, brought the atmosphere back onto an even keel. When he asked her the secret of her excellent stock, she was our best friend again.

After a Kuih Dada – a small, sweet and quite excellent pancake roll with coconut, brown sugar and ice-cream – we paid the modest bill and shuffled off into the Battersea drizzle amidst much waving. A stone's throw from Marco Pierre White's Harveys, Nancy Lam offers warmer hospitality, a better class of abuse and jolly good food, and all for a fraction of the price.

'What'll We Be Having, Then?'

Melvyn's Cousin Harry's Pigeon

One of the most crucial aspects of contemporary life touched on by Melvyn Bragg in his lengthy novel *Kingdom Come* is the problem of eating out. The hero, Douglas, a television arts producer with roots in Cumbria – and, as such, an imaginative creation of some stature – has just finished a long lunch in a London restaurant. The bill comes, and Douglas starts thinking. '30 pounds,' he says, 'was as much as my grandfather earned in his first year's employment – 82 hours a week . . . What sense is there in all that?'

Many diners have begun to experience similar dilemmas to that so vividly pin-pointed by Douglas. *I shouldn't be here*, they think as they flick a finger for another Muscat de Beaumes de Venise, *I should be down the pits*. Restaurateurs, sympathetic to their plight, are using a variety of ploys to make television producers and kindred spirits feel more at home. Two of London's most fashionable restaurants, Ménage à Trois and Eleven Park Walk, are situated firmly in basements: plans to lower the exuberant lighting and have the waitresses ride around on pit ponies have so far remained on the drawing-board. Douglas' creator, Melvyn Bragg, a Lloyd's underwriter, has overcome whatever qualms he may have had so successfully that, when dining at L'Escargot, he always goes *upstairs*; there a bill generally comes to the equivalent annual earnings of Douglas' grandfather, grandmother, both aunties and Cousin Harry's racing pigeon. No doubt Bragg draws comfort whilst confronting this paradox from the motherly figure of Elena, maître de at L'Escargot, who is happy to go from table to table throughout the night reassuring her customers that there is *nothing wrong* about them being there. Other restaurants employ more complex tactics.

Founded in the guilt-ridden Seventies, Langan's soon attracted every dormant puritan conscience in London and beyond. At the same cost as L'Escargot, but with perhaps a couple of great grandparents thrown in, everyone could relax at the bar, then eat well, all in glamorous surroundings, secure in the knowledge that some time around the brandy stage their now activated conscience would appear, alive and in person, in the grand Guignol figure of Peter Langan, looming up, falling over, spitting abuse in all directions. Having exorcised their guilt out of themselves and into the figure of the proprietor, these diners/victims could sit back, complete human beings ready to take whatever grievous insults were on Today's Menu. Other restaurants have attempted to imitate this cleansing wrath (notably the Brasserie in Brompton Road where each and every one of the waiters is adept at abuse) but they have forgotten an essential element: there must be a fair measure of pleasure *before* the pain is inflicted, or there will be nothing to be redeemed from.

If there is guilt to be overcome in the diners, there is also, in the new topsy-turvy social world, an innate sense of superiority in the staff toward their clients which must be, if not diminished, at least accommodated. Waitresses in many expensive restaurants now look and sound like Fergie, and have a consequent need to establish their claims to the throne upon which, by some temporary aberration, Douglas now sits. It was *my* grandfather who employed *your* grandfather for £30 a year on an 82-hour week: this is what they wish to make clear to Douglas as he wrestles with his conscience. Thus they employ a stunning combination of matiness and bossiness. 'What'll we be having, then?' the waitresses say at Ménage à Trois, parodying their own idea of a waitress and thus making it understood that, underneath, they are not waitresses at all. In other restaurants the Fergies are less subtle, moving their heads to stare at other tables, while taking the diner's order, or, if the diner hesitates for a few seconds while choosing his main course, huffing 'I'll be back in a couple of minutes' and belting away.

Preserving the Fergies' self-esteem is not Douglas' sole function in the new, confused restaurant: he must also show the chef (né cook) that he is loved as a chum, admired as a man, and venerated as an artiste. Menus no longer carry just a list of food on offer; they are jam-packed with ecstatic reviews of that food ('wrapped delicately in the crispiest lettuce') written, in his own handwriting, by the chef himself. So chummy is Mr Worrall-Thompson at Ménage à Trois that he signs himself 'Antony' with a little kiss. Chefs now abandon their kitchens early on in the evening to take up their rightful places reaping compliments and free drinks from Douglas and his friends. In Alastair Little's restaurant called 'Alastair Little' the chef, Alastair Little, walks casually about while the Projectiles crane their necks in his direction bleating 'Alastair', desperate that he should honour them with their christian name and a sit-down discussion about the spinach soup and what he has been up to recently.

The food, too, will further Douglas' angst. He worked his way up into society so that he could always eat the meat closest to the surface of the animal, and now, the more money he pays, the closer to the innards his meal becomes. Creatures they wouldn't have dreamt of eating in Cumbria are served up in a Soy, Ginger, Garlic, Star-Anise and Coriander sauce. Even animals are losing their direction in the social upheaval. What would Cousin Harry say? Douglas has just enjoyed his pigeon coddled in sour cream.

'White Shoes'

Bob Maxwell and The Trifles

L ooking back, everything about Maxwell seems to fit into place, like the neatest of jokes. It is almost as if in life he had been the personification of a solitary punchline – baffling, absurd, guffawing, exclamatory – and only in death did the rest of the joke become evident.

For instance, in 1982, no-one quite knew what to make of Maxwell's rare excursion into book-reviewing. 'Does it really make a valuable contribution to our society to destroy both in our own eyes and in those of the world at large our major national asset of incorruptibility in national life . . . ?' he asked in a review of a history of *Private Eye*. At the time, there must have been many who nodded their heads in agreement; now, their heads will be nodding, if not in embarrassment, at least in mirth.

Over the past week, the bleat of journalists saying 'Bah! Bah! I knew all along' has not proved especially savoury, but I think that *Private Eye* should take a cheer. In the past, the magazine has been criticised for making its attacks too personal, for savaging the superficial – clothes, manners, girth – at the expense of the grave. But if there is a motto in Maxwell's death it is that a villain adept at secrecy can only be uncloaked by the Sherlock Holmes method. 'You know my method,' says the great detective in *The Boscombe Valley Mystery*. 'It is founded upon the observance of trifles.'

In his public role, Maxwell may have been one of the Great Incorruptibles, but his trifles told a different story. He was a great wearer of flashy bow-ties, a sure sign, to my mind, of a charlatan. A close study of these bow-ties revealed many of them to have been manufactured from odd materials; some looked as if they were Aertex, others like some sort of bendy rubber.

His hats, too, were those of a conman, the hammiest of ham actors, always over-playing the sincerity. In Moscow, he would sport a fur hat the size of a koala bear watching football, a ridiculous bonnet-and-scarf combination bearing the day-glo imprint of whatever team he had just bought; in New York, a baseball cap, its rim rearing up in sympathy with his eyebrows. Those who preferred to judge Maxwell not by his hats and ties but by the impressive roll-call of the great and the good who chose to adorn his letter-heads might have been better to heed Oscar Wilde's old adage: 'It is only the shallow who do not judge people by appearances.'

Until last Thursday, I had always suspected that this was just another one of Oscar's teasing little paradoxes, but the following tale – chilling, and not, I must warn you, particularly humorous – has taught me its truth.

Three years ago, my wife was expecting our first child, and was searching for a suitable nanny to take care of the baby over the first month. A friend of ours had employed a monthly nurse who might, she thought, be suitable for us.

My wife interviewed the monthly nurse while I was out. 'What was she like?' I asked on my return. My wife said that she seemed all right, but . . .

'But what?' I sighed.

'There was something about her shoes,' said my wife.

'Her SHOES?' I barked. But my wife was insistent. The young woman was wearing shoes that were peculiarly off-putting – high-heeled and shiny white and too tight for her feet. We should try for someone else, she concluded.

'You can't judge someone by a pair of shoes!' I argued. 'You must approach these things rationally.' But my wife turned the girl down. Luckily, a few days later we interviewed someone else who proved to be perfect.

The tale now moves to last Thursday. At a party, we bumped into the friend who had recommended her monthly nurse. She seemed shaken. She had, she said, something awful to tell us. She had been contacted a few months ago by the police. They had told her that her monthly nurse was to be charged with causing grievous bodily harm to three children. The monthly nurse was now in prison.

Thus was our darling daughter saved by my wife's distaste for a pair of shiny white shoes. Never again will I argue for the rational approach, the excellent references, the names on the letter-head. 'I can never bring you to realise,' says Sherlock Holmes in *A Case of Identity*, 'the importance of sleeves, the suggestiveness of thumb-nails, or the great issues that may hang from a bootlace.'

'Why Are Other Poets So Glum With Me?'

Wendy Cope's Diary

*T*he Poetess At Last Recognises Her True Worth

The editor phoned and asked me
Is your name Wendy Cope?
Would you take some money
For a yard of old rhyming rope?

I said, 'When do you want it?'
He said, 'As fast as you can do'
I said, 'I'll start just as soon as
I've downed a bottle or two'

The editor said he'd like them
About all the usual stuff:
Lunch and bad weather and poets
And boyfriends cutting up rough

And having one too many
And feeling rather down
And having another too many
Vide: 'Tears of a Clown'

But when I quoted my prices
He said that cash was tight;
And instead he'd print Dorothy Parker
Who was no longer in copyright.

Why I Put Men In My Poems
I often write about men
And how they let you down
Which is all very handy
Because 'down' rhymes with 'frown'
And 'noun' and 'crown' and 'town'.
I also like the word 'men'
Because it rhymes with 'wren'
And 'then' and 'den' and 'pen'.
So I write to all the editors
Saying would you like a poem about men
– Again?
They say, 'Yes, but could you make it scan
This time?'
I say, 'Of course I can make it scan and I can also make
It Rhyme.'
So they cough
And let me off.

Another Poem About Men
I look in the fridge
And find it empty
But nothing rhymes with empty
So I look again
And find a hen
Which gives me the chance
To make this another poem about men.

Why Are Other Poets So Glum With Me?
Why are other poets so glum with me?
Where are their poetic loyalties?
Why do they grow snappy
And so very unhappy
Whenever I mention my royalties?

Which If Any Great Poets Might I Have Fancied?
I suppose I could have fancied Milton
Though his feet might smell of Stilton
Or maybe I could have gone for Keats
If he'd been better between the sheets
I could have had a date with Kipling
But his muscles were far from rippling

Dylan Thomas could have made me frisky
If his breath hadn't smelt of whisky
A crush on Shakespeare, I might have fear'd,
If it wasn't for that awful beard
I might have gone for Rupert Brooke
But he had that awful pansy look
And I couldn't take the loopy stare
Of the also-bearded John Clare
And the creepiest guy around
Must surely be old Ezra Pound
Wordsworth and his daffodils
Could never give me the thrills
And the great Alexander Pope
Doesn't appeal to Wendy Cope
Leaving me with Edith Sitwell
Which doesn't make me feel a bit well.

What Do You Think?
A man called Desmond
A bloke called Ron
A boy called Andrew
A guy called John
They all vanished, for better or worse
And all I had asked them
Was what they thought of my verse.

*Buses I Have Written Poems To Past Lovers On
In The Past Fortnight*
56, 14, 29, 11,
19, 23, 24, 8,
17, 9, 44, 7,
4, 12, 18 (late).

Without A Punchline
Just occasionally, I write poems which
Don't have any sort of rhyme at all.
Instead, they just meander on
And then finish without a punchline.

Things I Must Do Today
Fetch my laundry
Darn my socks
Put my old sheets

In a box.
Have a drink,
Make some toast.
Go shopping for
The Sunday roast.
Watch some telly
Sip some tea
Give the milkman
Thirty pee.
What a lot
Of boring labour
But apparently not
To the man at Faber.

'With a Hyphen or Without?'

The British Pedants' Association Annual Fun-Day

'I always greatly look forward to The British Pedants' Association Annual Fun-Day,' I said to a fellow-member as the hall began to fill up.

'Wouldn't "I always look forward greatly" be preferable?' he replied, 'Or even, "I look forward greatly always".'

'Forgive me overhearing,' chipped in a passing pedant, 'But, quite regardless of grammar, it would not be strictly true to say that you *always* greatly look forward to The British Pedants' Association Fun-Day. On the Fun-Day itself, you would no longer be *looking forward* to it, as you would already be present at it, the 'it' referring, of course, to the Fun-Day.'

'Unless you were looking forward to *next year's* Fun-Day,' countered the first pedant.

A bell rang for silence. 'Absurd to ring a bell for silence,' whispered the first pedant, 'when the noise imparted by the aforesaid bell itself contributes so generously to the prevailing noise.'

'Welcome, one and all,' said the Chairman.

'On a point of information, Mr Chairman.' A woman at the back of the hall rose to speak. 'On a point of information, is there any reason to welcome *one* and *all*? Surely the term "*all*" incorporates the term "*one*", thus making any need for the term "*one*" redundant.'

'Welcome, all,' said the Chairman.

'On a point of information, Mr Chairman.' Again, the woman in the back leapt to her feet. 'Welcome all WHAT?'

One and a half hours later, the meeting got underway. It started, in traditional fashion, with a move by the Apostrophe Action Group to have an apostrophe incorporated into the title, making it The British Pedants' Association. This was countered by an angry move from a reformist splinter-group to place the apostrophe after the 't' of 'Pedants', making it The British Pedant's Association.

'Oh dear,' sighed the Chairman, 'Tempers are continuously flaring.'

'*Continually* flaring,' chorused one half of the hall. 'Our dictionaries define 'flare' as "a sudden outburst of flame",' chorused the other half of the hall, 'so it could neither be "continuous" or "continual".'

' "Nor" after "neither" not "or",' screamed everyone else.

The Chairman, wishing to avoid a scene, hastily moved the meeting on. 'This year, our Fun-Day consists of a boat-trip,' he announced.

'With a hyphen or without?' asked the woman at the back, but everyone had already begun to take their seats on the coach, within which a new spirit of jollity prevailed as we joined together to sing hearty renditions of 'Maybe It Is Owing to The Fact That I'm a Londoner', 'Here We Are Going, Here We Are Going, Here We Are Going' and 'She Loves You, Yes, Yes, Yes'.

Once on board, a group of us made our way to the bar. 'I'll have something long,' I said to the barman, who passed me a ball of string. It emerged he was a branch-secretary of The British Pedants' Association. The waiter came to take our orders for lunch. 'Do you have Frogs' Legs?' I wondered. 'No, sir, I was born like it,' he replied.

Wishing to take a break from such an excess of pedantry, I went up to the top deck of our boat, HMS Boat. There I began to throw a few nuts to the seagulls, who would swoop down in order to read the ingredients on the packet before gingerly pecking at each one. I was chatting to a fellow pedant about how very untidy the waves were when I noticed with horror that we were fast approaching a rock.

'Land Ahoy!' I yelled to the Captain.

'Slang,' he replied. 'And, I might add, there is no verb in "Land Ahoy!", so that it does not, in any strict sense, constitute a proper sentence.'

'SOS!' I screamed, 'The rock is coming closer!'

'Correction,' said the Captain, 'It is *we* who are coming closer to the rock, not vice-versa.'

When the crunch finally came, the Captain shouted, 'All hands to the deck!' As I swam away, I watched the boat sink with the palms of hundreds of pedants fixed doggedly to her deck. 'It is the way they would have wanted to go,' I thought to myself as their pedantic bottoms disappeared beneath the waves. 'Or, on second thoughts, should that be "It was the way they would have wanted to have gone"?'

'Yes or No?'

Lord Young and Michael Miles
(Political Sketch 9)

In many respects, Lord Young of Graffham bears an uncanny resemblance to Mr Michael Miles, the influential television quizmaster who became widely known in the mid-to-late 1960s for his popular programme, *Take Your Pick*. Within this extraordinary similarity – up until now largely ignored by political commentators – there might well lie a clue to the character of the present Secretary of State for Trade and Industry. Yes or no?

Yes. Gong! It was, of course, one of Mr Miles' guiding rules that his contestants should never utter the words 'yes' or 'no'. If ever they did, the gong would bang, and off they would be led. Lord Young sticks rigidly by Mr Miles' principles, applying them to himself with an even greater rigour than he demands of others.

Yesterday, the quizmaster was to become the quizzed when he was due to be called to account for himself in a Private Notice Question from Lord Shackleton. Lord Shackleton believes that Lord Young deceived the House when he implied that there was no deadline to British involvement in the Canadian Radarsat satellite project. Lord Young says he did not. Yes or no?

A few minutes before he was due on, Lord Young trotted into the Chamber of the House of Lords with a brisk and confident air, nodding this way and that to the ranks of panellists, his traditional red clipboard nestling in his hand. Lovely you could make it, his expression seemed to suggest, I'm sure we're due for a lot of light-hearted fun.

It is customary for major stars to be preceded by a warm-up artiste, often a comedian, to encourage a bit of animation in their reactions. While Lord Young made a few last-minute adjustments to his over-neat double-breasted suit, it fell to Lord St John of Fawsley to dust down an old gag or two. The DTI building, he drawled, was one of the most hid-e-ous structures in London, even in the Kingdom. Could it not now be demolished? Boom! Boom! The Government spokesman couldn't agree. Well, said Olde-Tyme trouper Lord 'Uncle Bob' Mellish, if it wasn't the worst building, could be say what was worse? Boom! Boom!

By now, the House was beautifully warmed up, so much so that steam could be seen to rise from some of its most prominent members. Lord Young had finished wiping his spectacles and was now folding and refolding his handkerchief, ready to pop it back, crisp and clean, into his top pocket. He rose, stretched both arms out and prepared for his inquisition. In front of him sat his opposing panellists, all with their gongs to the fore.

Lord Shackleton said that he would not accuse Lord Young of misleading the House, a trick statement really meaning that he would accuse Lord Young of misleading the House. 'I did not mislead Your Lordship's House,' declared Lord Young. The position on the Radarsat project was very simple, he said: 'We will make up our minds in good time.' His bright, somewhat over-large white cuffs seemed to twinkle in the sunlight.

'I accept Lord Young's expression of regret that the House was undoubtedly misled,' chipped in Lord Shackleton, who was fast revealing that his own knowledge of techniques employed on *Take Your Pick* was virtually encyclopaedic.

'Excuse me,' Lord Young, his face reddening, his cuffs a-quiver, leapt to his feet. 'Excuse me but I did not mislead the House. I stand by each and every word I said.'

Lord Shackleton then seemed to say that he had not meant to say what he had said about what Lord Young had said he hadn't said, but then he ruined it by saying again what he hadn't meant to say. 'Of course I withdraw that remark. I just hope the Noble Lord will come a bit cleaner,' he said, adding: 'It is within the knowledge of the House that the House was deceived.'

By this time, the Conservative benches were banging their gongs, demanding that the temporary quizmaster be dismissed. Lord Young sat back, his ordeal over, his smile somewhat less avid than usual. And as for Lord Shackleton, he received the due punishment meted out to so many offenders in our society. Lord Longford sidled over and patted him on the back.

12 April 1988

'Yuletide Greetings'

Larry, Do-Do and The Kids

'Hi, y'all from Do-Do, Larry and the Kids!
'For us, there's never been a happier, more prosperous twelve months, our dreams all blossoming in the sunshine of good fortune.'

This year, we celebrate a marvellous new addition to our home with the arrival of Jeff's dear Mom, Granmaw Du Lally, after the Committee of Janitors decided she was better suited to around-the-clock supervision in the home environment. 95 years young, this Yuletide she's been bursting with good cheer, treating our neighbours to her spirited rendition of 'Gloria in Excelsis Deo', the four-hour version with harmonica accompaniment. Granmaw has even on occasion taken charge of the kitchen, producing good ol' home cooked dishes just like Granmaw thinks she used to cook 'em, such as Char-Broiled Salad and Gin and Bourbon Soup. Her laughter can best be described as infectious.

'And so to the youngest!!! This year, Ricky walked off with all the prizes in the kids' talent contest. Eventually the judges found them on him and gave them back to the winners, but Ricky was, as always, very good about it. In the Fall, he became Hero of the Hour when he successfully beat off a mugger, returning home with a reward of 200 dollars. He told us that the mugger was an ageing felon brandishing an open wallet, but luckily Ricky was carrying a gun.

'Our children grow older and more mature with the passing of each day! Daughter Charlene found that the boundaries imposed by an academic environment were too restricting upon her growth as a person so she now pursues her interest in gastronomy in the home environment. She regularly hears the call of the open road, and instinctively knows when the Mobile Pizza Van has pulled up in the driveway. Her marriage was the highlight of our year. Mr Moon delivered a truly beautiful address, and with the aid of Larry's trusty binoculars we were able to be pretty sure which one Charlene was. Daughter Diane is now aged 16 and wearing her first make-up, every bit the young lady, with her second due in the spring.

'Son Andy continues to grow internally with his daily visits to the analyst, and has taken to re-birth like a duck to water, his primal screams acting as a valuable alarm clock for those of us wishing to rise at 3 a.m. He has now, he informs us, emerged from re-birth, and is entering into his original trauma as a spermatazoon, spending much of his day rushing headlong into doors with great gusto.

'Last but not least, Wally is now 24 and has never been happier, though the doctors tell us they can't go on increasing the dose indefinitely. He is thrilled to bits that he has had firm offers for his book from many publishers, both here and in America, but he is insisting on an author who won't sensationalise things, and who will show the world that deep down he intended nothing but the best for his victims. Norman Mailer has even expressed an interest, but only if the final toll is in double figures – so fingers crossed, y'all!

'And so to the adults! This year, Larry received well-deserved promotion from his firm, allowing him to operate full-time from home, with fewer day-to-day burdens and less worries about income tax, company cars and so on. He tells me he has become quite fascinated with the ancient art of constructing ships in bottles, and he has already succeeded in building up quite a collection of empty bottles in his den, where he shuts himself away for so much of the day, always emerging with a song in his heart and a swagger in at least one of his steps. No sign yet of a ship in any of the bottles, but it's still early days.

'It's been an exciting year, too, for Mom – that's me, folks! I have succeeded completely in giving up smoking tobacco. I now chew it instead. Our vacation this year was the greatest ever. Who'd have thought jogging could be such fun? Whaddyaknow? I lost a full 80 pounds over the year, and I can now fit into lots of things I could never manage to before, like the Renault and the downstairs rest-room! Yes, it's been a year of achievement and progress for the Du Lallys – and we sure hope it's been half as good for you!'

'Zap'

Sardine Tin Labels From Norway

Reading *The Daily Telegraph*'s books page last week, I could not but grieve for the way the world dwindles daily for the humorist. An epidemic of jocularity is sweeping the country. We are all Mad Cows now. The trouble is not that there is nothing to laugh at, but that there is everything to laugh at. Jokes are fast running out, for a joke must transform real life in some perverse way, and real life has begun to perform the same operation perfectly professionally upon itself.

The book review that caught my eye was of *The Oxford Book of Canadian Military Anecdotes*. Now, the ever-increasing dullness and oddity of Oxford books is an old favourite among humorists, who are always trying to think up new and hilariously tedious 'The Oxford Book of . . .' titles. The real life Oxford Book of Death set us back a bit, but *The Oxford Book of Canadian Military Anecdotes* has dealt us a blow from which it will be hard to recover. Already there are reports in from the North that up to 10 humorous jobs have been lost, and a joke factory is to close.

But the joke in the *Telegraph* did not end with the title. I was wondering why the *Telegraph*'s literary editor, usually a very sensible fellow (as those of us who have books out this year will all agree) should have granted such a lot of space to such an obviously boring book. I then noticed the by-line. It was 'Conrad Black', who is, well, blow me down, the Canadian proprietor of *The Daily Telegraph*. So not only was this a first-class joke about OUP books, it was also a first-class joke about the newspaper proprietors, and not a joke-monger in sight.

Esoteric art exhibitions with wacky titles are another simple way for a humorist to raise a laugh. But there seems to be no point anymore in going to all that trouble because real life continues to win hands down. In *The Times* list of recommended art exhibitions this week there was one at the Design Museum titled 'Sardine Tin Labels From Norway', on until June 17th.

And so it goes on: on Wednesday, it was announced that the new Stephen Sondheim musical would be called *Assassins*. Leading characters would include Lee Harvey Oswald and Sirhan Sirhan, and there would be a final chorus in which the assassins turn to the audience singing, 'We've done our bit – now it's your turn'. Just as I was adding this to the claim by the editor of the *Times Literary Supplement* in last week's *Spectator* that there had once been a musical about the Kray brothers, I read of yet another musical, called *The Death of Klinghoffer*, about the wheelchair-bound tourist who was murdered by terrorists on the Achille Lauro in 1985.

From time to time in these pages, I like to parody the memoirs of politicians, highlighting their conceit, their pomposity, their simple delight in themselves. Over the past couple of years, the job has become abominably hard, for each politician seems far more adept at parodying himself than I could ever hope to be. Who could capture the complacency of Callaghan better than he does himself, in this sentence from his memoirs, summing up his feelings on the outcome of the disastrous 1979 General Election. 'It demonstrated how much steady understanding and support existed for what we had tried to do'. And who could better parody the idea of Christmas at the Benns than Tony Benn himself, in this extract from his *Diaries* for Sunday 26 December 1976? 'Caroline gave each of us a copy of the Communist Manifesto in our stockings, published in English in Russia, and she gave Josh a book called *Marx for Beginners* and gave Hilary Isaac Deutscher's three-volume biography of Trotsky'.

Though Graham Greene only came second in a *New Statesman* weekend competition for parodies of Graham Greene, I suspect he was trying too hard. He should have sent in the first paragraph of *The Honorary Consul*: 'Doctor Eduardo Plarr stood in the small port of Parana, among the rails and yellow cranes, watching where a horizontal plume of smoke stretched over the Chaco . . . It was an evening which, by some mysterious combination of failing light and the smell of an unrecognised plant, brings back to some men the sense of childhood and of future hope, and to others the sense of something which has been lost and nearly forgotten'.

Similarly, a Ruth Rendell first paragraph competition would undoubtedly be won by Ruth Rendell: 'It was the first dead body he had ever seen . . . Something unpleasant had happened to her face; it was swollen and a greyish blue colour, and her eyes protruded under strained shiny eyelids' (*Master of the Moor*). And no-one can quite capture the full pedantry of the final, nit-picking lines of an Anthony Powell review quite so well as Anthony Powell: 'The note on p90 should read Lady Diana Bridgeman, not Bradford; the Princesse de Caraman-Chimay on p430, the same as she on p559, was nee Hennessy, not Hamilton; the dog that acted in *La Dolce Vita* belonged to Iris Tree, not Mrs Taffy Rodd'.

There are already murmurings in the joke-mills of a national strike by humorists. We will down exclamation-marks until the world pulls its socks up and acts seriously once more. But the situation is looking bleak. News just in confirms that Radio One disc-jockey Mike Read, prevented by the Betjeman Estate from putting on a musical called *England's Teddy Bear* about Sir John Betjeman, will be presenting a new musical about Rupert Brooke in the West End this autumn. Already, massed lines of humorists are gathering at Beachy Head, ready to leap.